THE FIRST R

THE FIRST R

How Children Learn Race and Racism

DEBRA VAN AUSDALE AND JOE R. FEAGIN

ROWMAN & LITTLEFIELD PUBLISHERS, INC.
Lanham • Boulder • New York • Oxford

ROWMAN & LITTLEFIELD PUBLISHERS, INC.

Published in the United States of America
by Rowman & Littlefield Publishers, Inc.
4720 Boston Way, Lanham, Maryland 20706
www.rowmanlittlefield.com

12 Hid's Copse Road, Cumnor Hill, Oxford OX2 9JJ, England

Distributed by NATIONAL BOOK NETWORK

British Library Cataloguing in Publication Information Available

Library of Congress Cataloging-in-Publication Data

Van Ausdale, Debra, 1954–
    The first R : how children learn race and racism/Debra Van Ausdale and Joe R. Feagin.
        p. cm.
    Includes bibliographical references and index.
    1. Social interaction in children. 2. Racism. 3. Prejudices in children. 4. Child
development. 5. Child psychology. I. Feagin, Joe R. II. Title.

HQ784 .S56 V36 2001
305.8'0083—dc21   00-042563

ISBN 0-8476-8861-5 (cloth : alk. paper)
ISBN 0-8476-8862-3 (pbk. : alk. paper)

Printed in the United States of America

♾™ The paper used in this publication meets the minimum requirements of American
National Standard for Information Sciences—Permanence of Paper for Printed Library
Materials, ANSI/NISO Z39.48-1992.

CONTENTS

ACKNOWLEDGMENTS

We are grateful for the cooperation of many people who gave us their time, attention, and respect while we were developing this research. Most of all, we are indebted to the children who embraced and accepted the first author (Debra Van Ausdale) as part of their daily lives. Without their willingness to include her, none of the insights we have gained through this project would have been possible. We are also thankful to the teachers, parents, and administrators at the day care center and to our many colleagues who offered us understanding and support as we did this research and wrote this manuscript.

Any list of those who have been helpful and supportive is necessarily incomplete, but we would like to give special thanks to Hernan Vera, Karen Pyke, Diana Kendall, Barrie Thorne, Bernice Barnet, Nijole Benokraitis, Karyn McKinney, Kendall Broad, and Jessie Daniels for assistance in various ways, including comments on drafts of the manuscript. Marjorie DeVault and Gary Spencer provided special insight and support for the continued development of the ideas in this book. We would also like to thank our editor, Dean Birkenkamp, for his endless support, enthusiasm, and patience.

Watching little children indulge in hateful rhetoric and hurtful interracial activity was the hardest thing Debi had ever done, and there were many occasions when she wanted nothing more than to leave the field to cry. Yet watching them grow in understanding themselves and others was a constant source of wonderment. We have learned much about the social world from them.

1

YOUNG CHILDREN LEARNING RACIAL AND ETHNIC MATTERS

Carla, a three-year-old child, is preparing herself for resting time. She picks up her cot and starts to move it to the other side of the classroom. A teacher asks what she is doing. "I need to move this," explains Carla. "Why?" asks the teacher. "Because I can't sleep next to a nigger," Carla says, pointing to Nicole, a four-year-old Black child on a cot nearby. "Niggers are stinky. I can't sleep next to one." Stunned, the teacher, who is white, tells Carla to move her cot back and not to use "hurting words." Carla looks amused but complies.

Later, after the children awakened and went to the playground, the center's white director reports to the first author that he has called Carla's parents for a meeting about the incident: "If you want to attend I would really like to have you there. . . . I want you to know that Carla did not learn that here!" At the meeting both parents—the father is white, and the mother is half-white and half-Asian—were baffled when told of the incident. The father remarked, "Well, she certainly did not learn that sort of crap from us!" The teacher immediately insisted that Carla did not learn such words at the center. Carla's father offered this explanation: "I'll bet she got that from Teresa. Her dad is . . . a real redneck."

Like most of the children we observed, Carla is not the unsophisticated, innocent child of many adult imaginations. This three-year-old knows how to use racial material, such as the hurtful epithet, which she has learned from other sources. But she is not just imitating what she might have heard in some other social setting. She applies this particular bit of racial knowledge to a distinctive and personal interactive encounter. The range of concepts she has linked together are remarkable. She has not acted indiscriminately, using an ugly name only to foster a reaction in the other child. Instead, Carla uses "nigger" to explain and justify her action

1

to an interested onlooker, the teacher. This shows a level of forethought. She has considered what a "nigger" is, to whom the appellation applies, and why such a label is useful in explaining her behavior to an adult. This is not the thoughtless blunder of a sleepy child.

The origins of Carla's racial knowledge, while certainly important, are not our focus in this study. We conducted observations of the children solely at school during school hours. We did not formally interview or question the children, nor did we seek out explanations from parents, teachers, or other adults who were significant in these children's lives. We wished to discover how children themselves perpetuated racial and ethnic patterns, away from the prying eyes and controlling activities of adults. Most white adults, including many scholars, believe that very young children are incapable of seriously understanding the implications of race and racism. In contrast, most Black adults and other adults of color are of necessity much more aware that their young children are forced to deal with racial matters. Even when children do employ racial concepts, white adults and analysts tend to dismiss the significance of their actions. "They're just kids; they don't understand" is the typical response to the behavior we describe above. Yet racist practice is still perpetuated across generations, and racist attitudes and beliefs continue to hold sway in our society. As we will demonstrate throughout this book, three-, four-, and five-year-olds often hold a solid and applied understanding of the dynamics of race.

The reactions of the key adults in this story illustrate the strength of adult beliefs about the conceptual abilities of children. Their focus is on child as imitator, not as creator or master of language, and the principal concern of teacher, parents, and administrator is to assure each other that the child did not learn this behavior from them. This commonsense conceptualization of children is the long-standing norm among adults, including researchers and legislative officials. Most adults go into denial when it comes to acknowledging racist attitudes and actions among children. Take, for example, this 1967 report of the Plowden Committee, on children in public schools in Great Britain. The committee concluded that

> Most experienced primary school teachers do not think that colour prejudice causes much difficulty. Children readily accept each other and set store by other qualities in their classmates than the colour of their skin. Some echoes of adult values and prejudices inevitably invade the classroom but they seldom survive for long among children. It is among the neighbours at home and when he begins to enquire about jobs that the Coloured child faces the realities of the society into which his parents have brought him. (Plowden Report 1967, paragraph 179)

While this report is several decades old, little seems to have changed in much scholarly and everyday understanding of children's worlds over the intervening period.

Much recent work (for example, Wardle 1992) continues to suggest or assume that children, as we will see in more detail below, are more or less naive and innocent about racial and ethnic matters. Most adults refuse to accept that little children would make knowing use of the ugliness inherent in racist epithets, emotions, and behavior. Most parents do not believe that small children can understand what such language implies. When children do employ racial or ethnic terminology, they are assumed to be mimicking some other adult's behaviors and, often, *not* those of their parents or other caregivers. Most important, racist talk and behavior among young children is usually dismissed by adults as being of little consequence and is not taken seriously until children are older. The young child, it seems, always learns about racism somewhere else, in a place where the adults making the judgments do not reside. Additionally, if the fundamental premise of the Plowden Committee were correct, that is, if adult prejudices seldom survive for long among children, it would seem that racism would be a thing of the past after the passage of more than thirty years. It should have slowly eroded away, extinguished by children's inability to comprehend it. Obviously this is not the case.

In particular, white adults abdicate their responsibility to recognize and combat racism when they deny that race and racism can even exist in serious forms among young children. This denial, which is likely rooted in often deeply held convictions that children are untutored in the ways of adults, is counterproductive, since, as we will see in our data, it rejects children's considerable and ever-growing knowledge of the world and thus creates a set of adult-centered excuses. From this perspective a young child who does use racist language is said to do so out of naivete or ignorance. Conversely, one who does *not* use such language is assumed to be lacking in such knowledge. Either assumption allows adults to ignore the possibility that children are actively reproducing in their everyday lives the matters and realities of race and racism. Neither situation is reasonable, however, since racism remains systemic in U.S. society. When adults indulge in such denial, they neglect children's present, active reality and fail to understand how children's actions also create and re-create society.

We use the term *adultcentric* to mean that adults interpret children's activities in comparison to adult conceptions of what children *should* be doing, rather than what they are *actually* doing. This holds whether we are discussing everyday life or scholarly theories. When children's conduct does not fit within adult preconceptions, their activities are often rejected or explained away. Generally speaking, adults evaluate children using a deficit model, assuming without questioning that children do not possess maturity or sophisticated knowledge of the social world. When young children demonstrate knowledge that exceeds their expected stage of development, they are usually deemed cute or precocious when their behavior is acceptable, or odd or naive when their behavior is unacceptable. Consider the example of an occasional report of a young child who, when faced with an emergency, dials 911 for help. The child is hailed as a hero, and the story often gains airtime on local news. Adult viewers may remark on how extraordinary it is that a young child would know what to do. Yet thousands of adults phone 911 each day but never make the evening news through their actions. Adultcentric thought permeates even psychological and social science theories about how children think and learn.

We are not suggesting that young children's thought processes and behaviors can be simply equated with those of adults. Nor are we reducing our perspective to one that views children as merely small adults who lack experience with the world. We are constructing a perspective that attempts to account for the discontinuities in theoretical understanding of children's activities, gaps that often result from the relative invisibility of children's activities. Children's lives remain substantially unknown to adults, both in research and in everyday practice. As David Oldman (1994) points out, much research about children is limited by reliance on adult-oriented and controlled perspectives and theories of development that reduce children to "not yet persons" and tend to either ignore children's experiences or redefine them under paradigms that reinforce traditional perspectives. Thus our work is directed at investigating the complex social constitution of children's lives.

SOME MAJOR THEORIES OF CHILD DEVELOPMENT

The adultcentric perspective on the child is central in much theorizing and analysis of child development, which generally maintains that very young children, those aged two to five, know little or nothing about such things as racial and ethnic matters because of their "egocentric" stage of cognitive development. Egocentric in this sense does not mean selfish, in the sense that children are egotistic. Rather, egocentric children are unable to really perceive any viewpoint or attitude except their own. They are generally unreflective as well. In his classic work on young children in three schools in England, for example, King (1978, 8) concluded, "If teachers are unused to reflecting on their own actions young children seem almost incapable of doing so." He was referring to children as old as age six.

In this school of thought, because they are not able to take the perspective of the other, young children are cognitively incapable of either feeling or expressing certain social concepts in a serious or meaningful way unless they receive active adult instruction. Meaningful understanding of major social abstractions such as race, ethnicity, gender, or class does not develop in children until they are at least grown to elementary school age. In effect, then, young children cannot "do" race or ethnicity in a serious or meaningful way. They generally do not know how to make use of racial or ethnic concepts, except in naive and rudimentary ways, or to organize their lives or to make decisions about everyday social interaction based on race. Conventional theories of child development draw on a wide range of research demonstrating that very young children are unable to recognize even their own racial group with any degree of consistency or accuracy. According to previous research, before about seven to eight years of age thoughtful use of racial categorization does not enter children's social repertoires (Goodman 1964; Porter 1971). Prior to this age, racial or ethnic concepts may be employed by children, but only in imitative or artless ways, with little or no awareness of the broader implications or social meaning.

The Piaget Tradition

The thought and research of Jean Piaget have perhaps done more than that of any other researcher to create and shape the field of child development. After an exhaustive review of Piagetian theory and research, one recent child development textbook (Siegler 1998, 60) sums up his impact this way: "Piaget's theory remains a dominant force in developmental psychology, despite the fact that much of it was formulated half a century ago. Some of the reasons for the lasting appeal are the important acquisitions it describes, the large span of childhood it encompasses, and the reliability and charm of many of its observations."

Not surprisingly, then, the interpretation of young children as generally incapable of seriously understanding concepts such as racial group and ethnicity often draws on Piaget's theories of cognitive development. In his career Piaget (1926; 1932) refined a theory of cognitive capability that divides the development of human beings into distinct stages: sensorimotor (birth to age two), preoperational (ages two to six), concrete operational (ages seven to eleven), and formal operational (age twelve and older). Piaget's primary notion is that children's systems of thought are fundamentally different from those of adults. This difference means that children are generally incapable of understanding information in the same way as adults. As a result, information that is not developmentally appropriate will not be understood, no matter how carefully it is delivered, because the child's system of thinking is qualitatively different from that of adults (Saunders and Bingham-Newman 1984).

Piaget's theory of cognitive development, and that of many subsequently working in his tradition, views children's lives as a series of movements from one stage of cognitive development to another, with movement motivated by a quest to achieve equilibrium with the environment. It is an assimilationist perspective, wherein a child undergoes a process of reconciliation between new experiences and past realities. It is also a linear process, with each stage following on another. New experiences are seen as challenges to an individual child's conceptions of how the world works. These challenges create cognitive anomalies, which then produce intellectual tension. That is, new experiences require that the child reevaluate the world. Piaget breaks with behaviorist theories of childhood development that see children as passive recipients of adult reinforcements and punishments. Children are active and involved in appropriating information from their environments (Corsaro 1979, 11). Children mature cognitively as they work to alleviate this tension, first by assimilating the new experience and then by fitting it into their existing mental scheme of thought. The world that must be accommodated is, of course, the adult world. Successful accommodation occurs when children are able to shift their thinking to adult forms of mental activity. That is, children's thinking remains incomplete until they begin to think like an adult. Until then, children are assumed to be mentally operating under either "preoperational" or "concrete" forms of thinking and are viewed as likely to misperceive objective information, especially abstract, social information.

The application of this interpretation of children's lives has a major impact on research design. The focus on cognition and the hierarchical nature of Piaget's stages are linked to an emphasis on individual intellectual activity. The concentration on individual skills leads researchers to neglect the social nature of children's lives in favor of identifying certain mental activities that may or may not have a clear connection to lived reality. In addition, influential theories of cognitive and moral development (Piaget 1932; Kohlberg 1969) have stressed that children do not show solid awareness of the significance of social and moral concepts until they are at least seven years of age, and sometimes much older. Egocentricity is the natural state of the child, particularly the young child, and it must be overcome before social abstractions can be dealt with and more objective, rational thought processes emerge. Without this full cognitive development a child cannot move to the significant level of moral reasoning and cannot attend to giving consideration to the views and concerns of the relevant others.

One limitation of Piaget's research now seems obvious. Piaget never investigated children in social settings not dominated by an adult. He insisted that the young child is generally unaware of social interaction and remains egocentric when interacting with others: "He [the child] plays in an individualistic manner with material that is social. Such is egocentrism" (Piaget 1932, 27). In a later work Piaget elaborates: "We must expect childish reasoning to differ very considerably from ours, to be less deductive and above all less rigorous" (quoted in Campbell 1976, 17). Such expectations persist today in much scholarly work and are pandemic in popular thought. This accent on children's *inabilities* is also revealed when Piaget warns the researcher to be aware that "childish idiom ought to display a discontinuous and chaotic character in contrast to the deductive style of the adult, logical relations being omitted or taken for granted" (quoted in Campbell 1976, 18).[1] When he and others in his tradition view children's behaviors and thoughts as "childish," they indicate an assumption that children cannot be expected to behave in an "adult" manner and thus cannot be held responsible for understanding the implications of apparently adult behavior. This conceptualization of children as quite different from, or much less capable than, adults in thought or action holds sway in many realms of contemporary thought, from social research concerns, to educational policies, to the legal system.

There are serious difficulties in applying conventional Piagetian theory to the investigation of children's social behavior. There is a focus on the inner workings of the child's mind, and children's behavior is interpreted by comparison with the expected behavior for a child at her or his stage of development. Like the height and weight charts that many parents use to gauge the physical growth of their children, cognitive theory locates children at stages and within a restricted range of intellectual abilities. This approach can shape educational action and interpretation. Those accenting this theory, such as many teachers, will expect young children to have very rudimentary understandings of the social worlds and be incapable of seriously comprehending the reality and meaning of their and others' social relations. Children that fall outside the range of anticipated growth for a stage may be seen as abnormal and problematic. Social events may be particularly prone to misinterpretation, since young children are thought to operate with a dual handicap: limited experience with the social world and age-restricted cognitive abilities. From this perspective, the child progresses in linear fashion through stages of development toward the ultimate goal of mature adulthood. Intellectual maturation is reached when a child can approximate adult levels of thought and uses adult-appropriate explanations of behavior. While this perspective on children has been shown to be useful for considering children's abilities to handle advanced grammatical or mathematical concepts, its application to social concepts and proclivities creates serious difficulties for understanding the lives of children. When such thinking is applied to theories seeking to understand the meanings and behaviors associated with racial and ethnic matters, it is far from satisfactory as an explanatory framework.

Generally speaking, adults operating in society are not subject to reinterpretations of their behavior in light of defined stages of intellectual development. Whether or not they actually have requisite knowledge of the social implications accruing to their behavior is not usually taken into account when evaluating that behavior. That is, other members of society assume that, generally speaking, an adult possesses enough knowledge to engage in reasoned and informed behavior. When an adult indulges in socially disapproved behavior, that behavior is usually considered by others as indicating that adult's state of mind. Adults cannot call other people epithets or other hostile names and expect to be held free of blame when other adults in their social worlds view such behavior as unacceptable. Young children, however, are not ordinarily subject to such judgment, and this often works to their advantage. It also adversely impacts adults' ability to evaluate accurately and fully children's social activity, whether those adults are parents, teachers, or scholars. Erving Goffman described this status of children as "nonpersons" in his investigations of public place behavior (Goffman 1963). Children are excused from proper public conventions of behavior, from doing much harm, just as are servants and other socially invisible social actors (Goffman 1963, 40). It is children's status as socially insignificant that cripples adults' ability to analyze their worlds accurately and enables them to effectively hide some significant activities from adult scrutiny.

Taking the Role of the Other

In this book we suggest that racially hostile and discriminatory be-havior among children deserves more attention. As we see it, what is es-pecially critical is the harm that accrues to children who are the targets of hostile comments, emotions, and discriminatory behavior. Racist behav-ior, intentional or not, usually causes harm to its target. Often this dam-age is not apparent immediately. The accumulation of damage over years of exposure to racial mistreatment will become more apparent as we in-vestigate how racism has an impact on social relations in the lives of preschoolers. The impact of one episode of verbal racist attack may not be immediately apparent. Its damage may be unclear or hidden, simmering below the surface. We will never know, for example, what the impact of Carla's words was for little Nicole. Nonetheless, recurring encounters with racial or ethnic hostility generally accumulate to a greater effect on an individual than a simple sum of the interactive incidents might suggest. When the wounded child hears negative language, experiences exclusion or avoidance, and must remain alert to combating rejection and negative stereotypes for long periods—and eventually a lifetime—the damage as-sumes critical significance, for the child as an individual, for her or his fam-ily and community, and for the larger society. Racial or ethnic mistreat-ment is more than a personal matter. A child who is a victim of such mistreatment may well share an incident with family, thereby lightening the burden but passing on the pain to family members, who may in turn share it with other members of the family or community. Over time, this sharing contributes to the collective knowledge about racial or ethnic mis-treatment that is often important for individual and community survival.

When conventional Piagetian researchers define young children's activ-ities as only or mainly egocentric, they view the child as highly individual, in-ternally oriented, and possessed of little ability to realize that her or his per-spective is not necessarily shared by others. The "preoperational" child functions with an intellectual handicap, for preoperational intelligence lacks structure and is not a unified system of thought (Saunders and Bingham-Newman 1984). For example, a child in this stage will provide "wrong" an-swers to questions about the spatial arrangement of objects. This is said to be because the child cannot mentally visualize an arrangement of physical ob-jects from a different, other-centered perspective. A young child must phys-ically move to a second perspective in order to "correctly" depict it.

This assumed inability to take another's perspective when dealing with the physical arrangement of objects is often extended to encompass children's capabilities in social interactions. The lack of intellectual unity and structure precludes mature awareness of social concepts. The emphasis here is on the importance of maturity. Since a young child lacks the ability to accurately visualize or describe even concrete objects, it seems reasonable to assume that abstract social concepts like gender and race will be equally difficult for children to employ. Egocentricity defines the realm of social relationships. Yet there is little empirical evidence to suggest that this is the case. When this assumed egocentric state is linked to children's supposed limited exposure to social situations, it becomes easy to assume that any social definitions that a young child constructs are bound to be transient reflections of an overall incapacity to grasp social functioning in sophisticated or mature ways. Constructs such as race, ethnicity, gender, and class are thought to require the development of higher-order ideas and are nonexistent or only mirroring imitation in the young child. The views that a child may express about such abstractions are dismissed as primitive imitations of adult behaviors rather than as reflections of the child's (or children's groups') significant interpretations of reality. The presumption of naivete or disability in mental functioning of the child too often informs traditional research and guides the overall design and interpretation of findings.

Further developmental hurdles facing the child include the Piagetian notions of centration, transformation, object permanence, and conservation of the absolute quantity and quality of objects. These ideas are central to numerous analyses of cognition and attitude formation. Such cognitive development theorizing has so far disproportionately informed research on the development of attitudes on racial, ethnic, gender, and other social statuses. This influence has too often resulted in an illusory portrait of the nature of children's behavior in everyday life, as well as a neglect of the racial–ethnic attitudes and behaviors of young children. Moreover, this neglect of how young children begin to incorporate racial and ethnic concepts into their lives exacerbates and extends the influence of racism in U.S. society. By neglecting how children learn about these matters, we neglect some of the reproduction processes that undergird the nation's continuing racist system.

RESEARCH ON CHILDREN'S
RACIAL AND ETHNIC CONCEPTS

Children and Racial Concepts

One difficulty in recent research on children and racial matters is a certain distancing of researchers from those they try to study. Indeed, most studies have used research methodologies centered around attitude testing, behavioral checklists, or modest field experiments. Occasionally, surveys of children's attitudes are undertaken, but usually not for children younger than about seven years of age. These surveys typically have a very limited scope and generally rely on simple yes-and-no response questions to gauge attitudes toward social issues.

This now substantial literature has developed over several decades and embodies some well-known findings about racial matters in the United States. For example, white children have consistently been found to prefer their own racial group to any other, and they do so from a young age (Clark, Hocevar, and Dembo 1980; Horowitz 1936; Lasker 1929; Morland 1966; Troyna and Hatcher 1992). Moreover, many African American children have been shown to share that preference, sometimes to the point of apparently misidentifying themselves as white (Spencer 1982; Spencer 1984; Spencer and Horowitz 1973). Dark-skinned children are regarded as devalued members of society by its youngest members, even when those young members are themselves dark-skinned (Aboud 1977; Weiland and Coughlin 1979; Williams and Morland 1976). Despite some evidence suggesting that racial relations among older children may be improving (Aboud 1988), low levels of cross-race friendship and little evidence of voluntary association between groups of children have been noted. Ordinarily, children do not try to develop relationships with those in other racial–ethnic groups unless they are directed by teachers or other significant adults.

Yet, in regard to racial and ethnic issues, surprisingly few research studies have made observations of children's actual day-to-day relationships with each other in order to inform knowledge of or theorizing about children. Only occasionally have researchers sought children's understandings directly, beyond brief responses to check-off tests. Only a few studies have actually interviewed children or made in-depth, long-term observations to assess their racial, ethnic, and other social attitudes. Fortunately, there is a slowly growing number of studies where the researchers are engaging in in-depth interviewing or direct field observation of children in their natural settings (Thorne 1993; Connolly 1998). Thorne (1993) has pioneered in research on children's understanding of gender. Holmes (1995) and Connolly (1998) have done the same in interviewing children about their racial understandings. Researchers such as Thorne, Holmes, and Connolly, however, have not examined younger children (under five years of age, for example) and have generally employed their field methods to study older elementary school or high school children.

Moreover, influenced by long-established research traditions, even some otherwise insightful field investigations have proceeded under the assumption that young children are uncomplicated and incapable of using major abstract concepts. Some researchers often proceed in their investigations from the apparent assumption that children are ignorant of racist behaviors unless actively taught otherwise, and the researchers rely on these assumptions in their research interpretations and designs—that is, the questions they ask youngsters are couched in developmentally appropriate terminology. For example, Holmes (1995) reports that her research entailed ethnographic field studies of young children and that she sought to discover the real meaning of race for children. Still, like previous researchers, she frames her work in cognitive development terms and evaluates children's responses to direct, adult-framed questioning about their attitudes. She straightforwardly asked kindergarten children if they thought there were "any differences" between Black and white children and requested that they draw pictures of different racial groups. This sanctioning adult's overt concern with racial distinctions was apparent to the children, to the point where some of them were reluctant to participate in Holmes's research and exhibited anxiety about her questioning.

Moreover, using Piagetian terminology in her interpretation, Holmes questions whether "race" is a useful concept for analysis of young children, in effect rejecting it because of the "arbitrary and imprecise nature of the existing biological and cultural definitions of race" (Holmes 1995, 4). She prefers to use "ethnic group" instead of "racial group" as a relevant way to describe the concept at hand and denote what are usually racial groups for the children. Thus, she specifically limits her understanding of children's conceptions of race. She further admits that, since she has never given her own race a moment's thought, she finds it "reasonable to suppose that, for children and adults, being a color is equated with just being a person" (Holmes 1995, 54). Given this stance, it is perhaps surprising that she reports from her field study that race is a meaningful part of children's lives. Still, she concludes that race, while an important variable in children's lives, provides them with no significant social dilemmas.

Most continuing research on children and race does not involve in-depth interviewing or participant observation in the field. An explicit emphasis on psychological testing is often coupled with models of children having very limited understandings of racial concepts (Goodman 1964; Porter 1971; Katz 1976). Moreover, much research exploring children's attitudes still relies heavily on traditional Piagetian theory and proceeds from the general assumption that, since young children's minds are naive or egocentric, they have little or no capacity for handling complex abstractions applicable to social interaction (see Aboud 1988; Ramsey 1987). Wardle (1992) summarizes cognitive development theory on children as depicting three- to seven-year-olds as egocentric, reliant on concrete rather than abstract knowledge, and possessed of no complex ideas about such things as racial identities. From this perspective, racial distinctions have little significance until children are able to use the appropriate concepts in the same way as adults would. Since children do not conceptualize race in the same manner as adults, they do not conceive of race either negatively or positively, as adults do. For the three- or four-year-old, matters of race are as uncomplicated as those dealing with what color to use for ducks in a coloring book. The color of people is as inconsequential as the color of ducks, according to this conventional cognitive model. No larger social understandings or meanings are attached to colors.

Major cognitive-developmental theories derived from Piaget's standpoint stress that children's expressed social attitudes reflect their stage of ego-centered cognitive development rather than actual social experiences, insisting that their attitudes on social phenomena are limited by their developmental stage. Some researchers utilizing this framework develop experimental techniques and statistical interpretations of the data obtained. The emphasis in psychological testing and experimental studies is on assessing the linear development of measurable attitudes that are assumed to develop to a logical, adultcentric endpoint. Research on racial attitudes in young children driven by this perspective centers on children's abilities to accurately process age-appropriate racial information provided by adults in narrowly focused testing scenarios. This mainstream approach position is exemplified in Bigler and Liben's (1993) study of children's racial attitudes. Their work used pictures and stories, designed in advance by adults, depicting white and Black characters in stereotypical scenarios as seen by adults. These were presented to children in a testing situation. The children were first told stories about these pictures; then the investigator asked them to look at another set of pictures depicting people of various racial groups, ages, and genders. The cognitive task for the child was to "accurately" sort these pictures of imaginary individuals into groups of "people who go together." This activity, coupled with the children's responses to an oral test of racial attitudes, was used as an indicator of racial prejudice.[2]

In such adult-centered research the accuracy of the child's description is determined by his or her ability to approximate the standards that adults have predetermined. Such research generally does not account for how the children themselves, among themselves, define or view a racial group—their own or that of the others. Nor does it try to determine the criteria children use to resolve what racial or ethnic group an individual child belongs to. This adult-oriented technique focuses on prejudice predefined in line with adult forms of understanding and thus does not require research on how children in practice define and shape their views on racial matters. All the children must do is respond to adult-provided racial tests or markers, which may or may not be pertinent to the children's expanding knowledge of the socio-racial world. Such research often seems more concerned with obtaining reproducible results than for understanding the nature and development of prejudice and of the variety of racial–ethnic distinctions and concepts among children in situ. The everyday realities of life for children and how they live it are neglected in the interest of obtaining a snapshot of individual attitudes in a brief and, too often, superficial examination of the suspected state of mind of individual children. These researchers center their interpretation of the data on the deficit model of intellectual functioning assumed to be central in the "preoperational" young child. Under this model, children lack essential knowledge, information assumed to be critical for accomplishing adult behavior.[3]

Another limitation of the traditional psychological testing or experimental method—or, in fact, any research asserting implicitly or explicitly the sanctioning authority of the adult researcher—is that children know they are being tested by sanctioning adults and are in all likelihood responding by searching for the "right" answer. That is, they are responding by providing researchers with what they expect, as Piaget himself pointed out. Children often know that our research activities are not just the games we present them as, but are intentional information-gathering operations for adult purposes. When it comes to much research on race, the right answer the children are expected to give is that "we are all the same inside" (see Holmes 1995). For youngsters engaged in a structured question-and-answer activity with a powerful adult, the motivation to please the adult is strong. Researchers are misguided if they think children are unaware of these intentions. Adults rarely engage in such "games" with children unless they want information. Furthermore, when the topic of such a game is a forbidden or socially loaded one, children become even more alert and are likely to be circumspect in their responses. Indeed, drawing on discussions with hundreds of children on racial questions, Hughes (1997, 123) concluded that "children think race but believe that they should not." They know that many adults frown on dis-cussions of race, at least on the part of children.

Thus, assumptions about what children know, or do not know, have too often handicapped research on children. In one important study, Aboud (1988) relies on a cognitive-deficit model to frame an examination of prejudice in children, in spite of her declaration that research should not brush off children's attitudes as reflections of parental attitudes. Para-phrasing Piaget, she asserts that "certain components of the definition [of racial attitudes] are too sophisticated to exist as such in children. For ex-ample, the psychological structures of children are generally simpler than those of adults, in the sense of being less differentiated and less inte-grated" (Aboud 1988, 4). Although many studies show that young chil-dren display racial prejudice, Aboud (1988, 4) warns that researchers should "expect the structure of prejudice to be simpler in children, per-haps less organized and perhaps less categorical when they are very young." Such expectations seem to lead many scholars to discover what they expect to discover: that racial attitudes and prejudices in children are, if not rare, at least quite different from those in adults—that is, they are much less formed and very rudimentary. Moreover, a finding of less racial prejudice is often transformed by many adults who are reluctant to ac-knowledge any prejudice in children into "no" significant prejudice.

Traditional research presumptions that children are unable to seri-ously discern or understand complex social relationships are often linked to measurements of children's knowledge about social concepts that rely on predetermined levels of cognitive functioning and development. The instruments used represent children's performance in structured "age-appropriate" terms. Appropriateness is determined by the same theories of development that declare that children below certain ages (ordinarily, under seven) are not sufficiently developed to perform successfully on at-titudinal and related tests designed for adults or older children. One re-sult is that tests and scales are reconstructed and simplified to ensure that young children are not confused by inappropriate material. Although these instruments are designed with an eye toward discovering the extent of children's abilities to discern and describe social concepts, what they often produce is a detailed account of children's inability to respond to tests at an adult level of understanding. The logic driving such research seems to be this: Because young children are more or less egocentric, they do not have a sustained ability to take another's point of view. Fur-ther, young children do not have the ability to understand complex so-cial behaviors. By extension, because young children cannot comprehend complex behavior, they cannot understand categorizing along racial lines, since this entails the active, intentional, and socially based behaviors of older children or adults. Since children cannot behave in these socially specific ways, they cannot understand the complex implications of established racial and gender arrangements. As we have noted, the young child's racialized and gendered behavior, under Piagetian analysis, is defined as preoperational. Thus, it is not a function of serious cognitive action, and it can easily be downplayed by the researchers.

In addition, some research on racial issues focuses on the development of racial understandings among adolescents or adults (see Arce 1981; Cross 1991; Helms 1990; Kim 1981; Phinney and Rotheram 1987). In this developmental literature younger children's attitudes on race are ignored or viewed as unimportant for understanding adults' attitudinal development (Cross 1991), or they may be explained away as imitative of family surroundings (Kim 1981).[4] Adding racial distinctions and concepts to the developmental picture creates a conceptual problem for some developmentalists. They often assert that in general children's early experiences are important for later development, yet also insist that early experiences with *racial* distinctions are not so consequential. The development model accenting early experiences is applied to most behavior except that of racial experiences and behavior, which are usually held to belong solely to the province of older people. In this literature children are often seen as capable of developing working hypotheses on some complex social behaviors, such as understanding social status and friendship. Yet, when it comes to racism, children are depicted as mostly or entirely blameless or ignorant.

AN ALTERNATIVE PERSPECTIVE ON RACIAL LEARNING

If one observes children carefully in their own settings and in peer group interactions, as we did, it is apparent that a partial, developing understanding of the adult dynamics of racial–ethnic relations does not hinder children from developing their own complex racial and ethnic dynamics in interaction with others, be they young or old. While some scholars have argued that young children do not understand the economic or political significance of racially based stratification (Hughes 1997, 121; Hirschfeld 1997, 81), a highly developed, well-thought-out racial ideology is not necessary for children to make and develop complex racial distinctions in their everyday behavior. The nature of coping with daily life can be an important factor. As some researchers (Miller, Galanter, and Pribram 1960) point out, any plan of action for behavior that a social actor might choose is drawn from a set of potential plans, all developed out of the experience of everyday living. Commonsense procedures, drawn from encountering facts of social life, are used to generate explanations for how life is handled on a daily basis. For children, attention to racial or ethnic distinctions arises from their salience to interactional situations at hand. They are meaningful to children because they are significant in *their* social worlds. The very real images of racial and ethnic groups are available to the children through direct observation of the world around them, and these images are grounded in the dynamic social structure of the society—as seen around them and in the mass media—and in their past and ongoing interactions with other adults and children. Many choices of action accumulate over a period of time and constantly reinforce race and ethnicity as developing, working concepts for children.

The Sociocentric World

We see our work as part of an emerging literature that treats children, including young children, as more than empty vessels into which adults put their own ideas, concepts, and attitudes. As we have noted above, there is a slowly growing number of researchers who are doing studies of children—less often young children—in their own natural settings and who are focusing on how children create their own meanings in interaction with one another, without assuming what children are capable of knowing or not knowing. We have in mind here the "interpretive reproduction" work of the pioneering developmentalist Bill Corsaro (1979; 1981; 1997), who has researched children interacting in their natural settings, and the fine work of social psychologists Troyna and Hatcher (1992), who have studied British ten- and eleven-year-olds in everyday interactions about racial matters. Here, too, we would place some of the cutting-edge work in developmental psychology and psychological anthropology, such as that of Rogoff (1998) and Hirschfeld (1997). Writing of the emergence of "sociocultural theory," Rogoff (1998) argues strongly that cognitive development occurs as new generations collaborate among themselves and with older generations. Indeed, Rogoff (1998, 680) has noted the uphill struggle necessary to make this point central to research and analysis: "The idea that cognition is a process involving more than the solo individual is still new to many cognitive developmentalists." Hirschfeld (1997) accents the ways in which children construct their own culture, including adult-like understandings of race. We especially have in mind here the pioneering fieldwork of Thorne (1993), who observed how fourth- and fifth-grade children actually "do gender." Hopefully, this emerging wave of research can become a flood as we move to deeper and better understandings of the everyday, natural worlds of children of all ages.

In making sense out of the social contexts of children's learning and use of racial and ethnic concepts, we have found certain aspects of the conceptual frameworks of George Herbert Mead and Lev Vygotsky more useful for investigating cognitive and behavioral development than that of Piagetian thinking. Mead (1934) accents the social, and not the individual, world as being primary for human beings. The whole society is prior to the part, the individual, and thus the part is generally to be explained in terms of the whole, and not the reverse. Most important, human beings are generally reflective about their actions and are thus able to choose among a diverse range of possible actions. Mead used the idea of the "social mind," that is, the idea that human knowledge develops mainly within the settings of human interaction. As Sjoberg and Vaughan (1993a, 58) summarize it, how human beings

> reflect about their social world is grounded in the social process. The logical modes of reasoning persons employ, their domain assumptions, and their social memory are shaped by human interaction. . . . The social mind permits human agents to respond in a proactive manner and thereby to cope with and at times remake the . . . structures that mold their thought processes in the first instance.

Note that in the Mead tradition the social mind involves social memory. The ways in which we learn and develop are shaped by the social memory of past experiences and interpretations; this memory provides tools that both children and adults use for their social and personal lives (Sjoberg and Vaughan 1993b, 135).

Yet another aspect of the social mind is the way in which it helps to shape one's sense of the larger social order. Indeed, the reflections and interpretations that we make of the social order include our attempts to justify that order, including its moral norms, hierarchies, and inequalities. Such justifications take place especially when we are challenged by others, for both adults and children, as we saw in the opening example of Carla's justification of her discriminatory action. Children, like adults, become *human* beings in interaction with other human beings. The view of one's social identity, as well as of one's group, comes from everyday interactions with others. This social-mind perspective rejects the traditional individual-centered views in Western thought, including that of the mainline Piaget tradition. In our analysis, young children are no less able than adults to interact and learn from interaction. Within the contexts of interaction they deliberate and decide on actions, often of a very sophisticated kind.

Relatively recently, the work of Lev Vygotsky has been utilized by a number of child development researchers (for example, Corsaro 1997; Rogoff 1998) to give much more attention to the collaborative and interactional contexts in which children learn. Vygotsky's major work did not capture much attention in the United States until the late 1970s and 1980s. Vygotsky (1978) depicts human beings, including children, as social actors solidly involved in reflecting upon and creating the patterns of their own lives. There are several components to Vygotskian theory that contribute to its usefulness in the sociological analysis of children's racial and ethnic relations and understandings. First, most parts of a typical child's mental and conceptual development are social: "All higher functions originate as actual relations between individuals" (Vygotsky 1978, 57).

From this perspective, interaction is critical to, if not prior to, the development of the sense of the individual self. Activities that start as external and detached become part of the child actor's internal makeup through mental and actual reconstruction of the activity over time, incorporating and re-creating social events in a long series of developmental steps. Human experiences originate, to a substantial degree, in interaction with the relevant others. For Vygotsky, it is children's participation in a broad array of cultural and societal activities that enables them to learn the social tools available for their own learning efforts (see Rogoff 1998, 683). Interestingly, in some of his early writings in the 1920s Piaget himself speculated on the importance of children cooperating with their peers as part of their cognitive development, yet this idea "did not become a major focus of his theory or research" (Rogoff 1998, 684). In addition, in his limited speculations, Piaget notes interpersonal contexts and not the larger cultural and societal contexts of children's learning that were central to Vygotsky's analyses.

Vygotsky also posits that children's development does not proceed in a straightforward, linear manner. Instead, cognitive development proceeds in fits and starts, at times regressing a bit and at other times exploding in several directions at once. This seems to be a type of "punctuated equilibrium," a term one might adapt from evolutionary biology. As children collect experiences with others, the richness and complexity of those experiences will impel and reshape their cognitive processing and organization. Casual observation of children verifies this idea. Parents often report that their growing youngsters seem to have forgotten what they learned only a few weeks ago or that suddenly children appear to gain maturity and thoughtfulness that seemed impossible only days before. This seemingly capricious nature of development is much more clearly understood if we assume that development is intimately tied to everyday, accumulating, lived experiences rather than being a stage-bound, rigid function of age. Incorporating children's social experiences thoroughly and centrally into our explanatory scheme enables us to account for the nature of children's racial awareness in a much more direct fashion. Accenting the development of their "social minds" also allows us to view individual children as actors in their own developmental progress, rather than seeing them as mere imitators of the significant adults in their lives.

Like much of the child development literature, much in traditional social science analysis has conceptualized the socialization of children as a process in which complete adults instruct and train incomplete children, who thus imitate and mirror adults (Mackay 1974). As we have noted for Mead and Vygotsky, this notion that children imitate adults has an important element of truth. We human beings do not create our personal and social worlds out of nothing. We take the elements found in our social environments—what we call the tools from the social toolbox—and use them for our own purposes. Indeed, contrary to certain traditional Piagetian approaches, young children make use of social tools in rather early stages of childhood. There are a limited number of social tools available for children, as there are for adults, and few children invent entirely new tools of their own.

Nonetheless, the idea of imitation and modeling is inadequate for describing the full-fledged developmental lives of young children. Children, like all human beings, actively reshape, blend, and synthesize elements of the preexisting patterns found around them—in families, other social settings, and the mass media. As evident throughout this book, most children are in no sense the passive receptacles of adult socialization. They take an active part in their own socialization, interacting with other children and with adults in this ongoing process. While children do learn much from others, their originality and inventiveness—in effect, their distinctive personalities—are developed in personal and interpersonal experimentation with the tools provided to them.

This is a critical point worth underscoring. The children we observed in the day care center are actually *doing* life. They are not going through some waiting period during which their main goals are to mirror quietly or aggressively the ways of adults, delaying actual socializing, understanding, and performance until they are older. The children we observed take various bits of racial and ethnic information from the surrounding world and then experiment with and use that information in their everyday interactions with other children and with adults. Often, the information with which they are dealing is "hot," in the sense that adults—especially white adults—consider that information to be inappropriate for "naive," young children to use. It is perhaps surprising that many adults often take the position that children *do not know* about racial matters and similar controversial subjects, for most of these adults themselves hid controversial actions from their own parents. Moreover, young children sometimes play an important part in exposing and bringing to the fore certain social realities, to the discomfort of most parents, such as when they speak in unedited terms about what adults wish to hide. Most of the young white children in our study are helping to build, or rebuild, a racialized society with their own hands with materials learned from the racial order of the adult world surrounding them.

The importance of the social connection, context, and mind cannot be exaggerated. Karl Marx (1971, 77) was one of the first social thinkers to capture this point well: Society does not consist of individuals; it expresses the *sum of connections and relationships* in which individuals find themselves. How people, including children, understand the world begins within their connections to the others in their lives. Nowhere is this better pointed out than in the work of Maurice Halbwachs (1950), especially in his essays on collective memory. According to Halbwachs, for almost all human beings there is no possibility of being *dis*connected from the social world. Human thoughts, even the most private and isolated, are collective, "since we always carry with us and in us a number of distinct persons" (Halbwachs 1950, 23). Human experiences are perceived through the many lenses provided by others' connections to us through time. Nor are connections limited only to those others in our immediate social context. As Mead also reminds us with his concept of social mind, people draw information about the world from others they have never met, others who may have more indirect influences. For example, most Americans today rely on the various mass media to obtain information about our world. We literally cannot collect much of this vital information on our own. In addition to mere data, we collect the opinions, attitudes, and social connections of writers, commentators, and journalists who produce our raw information. Data rarely arrive in our lives without being filtered through someone else's experiences. We adults are as much constrained and enabled by others in our lives as children are by adults.

The Piaget tradition has seen some dissent on key concepts. Since at least the 1970s, a few child development researchers have conducted research that raised questions about aspects of the Piaget theory of egocentricity. For example, in her experiments Helen Borke (1971; see also Maratsos 1973; Siegler 1998) found that children as young as three showed an awareness of other people's feelings and could identify situations evoking different emotional responses. She concluded that "children are not totally egocentric but have some capacity for responding empathetically to another person's perspective and point of view" (Borke 1971, 263). Also, research on children's perceptions of reality shows that when children are presented with experimental choices that reflect their experiences, by the age of three they can clearly distinguish between reality and the nonreal (Woolley and Wellman 1990; Siegler 1998). When egocentric positioning is not afforded primacy in the understanding of young children, a different image of children's abilities in the social world emerges.

Children are adept at making sense of their world within the limitations of their own cultural and behavioral experiences. Our data in later chapters show how racial and ethnic concepts, understandings, and proclivities are integral components of the social toolbox available to young children. Like adults, children are not limited to what is taught to them directly and do not have to actually experience events in order to appreciate their significance. The toolbox of others' experiences and social knowledge is usually open, and its contents are available to almost anyone. Once most young children recognize the importance of racial and ethnic distinctions as meaningful concepts, they begin to reconstruct them into substantial intellectual and interactional devices of their own making, equipment suitable for use in their social milieu.

In addition, the importance of language, both spoken and that used in thought, is accented by Vygotsky and those working in his tradition. Culture, inculcating as it does prior human perspectives and ongoing practices, has a major shaping impact on the formation and evolution of the human mind. One key aspect of this culture is language and the concepts that language reflects and embeds. As children learn to use a home language, they develop their abilities to deal with the external world and in the process learn to think—mostly in terms of the concepts and metaphors carried in that language (see Lakoff and Johnson 1980). As shown throughout this book, the thinking of children about racial and ethnic matters is constantly interwoven with the use of language. As the children's bodies and minds grow, they gather, use, and adopt language and related concepts from their cultural heritage. This provides tools to manipulate both their physical and social worlds.

A key part of our argument is that children learn *by doing*, not just by parroting the views of adults. The cultural past of racialized language and thought is constantly pressed on children from the outside, but it is the active construction of racial concepts and ideas that is central to their lives. In everyday social interaction children utilize the surrounding culture's features and tools in their own ways to create individual and social realities. This use of culture in interaction reinforces the meanings of new ideas and concepts in their active minds. While most racial and ethnic concepts are initially conveyed from the outside, children internalize the concepts most completely when they use them in regular or recurring interactions where they can observe the effects that such usage has on other children and on adults. By using racialized language in social contexts, children develop their own individuality in relation to others, garner attention from other children and adults, and—at least in the case of the dominant-group children—develop a strong sense of power over others. The "doing" of racial and ethnic matters is what embeds these things strongly in their minds.

Periods of social time are requisites for the process of constructing concepts. The construction of abstract, complicated social concepts is accomplished through long-term interactional use of the concepts in daily social activity. The social memory must be individually incorporated. Appropriate social behavior is not learned overnight or even in a few years. It takes years of accumulating experience to become a highly functioning, social individual. Thus, all aspects of an individual's interactive history come into play in shaping how immediate behavior is transformed into thought, and thought into action.

Another component of Vygotskian theory that is supported in our data is the contention that child development is not a smooth process of orderly change moving to a definable goal of maturity. Rather, cognitive development is an uneven, often spasmodic adaptive process, which responds to internal and external stimuli and transforms social experiences into complex systems of meanings. Children can take giant steps forward toward integrating some social conceptions while simultaneously taking small steps backward for others. How racial, gender, or class notions become significant tools for social use is, at least in part, influenced both by children's positions in their own worlds and the meaning of these notions in the larger social world. If a social conception is powerful and affords its user authority in social interaction, it is fairly likely that it will become an essential component of the toolbox, often one with enormous social force.

Finally, and perhaps most importantly for understanding the development of racially and ethnically oriented behavior in young children, interactive *play* and the experimental world of play are central to this theory of development. Vygotsky views play as a more powerful determinant of learning than direct instruction, because of play's immediacy and importance for the child. Through play with others a child is connected to the social world, a tie that is a critical developmental need. As we see it, a central flaw in much mainstream analysis of child development is the conception of play as a child's "other world," an unreal world existing only in a child's mind or naivete. In Vygotskian terms, however, children's attempts to make sense of the world through manipulating it in play are very serious and can have long-term individual and social consequences. Indeed, in this sense "play" may not be the most accurate English word for this recurring activity of children. What they do is often more serious and adult-like than the term "play" suggests, especially since the commonsense understanding of play is that it is frivolous, insignificant activity. Indeed, adjectives used with "play" include "simple," "easy," and "naive." We are suggesting that this conceptualization must be abandoned if we are to come to a more complete understanding of social life (see Thorne 1993). Children become functioning humans in part through their interactive play with others. Action in play is a crucial factor for children, enabling them to learn about and operate in the social world by relying on internal constructs and meanings, as well as on external social stimuli. The various worlds of childhood are not separate or separable entities, and they likely contain no more fantasies than do those of adults. Learning to be social is often arduous work, not effortless play.

In our research and that of others in the tradition of studying children in their natural settings, we see young children actively and routinely constructing their own lives in association with relevant others. Peer groups are very important in this learning and constructing process. Rogoff (1998, 711) sums this up:

> Thus peers may fill important roles seldom taken by adults. Peer inter-
> action may foster exploration without immediate goals, which in the
> long run may lead to insightful solutions to unforeseen problems. Peers
> may also provide each other with engagement in building their own so-
> cial structure and opportunities to learn to take others' perspectives.

As peers, children can explore concepts, emotions, and actions more openly and equally, and usually with less fear of harsh sanctions. Moreover, most children are good historians and natural interpreters of everyday life. They remember a great deal, as many adults learn to their regret, and reintegrate that in their current and later lives. Indeed, most children become practical experts about social interaction. In interaction with their peers and with adults, children strive to learn about and provide meaning for compelling social phenomena. Racial and ethnic distinctions are among such phenomena. One motivating force lies in developing the ability to act independently of direct stimuli. The development of independence, the creation of willful behavior, informs both what the child will perceive as a compelling social stimuli and how this perception is put into action. Through experience, meaning moves beyond the recognition of shape, color, and size and proceeds toward recognition of relations and critical symbols.

Studying Children in Their Natural Worlds

In this book we accent the study of children's experiences in their actual social worlds. As several researchers (Lee 1975; see also the literature summary in Rogoff 1998, 708) have demonstrated, even an infant can be seen to be sociocentric if the researcher focuses on actual interactive experiences of babies. Babies put social skills to work almost immediately, engaging caretakers in a process of give and take and ensuring that needs are met. Lee describes these experiences and details the social nature of, for example, pointing at an object, a behavior that babies are masters of by the end of their first year. Pointing at an object with the intent of calling another's attention to it requires the baby to be aware of the necessity of drawing someone else's notice. That is, this suggests that the baby can assume the perspective of the other, determine that the other is unaware, and decide that their notice is important. These tasks, following a strict Piagetian logic, should be beyond the cognitive capability of infants. An examination of a baby's behavior, however, will reveal that they often point purposefully—strong evidence that they are attuned to the mental state of those around them.

Significantly, not one of the most heralded classical social theorists, such as Karl Marx, Max Weber, Emile Durkheim, Georg Simmel, and Maurice Halbwachs, paid attention to the sociology of children and childhood. Even Halbwachs, the master of social memory, declared that a young child was "not yet a social being" (Halbwachs 1950, 35). For these male social scientists, socialization and the reality of social statuses and categorizing seem to develop and flourish without significant beginnings in early childhood, at least not beginnings that need much conceptual or theoretical attention. Interestingly, the work of early women sociologists such as Jane Addams took childhood and children's socialization very seriously. Her important book *The Spirit of Youth and City Streets* (1909) and other neglected writings on children by early sociologists are finally being rediscovered and reconsidered (see Deegan 2000).

Since the 1980s, several social science researchers have expanded development theory in the direction of a better understanding of the sociocultural contexts of child socialization and development. For example, the "interpretive reproduction theory" of researchers such as Bill Corsaro and his associates (see Corsaro and Miller 1992) does not reject the constructivist aspects of Piagetian theory but argues for greater research and conceptual attention to collective processes and interpretive reproduction done by children in their own social worlds. The more child-centered theoretical frameworks place children solidly in the social world and suggest that their own interactions provide both the origin of mental functioning and the various meanings for social concepts (Peterson and McCabe 1994). These researchers stress the need for child-centered research. Corsaro (1979) pioneered in showing how young children are informed actors within the social production of everyday life. Sullivan, Zaitchik, and Tager-Flusberg (1994) demonstrate that three-year-olds maintain complex mental-belief systems, and Dunn (1993) illustrates how children maintain complex networks of relationships. Significantly, studies of gender understandings among children (Thorne 1993; Bem 1989) suggest that the more traditional researchers underestimate children's abilities to negotiate social constructs. Young children behave in gender-specific ways, and they can describe and explain gender categorizing and positioning in some detail to an interested adult.

Still, this new child-centered approach accenting studies of children in their own natural settings has not as yet systematically examined racial or ethnic concepts, understandings, actions, and emotions among younger children. Thus, Corsaro's (1997) excellent overview book barely mentions children learning about racial concepts and behaviors.

Influenced by this new focus on young children as independent actors and constructors, we argue that children as young as three and four employ racial and ethnic concepts as important integrative and symbolically creative tools in the daily construction of their social lives. There is scattered support for this argument in the research literature, although it is just beginning to be better theorized. Research studies indicate that children as young as three can have negative biases toward others of different racial groups, even if they have never seen a person of another group (Ramsey 1987). White children as young as three and four have been found to prefer stimuli showing other whites (Aboud 1988; Hughes

1997, 122). Hirschfeld (1997, 84) found that most three-year-olds and virtually all four-year-olds could match pictures of children of different racial groups (who were said to be raised by adoptive parents of another race) with pictures of their birth parents; "clearly, children naturalize race." Other studies (Bigler and Liben 1993) have found that children can also attribute an individual's ability, or lack of ability, to their racial group, even in the face of contradictory evidence presented to them.

The few researchers who have observed children's actual behavior outside of laboratories or of structured research settings in schools have found that children are strongly aware of racial and ethnic matters in their everyday lives (Spencer 1987; Troyna and Hatcher 1992). From interviews with five- and six-year-old children in a multiracial school in England, Paul Connolly concluded that they have substantial competence in dealing with racial matters. He views their racial understandings as complex and sophisticated and takes them seriously. Focusing heavily on the discourses of these children in interviews with an adult researcher, Connolly (1998, 187) reports that the children were able to actively "appropriate, rework and reproduce discourses on 'race,' gender and sexuality in quite complex ways." Connolly's work is important in dealing with race and gender, yet it has the methodological limitations associated with the (sanctioning) adult researcher versus child subject approach (see below). Our own work, as shown below, goes beyond Connolly's and similar fieldwork methodologically and focuses on much more than discourse by examining the everyday behavior of children interactively doing race and ethnicity.

Over the last few decades substantial research on race and children has involved studies of Black children, with particular interest in determining the young Black child's level of awareness of racial group and level of self-esteem (see Clark and Clark 1939; Clark and Clark 1947). If three-year-old Black children can recognize the existence and nature of two disparate cultures and function in both, and there is ample evidence that they can, then it is reasonable to assume that they can use racial concepts in the conduct of their everyday lives. Further, if three-year-old Black children have these capabilities, there is good reason to expect that children in many different groups can recognize, use, and precisely render the complex meanings of race and ethnicity in their social worlds. If, as a wealth of research demonstrates, young Black children are able to realize that they have a place in society and that this status is denigrated, then it is reasonable to assume that young children in general, regardless of skin color, are able to comprehend complex social concepts. That is, if Black children as young as three can be what Cross (1991) calls "biculturally compe-tent," then a similar competency might be assumed for other groups, such as white immigrant children, Native American children, and Latino Amer-ican children. Furthermore, because virtually all children—of all racial and ethnic backgrounds—are immersed in the disparate worlds of childhood and adulthood, they might be described as already functioning bicultur-ally in two divergent worlds at early ages. Children accommodate the rel-atively huge cognitive tasks of recognizing the existence and nature of both their own and the majority of adult cultures and selecting appropri-ate behaviors for conducting themselves in each. They usually accomplish this very early in life.

CONTENDING WITH AN ESTABLISHED RACIST CONTEXT

Understanding the daily behavior of children, their "doing racism," re-quires knowledge of the larger societal context. It is not enough just to look at the microworld of their everyday interactions, for the larger con-text constantly "crashes in" on this everyday world, as shown in many ex-amples in the chapters to follow. Life is a moving feast, but it has its con-straining structures and indelible markers, many of which can resist change for long periods of time. As we observe children's behavior, we see them operating within the constraints imposed from outside—from adults and their own playmates. As Connell (1985, 267) has pointed out, the constraining and channeling power of social oppression is very important. The system of racism in U.S. society is something that people, including children, constantly bump up against and find to be constantly pressing on their everyday lives. For children of color in particular, this hard and harsh reality is complex and nuanced, and it is realized in the everyday practices and actions of other people, including white parents, teachers, and other children.

Throughout this book we develop insights toward a more general the-ory of racial relations, which in most cases is a theory of racist relations (see Feagin 2000). We see how children learn and express racial concepts and at-titudes and how they implement these in practices. Their interracial and interethnic relations are socially produced. What Connell (1985, 269) says for social relations generally applies to racial relations: "The social is radically un-natural, and its structures can never be deduced from natural structures."

Today, many white adults openly argue that racism targeting African Americans and other Americans of color is no longer a major problem central to U.S. society—that really serious racism was mostly taken care of by the civil rights laws and civil rights movements of the 1960s. If there is any serious racism left, it is said to be limited to isolated instances or scattered extremists on the fringe of society. Indeed, many whites couple this broad societal view with the related assertion that "I am not a racist," often while they assert in the next moment some negative view about the racial "others." Today, the majority of white Americans seem to be in denial about the seriousness of racial prejudices, emotions, and discrimination in their own lives, the lives of their friends and relatives, and the larger society. This often loudly proclaimed denial takes a number of forms. As evidenced in later chapters, the white adults with whom we came in contact often suggested some version of this denial, if only in proclamations about children's innocence about racial and ethnic oppression.

Yet, the realities of everyday life in the United States dramatically refute such denials of the persistence of racism. Racial discrimination and segregation are still central organizing factors in contemporary U.S. society. The impact of discrimination is readily apparent, and even a casual observation of American social organization will reveal its continuing presence. For the most part, whites and Blacks do not live in the same neighborhoods, attend the same schools at all educational levels, enter into close friendships or other intimate relationships with one another, or share comparable opinions on a wide variety of political matters. The same is true, though sometimes to a lesser extent, for whites and other Americans of color, such as most Latino, Native, and Asian American groups. Despite some progress since the 1960s, U.S. society remains intensely segregated across color lines. Generally speaking, whites and people of color do not occupy the same social space or social status, and this very visible fact of American life does not go unnoticed by children.

We do not have the space here to document the full range of institutional and individual racism, but we can provide some research data demonstrating the continuing reality of systemic racism in the United States. By "systemic racism" we mean much more than just negative attitudes toward a racial–ethnic outgroup. This term encompasses many dimensions of white-determined racism: the white attitudes, emotions, practices, and institutions that are central to white domination of African Americans and other Americans of color. Racist attitudes and discriminatory practices deny African Americans and other Americans of color the opportunities, positions, and privileges that are available to whites as a group (Feagin and Vera 1995). In North American history systemic racism began in the early 1600s, with white colonists killing

Native Americans for their lands and enslaving African Americans to work those lands. This system of racism was legally recognized in the 1787 U.S. Constitution, was perpetuated after the end of slavery for more than a century (until 1969) under legal segregation, and continues today in the many forms of discrimination targeting African Americans and other Americans of color.

Negative racial attitudes directed at African Americans and other Americans of color remain commonplace. For example, an Anti-Defamation League (1993) survey asked white respondents to evaluate eight anti-Black stereotypes, including such items as Black Americans "prefer to accept welfare" and have "less native intelligence." Three quarters of whites agreed with one or more of these blatant stereotypes, with more than half agreeing with two or more of the stereotypes. Other surveys have shown similar patterns, with large proportions of whites openly expressing anti-Black, anti-Asian, and anti-Latino attitudes to pollsters and survey researchers (see Sniderman and Piazza 1993). Moreover, these results are likely underestimates of the situation, particularly given that some research indicates that adult whites often hide their true feelings on racial matters. The actual picture of anti-Black attitudes among whites is likely to be even more disturbing than these high figures indicate (see Bonilla-Silva and Forman 2000).

The research data also indicate that discriminatory practices by whites are still commonplace across the United States. One study in Los Angeles asked one thousand Black workers about discrimination and found that within the past year six in ten reported discriminatory barriers in their workplaces (Bobo and Suh 1995). Job discrimination was also reported by Asian and Latino workers. Moreover, a federal survey using 3,800 test audits with matched Black and white testers in two dozen large cities estimated that Black renters faced discrimination about half the time and Black homeseekers faced discrimination about 59 percent of the time, when compared to the treatment of the paired white testers (Turner, Struyk, and Yinger 1991, ii–viii). Recent housing audit studies in a half dozen U.S. cities have found high rates of discrimination against Black, Latino, and Asian Americans in rental housing (Feagin 2000).

The bottom line on systemic racism is that white Americans, especially white men of European heritage, still control 95–100 percent of the top and better-paying middle-level positions in most of the major economic, political, and educational organizations across U.S. society. One 1980s study found only twenty Black men and women, together with 318 other (mostly white) women, in the 7,314 most powerful positions across these various institutions (Dye 1986, 190–205). White men make up 95 percent of those with substantial power. More recent studies continue to confirm this pattern of white, or white male, dominance in most institutions and many better-paying job categories (see Feagin 2000).

Historical and contemporary data make it clear that not only white Americans but also Americans of color have been greatly influenced in thought and action by the racialized contexts in which they build lives and communities. For several centuries now, white Americans have constructed an extensive and institutionalized system of racial subordination for non-European Americans. While this racialized system has been most fully developed by whites for Black Americans, beginning in the 1600s, it has been applied to other Americans of color—including those entering this white-dominated society from the mid–nineteenth to the mid–twentieth century, the era when large numbers of Asian and Latino Americans immigrated. These Americans of color came into a system of anti-Black oppression already well embedded in most U.S. institutions. Not surprisingly, then, whites' prejudices and discrimination directed at these latter non-European groups have been greatly shaped by the centuries-old anti-Black system. In addition, for some decades, newer groups such as Asian and Latino Americans have not only faced severe racial stereotyping and discrimination at the hands of whites but also themselves sometimes adopted certain anti-Black ideas and propensities from the white racist context. As we view it, this type of anti-Black prejudice and discrimination has emerged out of the context of systemic *white racism* and is thus, if indirectly, a manifestation of that white racism. More broadly, the negative prejudices and propensities that one group of Americans of color direct toward yet another such group are often shaped by or assimilated from the surrounding white racist context in which they live.

It is within this highly racialized and white-dominated institutional context that the parents of our children, both white and not white, operate and come to their racial attitudes, their racialized views of the social world, and their proactive and reactive behaviors in regard to race. Adult whites learn to do racism—to think, feel, and act in racist ways—within a social and historical context, while those who are not white learn that they must constantly contend with racial hostility and mistreatment in their everyday lives. Moreover, each new generation of children—white, Black, Latino, Asian, and Native American—also comes of age in this framework of systemic racism. Much racial socialization is unconscious, however, barely discernible to them as a component of everyday life. Thus, the unearned privileges and benefits of being white are undiscovered by most and denied by virtually all (McIntosh 1988). Yet the structure is in place, and our children are deeply infused in it and it within them. Learning about racial matters begins early and progresses throughout life, as children begin to identify, accommodate, and engage the various social tools, options, patterns, and statuses available to them.

LEARNING AND PLAYING RACIAL IDENTITY–ROLES

Traditionally, sociologists have distinguished between social statuses and social roles. A status is a socially defined position with attendant obligations and privileges, while a role especially encompasses the active and performing aspect of that position. There are different conceptions of role in the theoretical traditions of the social sciences: Roles are the performing aspects of status positions that are set within a social and cultural framework; roles designate the behavior of those in these status positions; and roles involve shared expectations for role performance by those inside and outside the roles (Biddle 1992, 1682). Individuals accept or reject imposed role expectations in their role performances and by accepting them help reproduce the social structure, which in its turn shapes role performances.

A major problem with this "role" language is that typical social roles, such as those of teacher, student, or doctor, involve situated positions and identities (West and Zimmerman 1987; Biddle 1992; Farmer 1992). Thus, one learns or performs such roles in particular settings. However, if one were to speak of "racial roles," such roles are different from those of teacher, student, and doctor, for the former (like "gender roles") involves a status and identity cutting across many social situations and institutions. Ascribed roles—such as racial and gender roles—stay with people in all situations for their entire lives. They do not appear and disappear from one situation to another. This is in part because of outsiders' role expectations. For example, a Black female child carries with her the racial classification, as she passes from home to school to playground to grocery store. While she is not always in the role of student or shopper, she is always socially constructed as Black or Black female by those whites who encounter her. One can resist the expectations, but the pressures are always there.[5]

Given the crosscutting character of being subordinated as a Black person or other person of color in U.S. society, and the crosscutting position of those defined as "white," conventional "role" language is not sufficient to describe what is happening in the everyday lives of white

Americans and Americans of color. When it is used in regard to conditions of oppression, such as those involving race or gender, this role language has the advantage of accenting the learned character of much that is associated with race and gender in this society, and it suggests that there are important continuities to oppression. However, conventional role language does not accent the deep psychological meanings associated with both race and gender (Stacey and Thorne, 1985).

Given this situation, much recent research on racial issues has accented instead the idea and term of racial "identities" (see Omi and Winant 1994, 88–89). This is often coupled with discussions of the psychological and unconscious dimensions of race for whites and people of color. As shown in later chapters, children, as relatively new members of social institutions, are engaged in a highly interactive, socially regulating process as they monitor and shape their own behavior and that of other children and adults in regard to racial matters. They not only learn and use ideas about race and ethnicity but also embed in their everyday language and practice the understood *identities* of who is white, Black, Latino, and Asian. These (and other) identities and their associated privileges and disadvantages are made concrete and are thus normalized. They are normalized, moreover, not only in the performance of "roles" and "scripts," but also in the deeper psyches and subconscious understandings of children and adults. The children perpetuate and re-create the structures of race and ethnicity not only in society, but also in their social minds and psyches.

It is also important to keep in mind, as we report in our field research accounts, that the understandings of identity involve both the socially constructed racial other's identity and the identity of the person or persons implementing that construction. Much of the social science literature has accented the ways in which white Americans view African Americans and other people of color in negative terms; there are hundreds of articles and books on how whites think about and stereotype people of color. Yet, there is relatively little research and analysis on what Feagin and Vera (1995) have called the "sincere fictions" of the white self—the ways in which whites see themselves positively, often at deep cognitive and emotional levels. For example, the term "anti-Black prejudice" suggests views of the racial others but does not take direct cognizance of the sentiments about the white self generated in interaction with others. The sincere fictions held by white actors often include positive images of whites as "intelligent," "powerful," "good people," or "not racist" and thus represent personal ideological constructions that reproduce societal mythologies at the individual level. In our later accounts we see that young white children early on develop not only negative images of the racial others but also positive images of themselves as whites.

While understandings of identity and self are very important in making sense of the U.S. system of racial and ethnic relations, there is much more to racial and ethnic relationships than these understandings. Too much accent on identity can play down the material, interactional, and action-oriented aspects of racial and ethnic realities. Such a view can be too individually focused for the purpose of understanding interracial matters. As we noted earlier, there is a social and cultural structure of racialized language, concepts, practices, and role expectations within which children operate. As children adopt, adapt, and make these shared expectations their very own, they apply them in active interaction with the physical and social worlds around them. They act, practice, and do race in these worlds.

In their omnipresent interaction with other children and adults, children not only create and re-create the racial hierarchy, but also embed in their own minds what the racial hierarchy is and what it means cognitively and emotionally for themselves as individuals. Given its origin in drama, the idea of a social role strongly suggests this performing, acting, changing reality of racism. This is why we wish to keep the concept of "performance" in a socially learned role as one part of our analysis of what children actually do in regard to racial and ethnic matters. Thus, being "white" in the United States involves not only a privileged status and strong identity, but also the carrying out on a regular basis of a white performance that hems in, hurts, and frustrates the lives of Americans of color. Our data show that while the cultural language of race and racial hierarchy is conveyed to children by adults, children internalize these ideas most thoroughly when they implement them repeatedly in their own actions and interactions with other children and with adult caregivers. Thus, the language and ideas of race empower white children to set themselves apart as "better" than racialized others, and by so doing they learn and perform the social practices associated with being "white American."

In a racist society there is a hierarchical racial order, with much for young children to learn. There are complex racial roles to be comprehended and lived. Yet the theoretical discussion of racialized roles has been rare in recent social science analysis. In contrast, the idea of "sex roles" or "gender roles" has over the last two decades spurred much theory and research about how men and women, and boys and girls, relate to one another in the oppressive system of patriarchal power. We know much about how girls and boys come to learn the gender schemas and roles appropriate to this sexist system (Connell 1985; West and Zimmerman 1987; Thorne 1993). However, many gender researchers have moved away from use of concepts and terms such as "gender roles" to concepts and phrases such as "gender inequality" and "patriarchy" to better capture the oppression in such arrangements (Connell 1985; Benokraitis 1997). The idea of "gender roles" too often suggests that such roles are limited or can be unlearned, when in fact gender oppression is pervasive and enduring across virtually all sectors and institutions in society.

Significantly, in some 1960s racial relations research there was significant discussion of what was called "playing the role of Negro." The focus was on how Black Americans come to learn and perform the role of the racial inferior (Pettigrew 1964, 3–4; Griffin 1961). As many Black writers have pointed out for more than a century, Black Americans have long had to act the "role of Negro" in front of sanctioning whites (Du Bois 1989 [1903]). Moreover, a considerable literature has developed showing that playing the inferior in a relationship constantly creates problems for adults' and children's self-esteem and self-identity (Pettigrew 1964, 7). How individuals think about themselves is often shaped by the actions and performances they undertake (Kaplan 1992, 1927–35). Black children, like Black adults, must constantly struggle to develop and maintain a healthy sense of themselves against the larger society that tells them in a legion of ways that they are inferior.

Not surprisingly, perhaps, little social science research has been done on what might be called "playing the role of the white." Pettigrew (1964, 3–4) has recounted the story of one Black child who came to play therapy sessions each week. The boy sat down at a table, put his feet up on the table leaning back in his chair, and crossed his arms majestically over his chest. He asked the therapist if she knew what he was doing. She said no, and he replied, "I've been playing white man!" This young child already knew what being white meant, including the appropriate action. As social scientists, we still know relatively little about how white adults and children learn the role and identity of being white. In this book we make some effort to remedy this situation.

Identity–Roles: Combining Ideas

In our analysis of the preschool data, we have delineated a number of important dimensions of racial and ethnic relationships—often, relations of oppression. These dimensions include (1) concepts and thinking, (2) spoken discourse, (3) everyday practices and performances that restrict or privilege, and (4) identities and psychological (and physical) embodiment. We see these various aspects of what might be called the "racializing process" in the accounts of our children in this and later chapters. Recall the opening episode with Carla. Carla clearly has in mind certain concepts of Black people as undesirable, and she suggests her concepts discursively. The "Black" identity of Nicole is established, and Carla's own identity is implied. But there is more to this account. Carla takes action to move herself and her cot away from the undesirable child. When the teacher intervenes, she goes further and aggressively rationalizes her action.

There is no one word in English that can accurately capture the various aspects of what Carla is enacting. Part of her action and discourse is playing out a white-normed role, while another part is about establishing racial identities and meanings and deeply embedding these identities and meanings in her and others' psyches. The racializing process here and elsewhere involves establishing what we will henceforth call, for want of a better term, racial "identity–roles." When we use this combined term, we often have two or more dimensions in mind—concepts, discourse, identity, and role performance or action. Each of these dimensions can be emotionally loaded, to varying degrees, and each can be outwardly or inwardly oriented—toward the other or toward the self.

In U.S. society, today as in the past, the "white" identity–role has to be learned, developed, and performed. Young white children begin learning this by observing the world around them. Over time they take on the language and behaviors of whiteness and use them actively in their own lives. For children, as for adults, the performance as a "white" person involves ever-deepening understandings of "white" self and society. Note that the requisite behavior need not be actively taught, as when children learn to talk by means of constant exposure to the social world. Few three-year-old children have ever had adults attempt to teach them the details of grammar, but most are masters of much grammar, with remarkably few errors occurring in their everyday speech.

As shown throughout this book, young children perform racial identity–roles. Their actions involve the use of racial and ethnic concepts, images, and terms from their environments, but they adapt, reform, and use these to comprehend and shape other children's and adults' behaviors. As in the case of gender, even young children often treat the racial and ethnic categories, identities, and roles as more or less permanent. Drawing on what they have learned from the surrounding social world, the children express in their own behavior how they view racial and ethnic categories and understandings. We agree with the tenet of Piaget's theory that suggests that some characteristics of people are seen as permanent by children. Yet children are not the only ones who succumb to the notion that race, gender, and other social categories and statuses are fixed, permanent parts of individuals. In their everyday behavior, most adults demonstrate that they also view these characteristics as enduring and essential parts of life.

As we see it, researchers should give more attention to the ways in which these identity–roles are learned and taken up. In our data we see white children experimenting with and learning how to be white and how to handle the privileges, propensities, and behaviors associated with the white position in society. We also see children of color learning how to deal with the reality of being Black, Asian, or Latino in a white-dominated society. Let us anticipate briefly an account from chapter 3. During playtime in the afternoon, we watch Renee (4, white) pull Lingmai (3, Asian) and Jocelyn (4.5, white) across the playground in a wagon. Eventually, Renee drops the handle, and Lingmai jumps from the wagon and picks up the handle. As Lingmai begins to pull, Renee admonishes her, "No, No. You can't pull this wagon. Only white Americans can pull this wagon."

In this account a white girl is asserting not only her personal privilege but also citing a generalized white American identity–role as justification for that privileged position. Her action goes well beyond an egocentric "only I can pull this wagon" to a more complex and expansive generalization that attaches her to white-group power. Renee is not merely imitating something she has heard elsewhere; she is applying ideas from the adult world to her own specific situations. Her understanding of racial identity and role performance seems deeply coded into her mind, for she reacted quickly. She links a racial awareness (white) with a spatial and national reference (American).

Recall our previous discussion of the point that the socially constructed racial other's identity is only part of the racial equation. Also in this equation are the sincere fictions that white actors, including younger ones, hold in regard to themselves. Here is an example of an active and very personal ideological construction that adapts the societal racist ideology. Renee is inventively making use of what she has learned, but she is not acting apart from her history and social milieu. She has embedded the performance of being white as part of her understanding of her self. Racialized identities are part of this mix, too. By acting out "whiteness," Renee is participating in the creation of an ongoing social structure at the building block level. This account thus shows the way in which the societal hierarchy of racial power is replicated and reproduced over time. Doubtless, the deeper meaning of this action by the white four-year-old was not lost on the Asian child or the other white child in the wagon. Like adults, children teach each other about racial meanings in both overt and subtle ways.

A typical white adult's reaction to this account might be that Renee could not have understood what she was doing. The mythology of color blindness extends from the adult world to understandings of what children are doing. Numerous mass media and advertising presentations of white and Black children have suggested them to be more or less color-blind, treating each other only as human beings and having little sense of racial differences or their meanings (see DeMott 1995). Yet this commonplace denial of what children really know and understand is likely another example of a general white denial of racism that is central to U.S. society. When one ponders the matter for a moment, it does not make sense to assume that children have no understanding of the racist system around them. Indeed, they are inundated with it most days of their lives. Many white adults engage in racist practices across the society every day, in myriad settings, and with widely varying others.

OUR FIELD STUDY

In our research the daily lives of children in a racially and ethnically diverse day care center took center stage. We gathered experiential data on how preschool children use racial–ethnic awareness and knowledge in their social relationships. We bypassed the standard methodological approaches to the study of children that distance them from the researcher. Instead, we went into the field for nearly a year and made unstructured field observations of children. We recorded their everyday behaviors in settings few adults are privileged to observe. In our field research we quickly learned that young children become experts about the issues that they develop and discuss in everyday interactions with other children. Indeed, they often became our teachers.

Our observations took place in a variety of preschool settings, from teacher-led reading circles to open free play on the playground, where adults may not be present. Our data come from extensive observations of fifty-eight preschool-age children over nearly a year in a large preschool in an urban setting.[6] The children involved in this study ranged in age from barely three to more than six years of age. Our analysis is arranged thematically rather than chronologically; hence, the children's reported ages at the time of each episode may occasionally appear inconsistent. This apparent incongruity is an artifact of our thematic analysis. Each child's age at the time of involvement in an event was calculated from his or her birthday and reported according to when the event happened. The first author conducted the fieldwork, ordinarily spending about ten hours a day, five days a week in contact with the children and their teachers, as well as with the numerous teacher's aides, substitute teachers, volunteers, and parents who were a regular part of the daily life of the center. The center's director had notified parents that we would be conducting the research project and had invited them to contact us with questions at any time.[7]

The preschool had several racially and ethnically diverse classrooms and employed a popular antibias curriculum. The school's official data on children in the classroom we observed was as follows: white (twenty-four); Asian (nineteen); Black (four); biracial (for example, Black and white; three); Middle Eastern (three); Latino (two); and other (three). While the classroom's enrollment was never more than forty, the total number of children active in this classroom varied throughout the year as children entered and left the center for a variety of reasons. We observed all the children who were enrolled over the entire eleven months of study and are thus presenting data for more than the maximum class size. Additionally, there were occasional visitors from other classrooms, and siblings would appear from time to time, temporarily increasing the population. Some of the children were born in other countries. A few had multiracial or multiethnic backgrounds.[8] To some degree, our preschool classroom represents the new demography of the United States, with its increasingly diverse population—more Americans of color and fewer whites than at any time in its recent history. While there are still many predominantly white or all-white preschool classrooms across the nation, the number of classrooms with a great diversity of children is likely increasing. Thus, our children are already interacting in a setting that will, in its significant racial–ethnic diversity, increasingly be the characteristic adult setting in many areas of the nation in the near future.

Our classroom was divided into distinct areas. One area contained the children's library, games, and an area where children stored personal belongings. A second area contained tables and chairs and a play area. A third part of the room contained tables, chairs, easels, and art supplies. Teachers used each of these areas for organized instructional activities. Outside the classroom was a playground with an assortment of toys. We recorded observations in all areas accessible to the children.

Most child development research has involved activities or settings contrived by researchers. Rogoff (1998, 697) has raised the question of the impact of the formal-researcher role on research. Using an approach close to that called the least-adult method by researcher Nancy Mandell (1988), Debra Van Ausdale, who did the classroom observations, made a conscious effort to play down or eliminate the researcher/adult role and to remain nonauthoritarian and supportive in her interactions with the children.[9] While some children were initially puzzled by her behavior, they soon accepted that an adult could actually not be in charge of anything or anyone. Unlike almost all other researchers working with children, Debi was able to operate as a nonsanctioning, playmate–adult. Debi's activities in the day care center evolved to become a combination of teacher's helper, children's playmate, and official lap for children who needed comforting. Debi was soon accepted by the children as a nonthreatening, uninteresting component of the preschool world. Initially, some children asked Debi what she was doing, and she offered the explanation that she was a researcher who wanted to understand how children play. In just a few days her status became that of both playmate and toy. Once satisfied as to her purpose in the classroom, children generally disregarded Debi unless they saw that they could put her to use to achieve some personal goal. Teachers also tended to ignore her, unless there was some task that needed to be done. In no case did Debi ask the children predetermined questions about race or ethnicity or overtly demonstrate that she was interested in researching these concepts. She kept her involvement with the children relaxed and nonadversarial, generally responding to children's questions and requests in a conversational manner.

The children did not respond to Debi as they did to sanctioning adults, such as parents or teachers. Indeed, the children would customarily stop activities when a teacher or other adult approached their play groups, particularly if they were indulging in some forbidden pastime. In contrast, when Debi approached most children's groups, they continued their activities. That Debi was successful in the least-adult approach was verified by the teachers themselves, when she presented a preliminary report on her observations of the children. After reading her accounts of what the children in their charge were doing and saying, the teachers' response was unanimous: "These aren't our kids!" They were baffled and disbelieving of the field data.[10]

Over some extended period of time, direct observation of children creating racial and ethnic concepts in their own milieus is likely to be better able to explain what these concepts really mean to them. Time is an important component of the analysis, because racial and ethnic ideas and behaviors may not be revealed in single instances but will more likely be episodic in a particular child's life, just as they are in the lives of adults. However, they are still very important in children's worlds. As Damon (1977, 49) has pointed out, "Many activities of profound theoretical interest occur infrequently in the course of children's daily social lives. This is particularly true if our interest is not merely in children's social behavior but in the social knowledge manifested by the behavior." Watching the children carefully, over a relatively long period of time, enabled us to obtain a clearer picture of the children's overall environment. In addition, as with adults, the children's racial and ethnic understandings are often reflected in ways that are not immediately apparent. Ultimately, they are reflected in a range of choices about what to do or not to do. They shape choices of playmates, toys, books, and places to play. They affect how overt or covert children's actions are. Thus, our general research goal is to examine deeply the use, growth, and elaboration of racial and ethnic meanings, the complex constructs that require time to develop.

CONCLUSION

In this book we examine when, where, and how children make use of racial and ethnic understandings and distinctions in their everyday lives. We develop insights into everyday worlds of preschool children and examine the meanings of a variety of expressions and actions. We see how the children take these materials and use them to actively construct understandings and actions in their own social lives and environments. We see them learning and achieving social identities and role performances.

One can see children's worlds of experience as threefold. In one sphere of activity children play, read, or study by themselves, without others present. In a second sphere, children can be seen interacting with and responding to a variety of adults—most especially parents, relatives, and teachers. In a third realm, children are interacting with other children, including peers and those who are older or younger than they are. Each of these worlds of children involves learning norms and meanings from others, in direct or mediated form, yet each also entails children experimenting and developing their own meanings and understandings from the materials presented to them and from their internal resources. How they combine these realms is of central interest to our project. Additionally, while the three realms overlap somewhat, the two child-centered spheres of activity are often separate from the adult-occupied sphere. Children are subject to the *direct* supervision of the relevant adults in only one of these important realms; much of their activity occurs beyond our gaze. It is important to understand that these multiple and sometimes very dissimilar social contexts become momentous in children's lives and that these contexts can occur sequentially, repetitively, or in an overlapping fashion. Children move through their experiences, gathering vital information about the world and its workings and applying that information to their dealings with the world. Even very young children quickly learn to move from one interactive context to another and become socially competent in the process.

This point is central to our argument—the primacy of social relationships. Society does not consist of individuals but expresses the sum of the relationships in which individuals find themselves, and this is true for children as well as adults. The larger social and cultural fields in which children find themselves are not of their own making; they are, initially, put into these fields without their input. They must then cope with the involuntary social fields created by their elders, and learn their meanings and negotiations.

As they proceed into preschool settings, young children learn to move from the social field of interaction that is the family to the new social field of the school, a field that most will operate in for the next fifteen or twenty years of their lives. Both social fields have many lines of force—with varying attractions and repulsions, lines and styles of communication, and learning settings. Note, too, that these two fields are both immersed in the larger field of the broader society. Yet very young children learn to cope effectively and, over time, successfully with all these social fields. Indeed, their very personalities, identities, and life-coping styles are framed and formed in these social fields. Nonetheless, the world of children interacting with other children is the social context that adults generally pay little attention to or regard as unimportant. In this book we pay primary attention to this social world, drawing on hundreds of daily observations of children. Our analysis of child-to-child and child-to-adult interaction reveals how children construct and experience racial–ethnic distinctions and concepts in their everyday lives.

There is thus a problem in traditional developmental theories of children's knowledge of such matters as race and ethnicity. Conventional child development and cognitive theories place too much emphasis on adult conceptions of reality, which, as we explore later, often embed serious misconceptions of children's social and intellectual functioning. When young children fail adult-framed tests of racial–ethnic knowledge or developed under-standings, the studies too often conclude that young children do not have the cognitive capabilities to understand race or ethnicity. An equally rea-sonable explanation of their failure is that these tests fail to tap the children's constructions and understandings of race or ethnicity.

Thus, we argue herein for a redirection of research energy toward ex-amining the nature of children's knowledge of race and ethnicity in their own interactive contexts. If the possibility that very young children can construct complex mental structures for racial and ethnic concepts is ac-cepted, the next steps include an examination of these questions: (1) How do children create and understand their own experiences with racial and ethnic matters? (2) How do they define racial–ethnic concepts and dis-tinctions? (3) Do they use these understandings and distinctions to define themselves and the identity–roles they play? (4) Do they use these under-standings and distinctions to define others? (5) Are racial–ethnic distinc-tions and concepts useful, manipulative tools that children use in their in-teractions, just like adults use them in their interactions?

NOTES

1. Piaget's investigation of children's allegiance to their country suggests some contradictions in his theory. In his investigation of children's understanding of "homeland," Piaget directed a series of questions to children on their knowledge of how town, canton, and nation fit together into a cognitive whole (Piaget and Weil 1951). He warns that his survey of children's attitudes should be interpreted cautiously, mainly because of his inability to ascertain the extent of parental influ-ences on children's attitude formation. He suggests that for children the recogni-tion that they belong to a particular national group comes in a slow process re-quiring much time and a high level of cognitive functioning. The notion of nationality (or ethnicity) presents cognitive theories of development with a para-dox: The later development of a sense of nationalism requires that an older child undertake to redevelop the egocentricity lost at an earlier stage of development. Thus, sociocentricity seems to require that the young-child's egocentricity come into use again, as justification for the belief that one's country is preferable to oth-ers. Piaget recognizes this apparent contradiction.

Given that nationalistic views can emerge at some point in an older child's life, and given that this is contrary to the shedding of egocentricity said to be nec-essary for maturation, Piaget poses two possibilities: The readiness with which the various forms of nationalism later emerge can be accounted for by suppos-ing either that at some stage there emerge influences extraneous to the trends noticeable during the child's development or else that the same obstacles that impeded the process of "decentration" and integration (once the idea of homeland takes shape) crop up again at all levels and constitute the commonest cause of disturbances and tensions (Campbell 1976, 38). Piaget opts for the second, more psychological possibility and leaves unexamined the intriguing first hypothesis: outside forces intrude and are accepted by the child. Egocentrism maintains its hold on Piaget's interpretation of children's attitudes, including their national and ethnic attachments.

2. Typically, the Preschool Racial Attitudes Measures II (PRAM II) is used to test preschoolers' racial attitudes, although a variety of tests is available (see Williams, Best, and Boswell 1975).

3. When research moves away from adult-centered explanations and concentrates on producing explanations for children's behaviors that accommodate the children's perspectives, contradictions become apparent. Experimental studies (Baillargeon 1991; Baillargeon and Hanko-Summers 1990; Baillargeon and DeVos 1991) demonstrate that Piaget may have been incorrect in his interpretation of infants' abilities to realize that physical objects have permanent existence when hidden from view. Infants, Piaget maintained, do not develop this sense of object permanence until they are about nine months of age and until this age "believe" that objects cease to exist when they cease to be visible. Piaget attributed infants' failures to seek a hidden object to their belief that the object no longer existed rather than to the equally reasonable conclusion that infants simply have limited physical ability to search. His focus on children's abilities to approximate adult levels of functioning as a measure of their maturity is based on his use of quantitative skills as the measuring rod. Baillargeon and DeVos's work (1991) demonstrated that the use of a manual search task as an indicator of understanding can be misinterpreted. They have shown how Piaget may have seriously underestimated young children's understanding of objects.

4. The presumption that young children are simply imitating their parent's attitudes and behaviors in regard to racial and ethnic distinctions is brought into question by some research. While many studies point to strong parental or environmental influences (Cross 1987), a few demonstrate that children's perspectives on other racial groups can develop in opposition to direct teaching by parents. Branch and Newcombe's (1986) investigation of children's attitudes as a correlate of parental attitudes found that the four- and five-year-old children of pro-Black parents expressed pro-white attitudes, in direct contradiction to their parents' expressed beliefs. These children were "interpreting their parents' attitude and belief statements in a way that was different from what the parents intended. Consequently, it remains a puzzle how to explain or predict the direction of minority children's preferences in the 4 to 7 year age range" (Aboud 1988, 126). Aboud used this study to contradict the arguments of those who overemphasize parental and community influences as mediators between children and society, but offered no important insights into how children create their own meanings.

5. Also, categorizations can interact, so that being both Black and female usually has a social meaning that is more than the sum of the parts.

6. Over time the center enrolled fifty-eight children; about half were girls, and half were boys. All the children's and adults' names have been changed. In a few cases, country of origin for a child or parents is also disguised to further protect their anonymity. For over nearly a year in the mid-1990s, Debi carefully took detailed notes about the children's activities that were transcribed, usually daily, into computer files.

An early version of a few sections of this book, including some of the children's accounts, appeared in the *American Sociological Review* (Van Ausdale and Feagin 1996).

7. Early in the process Debi conducted an open meeting to explain its purpose to parents and teachers, but only three parents attended. We received approval for our research plan from the university's human subjects research office.

8. For example, four visiting children were Black, thereby increasing the number of Black children in our accounts. The children, teachers, aides, and other adults in the study have had their names changed to protect their anonymity. We give the child's name, then in parentheses we list age and racial–ethnic background. If a child is listed as (4, white), this means that the child is four years of age and white. The racial–ethnic designations are based on those given by parents on school forms, but also include information gained through our observations for a few children with mixed-ethnic identities. In the text we use a shorthand code for racial–ethnic background. In a few cases we use broadly defined designations (e.g., Asian) to further protect a child's identity. The children possess various levels of facility with the English language. All but one of the teachers are white.

9. Debi positioned herself as a nonsanctioning adult, in part to develop an atmosphere of mutual understanding and trust with the children and in part to ensure that her observations of their activities recorded the most natural behavior possible. Because children often alter their behavior in the presence of an adult, especially if they are engaging in behavior that will likely elicit adult interference (see Gubrium 1988), her success in this role was critical. Debi convinced both the children and the staff that she was "not a teacher." She established herself as a combination of playmate and listener for the children and as a teacher's aide for the adults. Following Corsaro's (1981) recommendations, if she needed to behave as a sanctioning adult, for instance when children were in danger of physical harm if she did not interfere, she tried to remain as peripheral as possible to the authority structure. Usually she brought a teacher's attention to the situation. If imminent danger was likely she directly interceded, although this was rare.

10. Debi let issues arise naturally and did not interfere with the children unless a physical threat to them arose. While she did sometimes ask questions that might have been asked by other adults, she never threatened the children with sanctions for their words or actions, nor did she try to influence them to change their behaviors. She did not engage children in directed questioning of their racial atti-

tudes or behaviors, nor did she direct their activities or design activities to elicit racial or ethnic responses. Significantly, thus, children would often use "potty language" in her presence or would enlist her in evading teacher sanctions. In no case did she ask any children predetermined questions; she let issues come up naturally. However, she did accept if asked to participate in activities, whether these were teacher-directed or child-directed, and would engage in casual conversations with the children, much as the other adults in the center did.

2

USING RACIAL–ETHNIC
DISTINCTIONS TO DEFINE SELF

were they are young children imitating the image of what the "other" is

Dao (4, Asian) started school today. Since he speaks almost no English, he remains a detached observer of the classroom, interrupted only by the teachers' frequent attention to him. Debi notes his arrival and sits on a bench on the playground, watching the rest of the children chase each other. Chasing is a favorite activity, particularly in the afternoons, when resting time is over and snacks have been distributed. Robin (3, white) and Trevor (4, white) race past her, wearing towels around their shoulders and holding their hands up to their faces. They shout gleefully as they pull up and turn, running back to where Debi sits. "Look at us!" Robin demands. "Look. We are other people." Debi regards the two with a smile but says nothing. Both Robin and Trevor have placed their index fingers at the outside corners of their eyes and are pulling the skin back, making slits of their eyes. They are quite obviously mimicking the physiognomy of an Asian person. "Yeah, we are other people," Trevor contributes. Debi remarks, "I see," and gives them a smile, whereupon they both laugh and continue in their chase.

In this episode the performance of the two white children's play does not seem malicious. Dao himself is nowhere in sight, so they are not mocking him. They say nothing other than "We are other people" as they laugh and chase each other. Why are they doing this? Perhaps they have seen Asians on television. Perhaps there was a storybook they shared that sparked this imitation of "other" people. Or perhaps Dao's introduction to the classroom prompted them to experiment with this image of, and language about, *other* people. Where they acquired their ideas is one question, but what matters most is that they have found a way to define the other that incorporates racial characteristics. Obviously, it is important enough an idea

47

to be not only included in play, but shared with an interested adult. At the same time, they are implicitly defining themselves as white, since they must change the way they look to become "other" people. They are playing with the racialized identities of others and thus of themselves.

The obvious, physically grounded racial and ethnic markers of skin color, facial features, and hair color and texture were widely used within the children's interactions with each other. A variety of other, more subtle symbols also came into play, and often children created combinations of physical identifiers with language use, mode of dress, types of food, children's parentage, and their relationships with others outside the day care community. Children as young as three invented complex combinations of racial meaning, for themselves and for others, and incorporated social relationships and physical characteristics to produce explanations for how their world was racially constructed and maintained. The children varied the ways in which they employed their explanations, demonstrating that they were aware of the importance of context and that they were wrestling with a multiplicity of abstractions.

USING RACIAL–ETHNIC CONCEPTS
TO DEFINE NEGATIVE IDENTITIES

Other children at the center have also identified important racial markers, but they use them in a different way. It is early spring and three girls, Renee (4, white), Christie (4, white), and Amy (4, Black/white) are sitting in a circle, comparing the colors of their arms. Lynne, a teacher's aide, joins them. Renee remarks to Lynne, "Christie and Amy are the same color." Lynne agrees with Renee, then points out that Renee is darker than the other two girls. Renee first frowns at Lynne, then gets a worried look on her face. She asks, "Does that mean that I'm not white anymore?" Lynne begins to laugh and tells her, "No, silly, it means you are getting a tan." Renee doesn't look convinced, continuing to frown. Lynne leaves the group to attend to another child, and the three girls continue with their comparisons. "I'm darker, but I'm still white," Renee reassures the other two girls. They merely look at her without saying anything, and soon the group breaks up.

Renee's concerns about remaining white resurface in another episode about two weeks later. The children are outside and Renee is involved in a conversation with Mike (4, Black). She tells him, "Well, I'm just getting a tan. I'm really a white person." Mike regards her with some amusement, remarking, "OK, so, you're really a white person. I'm really a Black person!" He pushes her over and runs away, laughing. Renee chases him.

Renee seems to be unable to convince herself that despite her darkening tan she remains a "white" person. The worry is strong enough that she has brought up the subject with at least one other child. Keep in mind that these conversations are only those Debi overheard. There were likely far more episodes than this when Renee discussed her dilemma with other children or adults. Cognitive theory would analyze Renee's behavior as demonstrating that she is being unable to conserve color, incapable of understanding that skin color is permanent and unchangeable. During tests of their cognitive abilities, young children often display this inability to "conserve," or understand that some features of physical objects (including human beings) are permanent and immutable. Children also display a tendency to fantasize, drifting off into imaginary worlds where they can, through only the power of their imaginations, become other kinds of creatures. Almost any casual observation of a group of children at play will reveal some of them engaged in this imaginative activity. They can become bucking horses, knights in armor, Ninja turtles, or airplanes and are invariably deeply involved in this play. Indeed, such activity is necessary for development and shows that children can readily use their knowledge to create alternative realities. Adults view such imaginative play in children with some amusement and tend to dismiss the children's activities as harmless fun. Should an adult engage in such "play," however, the evaluation would be considerably different. A grown person who was openly involved in the imaginative world of Ninja turtles would be regarded with great concern and suspicion by other adult onlookers. Such is the vast gap between adult and child realms. But do young children truly believe that they become horses and airplanes? No. Children skate from their imagined realities out to the immediate world and in again, exploring possibilities. Do they understand that their play is imagination? In our experience, they usually do, and if asked they will tell you so. But for Renee, as is the case for most light-skinned persons, skin color is changeable. It is probably not the immutability of skin color as an indicator of membership in a racial group that is causing her trouble. She can see that her skin is darker than it was at the beginning of the year and that some sections of her skin are darker than other areas. Rather, her struggle seems to revolve around a desire to remain a white person in the social sense of that term. She is working with images of both self and identity. She insists on being recognized in the identity of a white person. This definition of being a *white person* is important to other children also.

The worry remains with Renee well into summer. She discussed her concerns with her mother, April, who shared that story with Debi. It seems that Renee had made what her mother considered to be a very strange request. She told her mother that she wanted to be Black and informed her that this desire would become reality since she kept getting darker and darker. April told Renee that this couldn't happen, that Renee was white and would remain white no matter how dark the sun turned her skin. This information made the child angry, the mother reported to Debi, and now she wanted Debi's input on what to do. When asked if Renee had ever had contact with any Black people other than those at the preschool, April said, "In fact, we lived with a Black family for a while, while Renee was a baby, and we have stayed friends with them ever since. Do you think she wants to be part of that family?" April looked concerned. Debi replied, "It seems more like she is playing with the idea of whether or not changing colors changes race too." April nodded but seemed amused and dismayed at the same time. It was a puzzle.

Renee seems to have learned about racial group and color from her early experiences with a Black family and carried her knowledge over to deal with her present situation. Changing skin color, due to exposure to the sun, prompted a long-term, deeply involved routine in Renee's life, creating a continuous and developing evaluation of exactly what skin color meant to her. She brought her thoughts and concerns to her friends, her mother, and eventually to one of the teachers, repeating her wish to be "Black" and reasserting in a variety of situations her conviction that this transformation was imminent. Skin color and its ramifications for family relationships occupied some of Renee's energy for a long period of time. She continually refined her understanding of skin color, extending it from herself to others and creating explanations for people's relationships based on their skin color. Her activity was not ephemeral. Rather, her racial understandings gathered more strength and social significance as she refined, expanded, and applied her knowledge in behavior. Moreover, her attitude toward the "race change" she was undergoing transformed over time, moving from great concern to acceptance to eventually becoming the favored status.

For Robin and Trevor, racial characteristics became part of a game, one that they shared with Debi. For Renee, racial characteristics became a more important part of her life, a phenomenon that was also shared with Debi over time. We did not observe Robin and Trevor continuing to make use of their understandings and images of other people in a manner as complex and central as Renee's. However, they may have done so in other settings beyond our observation. Clearly, racial and ethnic markers can become compelling for children as soon as they observe them.

my main focus isn't skin color but rather how a child's experience

THE SOCIAL SIGNIFICANCE OF SKIN COLOR

Adults use racial and ethnic understandings to define themselves. From the typical white adult's perspective, including that of many researchers, children are generally not expected to employ ideas about racial group or ethnicity as part of serious self-definitions until they are well along toward adolescence. In contrast to this perspective, we argue that throughout a life span the ideas, feelings, and language of racial group and ethnicity hold central importance in a person's self-definition and self-concept. For children, racial group and ethnicity become pertinent to self-conception and self-definition as they begin to interact with people inside and outside their families. Hence, racial and ethnic group membership assumes great importance almost immediately, because young children are not normally raised in isolation. Even youngsters who have very little contact with those outside their immediate families share the vicarious experiences of those members of the family who do foray further afield. Fathers and mothers bring home tales of work; older brothers or sisters share stories about school; extended family members visit and socialize; and there are almost always trips to the market, church, or other social settings. Even a baby gathers some information from these experiences.

The social milieu of schools becomes a critical component in this process. It is there that many children, especially most white children, may get their first opportunity to gain firsthand experience with people of other skin colors, nationalities, languages, and cultures. In school, children will likely begin to refine their preliminary conceptions of what racial–ethnic distinctions mean in their everyday lives. Increasingly, day care centers are the environments where many children begin to have their first extensive social experiences away from the direct control of adults. How children of various backgrounds manipulate and understand these experiences is shaped by the structure of the outside world as much as it is by each child's individual personality and early understandings drawn from family settings. The social meaning of skin color is elaborate and complicated, formed by a process of trying out various ways of using this meaning (Troyna and Hatcher 1992). One important use is for the developing definition of one's self and its counterpart, the definition of the "other."

The meanings that children create and use for skin color are neglected by sociology, although they have garnered some attention in psychology. Individually oriented studies of skin color and its meaning for young children are necessarily superficial, generally investigating little more than an individual child's ability to define or recognize color, or perhaps to distinguish between people of different skin tones. In testing,

skin color

USE SKIN AS a classifying feature, but does this suggesting R. understanding by C.

definition is deemed correct if the child identifies skin color accurately according to predetermined adult-oriented criteria. A child is considered to be aware of skin color when that child can differentiate people based on skin color as presented in an experimental situation. Beyond this experimental research, much of the research on children's lives was, and continues to be, derived from evaluations of their lives by sanctioning adults such as parents, caseworkers, and teachers (Baughman and Dahlstrom 1968). This evidence is somewhat secondhand, since it relies on an adult's interpretation of children's behavior. It is rather like creating a theoretical understanding of employees' lives by asking only their employers about them. Employers are likely to produce a good approximation, but it will still be far removed from the firsthand accounts of life that the employees actually experience.

An example of this adult-centered orientation occurred at the preschool during one teacher-led activity. A white teacher was conducting an activity with a group of four children. They were asked to choose, from several large photos of children belonging to various ethnic groups, which children looked "the most like them." This activity was drawn from the antibias curriculum in use by the school and was intended to foster the orientation and concepts linked to valuing diverse racial and ethnic others. The children had a wide exposure to such activities, and there were numerous posters and photos of diverse children all around the play areas and library. Debi was watching the activity from a nearby table, where she was in charge of dispensing scissors to children, and the teacher was aware that Debi was observing her interactions with the group of children.

The teacher spread the photos out on the table and announced, "OK, can you discover which of all these different people in these pictures most looks like you?" The children smile and reach for the photos, picking them up and showing them to each other. One boy, Joey (3, Asian), selects a photo of a dark-skinned girl wearing a red robe and announces, "Here's me!" at the top of his lungs. The teacher looks over to him and smiles, remarking, "No, honey, that's a little Black girl. Which people look like you?" Joey stares at her for a moment or two, then returns to his perusal of the photos. He offers no challenge to the teacher's decision, nor does he provide an explanation of his choice. Debi was unable to view the photo he chose at that point. Trevor (3, white) finds a photo of a smiling man in ethnic German garb and proclaims, "I got me." The teacher verifies that his choice is "correct," then beams at him and says, "Good going, Trevor!" He grins back at her and leaps from the table. Joey continues his search, while Rita (3, white/Latina) sorts through the pictures with him. Sarah (4, white) remains sitting quietly, swinging her legs under the table and looking bored. She makes no effort to look at the photos. Joey finds a photo of a group of smiling white women and silently offers it to Sarah. She studies it for a moment, then sighs and hands it to the teacher expectantly. "Good job, Sarah," the teacher congratulates her, not noticing that Joey produced this racial identification for Sarah. Sarah finally smiles and leaves the table. The entire exercise seems, to her, to be more an annoyance than a fun activity. Joey finds yet another photo, this time of a Native American man. He hands it to the teacher, smiling and announcing, "Finally. That looks like me." The teacher accepts this one and tells Joey that he made "a good match." He lets out his breath in a' big puff and erupts from his chair. The teacher is left with Rita, who sits helplessly looking at the spread-out collection of photos. "Here's one," the teacher remarks, offering a photo of a woman in traditional Mexican garb to Rita. The little girl looks at it for a moment, smiles, and says sweetly, "Oh, such a pretty dress. Yes, that's me." The teacher beams at her, and the child asks, "Can I go now?"

Throughout this activity Debi was quietly watching both teacher and children. The teacher, for her part, has been trying hard to ensure that the children properly identified themselves through the selection of racially or ethnically appropriate photographs. Her goal was to encourage the children toward recognizing that they have distinct and valuable ethnic group membership, a goal reinforced through the reading of special storybooks and the presence throughout the classroom of posters and other graphics that depict a wide range of peoples. She smiles at Debi and asks, "Well, they sure don't know much about that, do they? I mean, they really can't pick out what group they belong to. They're way too little." Debi then suggests that perhaps accomplishing this task will take some practice. The teacher nods vigorously, then remarks, "I just love doing this with them; it helps them to know who they are." Her focus is on assisting these children to make appropriate choices. She seems pleased with their responses despite the fact that only one of the four was successful under her criteria.

Also noteworthy here is the fact that of the four, only Trevor made a "correct" identification. It was evident that he focused on skin, hair, and eye color, for the man in the photo was as blond, blue-eyed, and pale as Trevor. The photograph he chose matched him quite well, although the rest of the depiction was not accurate, since we never observed Trevor in lederhosen. It is also noteworthy that Joey was interested in assisting Sarah to identify herself racially. His selection of a representation for her was right on the money, yet the teacher's evaluation of his effort was that he failed to "pick out" his racial group. Each child was quite obviously operating on their own criteria, despite the teacher's explicit directions and heavy involvement in their activity. Still, her evaluation of the situation was that the children simply did not comprehend race.

After the teacher left the table, Debi took the opportunity to observe the photos more closely. She was curious about why Joey would have selected a photo of "a little Black girl" instead of one of the numerous photos of Asian people. She located the photo and quickly saw his impeccable logic in the choice: Joey is wearing a bright red sweater today, and the child in the photo is wearing a deep red robe. Apparently, in Joey's thoughts, he found someone who looked like him, albeit because of the choice of clothing. Here the color of the clothing was his criterion. The teacher, however, seemed to be trying to get him to self-identify according to criteria predetermined by adults. By accenting categories, for well-intentioned purposes, she reinforces them. This concern that children meet adult expectations is one shared by numerous researchers working on issues of racial self-identification and is demonstrated by this teacher's course of action.

In this preschool classroom yet another young child had some doubt about the permanence of skin color. Trevor (3, white) asks Crystal, a classroom teacher, "Is my skin brown?" Crystal regards him for a moment, then says, "Well, it's sorta brown, isn't it. But you're white, honey." Trevor looks puzzled and continues to regard his own arm. He seeks further information and asks Debi, "Is my skin brown?" "Yes," Debi answered, holding her arm up to his. "Your skin is very brown. You must have been swimming." He studies Debi's arm silently, and she offers, "But you are not as brown as me. See?" He continues to study both arms, then says, "But if I go swimming all summer I'll be as brown as you." He smiles, then races off to find someone else to play with.

For Trevor, the issue is comparison of tans, not racial group or the social meaning of skin color. He is more interested in determining exactly how brown he can get, not whether or not he will change races. In fact, Crystal's use of racial terminology seemed to puzzle him. He wasn't concerned with whether or not he would stay brown, as Renee was. Rather, he was interested in exactly how brown his skin would become and how he might encourage this change. Once someone else agreed with him that he would get more of a tan throughout the summer he seemed happy and dropped the subject. He had verified his original concern.

Assumptions about how children see, or do not see, racial and ethnic markers can affect the best field research in distorting ways. Recall that

Holmes (1995) proposes that existing research methods have failed to assess accurately children's perspectives on race and ethnicity. She states that participant observation with young children in classrooms, informal conversations with them, and analysis of their artwork will enable scholars to discover what meaning children assign to race and ethnicity. Yet, as we have noted previously, Holmes (1995, 4) explicitly abandoned "race" as a research concept early in her effort, preferring instead to use "ethnic group" as the term of choice. Her reasoning is that children, particularly white children, have little interest in racial groups and have given racial concepts little thought. Initially, she based this interpretation primarily on her own experience: she admits to devoting no attention to the concept of race or whiteness and their meanings to her own life. However, when she reports the responses of African American children to her informal interviews and requests for self-portraits, being Black was a very important self-identifier. Indeed, she describes Black children's use of skin color to define themselves as a major difference between white and Black children in the classroom, with all of the Black children emphasizing the color of their skin when describing their self-portrait drawings. In contrast, none of the white children in her study referred to skin color. Despite the fact that Holmes's work was carefully crafted and consistent with existing cognitive theory, it demonstrates that even attentive researchers can succumb to the assumption that children do not see race. Holmes's fieldwork demonstrated that skin color, though not the sole factor in the beginnings of racial group relations, does play a central part in facilitating children's initial evaluation of self and others.

ACTIVELY CONSTRUCTING
RACIAL AND ETHNIC IDENTITIES

In another episode in the classroom, skin color again takes center stage. It is just after nap, and Mark, a white teacher's aide, is sitting with Lu (3, Chinese), Susan (4, Chinese), Corinne (4, African/white), and Mike (4, Black). The children are listening to a story read by another teacher. The purpose of stories after naptime is to delay the children from racing to the snack tables before their hands are washed. They are required to sit and listen until they are released, and this release is accomplished by allowing only a few children at a time to leave the room. This prevents them from lining up and destroying each other while they wait. A favorite device for delay is to play the "color of the day" game, where children must remain seated unless they are wearing a particular color of clothing. Jeanne, the teacher, finishes her reading and announces, "If you have something brown on, you can get up and wash your hands for snack."

The children look around and seem to collectively decide that this invitation includes brown skin, hair, and eyes. Mike jumps up, yelling, "I have brown skin on!" and rushes to the sink to be first in line for food. Upon seeing this, Corinne also smiles widely, yells, "Me too!" and dashes away. Mark, regarding Lu with a smile, leans over and tells her, "You have brown skin too." Lu retorts, "I do NOT!" She appears to be very indignant. "I have white skin!" Lu looks to Susan to support her. Susan verifies this, telling Mark, "Lu's skin is white, Mark, not brown." Mark seems surprised, then says, "My skin is brown from the sun." He waits for Lu or Susan to respond. Lu states, "Well, I'm white." Susan nods, remarking, "Lu, you have brown eyes." Lu looks her over and smiles, saying, "So do you!" Susan peers deeply into Mark's face, asking him, "Do I have brown eyes?" Mark gazes back, pretending to think deeply. "Why yes, you do have brown eyes!" he finally declares. "So we can both go get snack," Susan declares. All three of them rise and go to the next room.

The desirability of whiteness, of white identity and esteem, is again evident in the children's exchanges, although it takes on a somewhat different shape than the previously discussed case of Renee. Renee is worried that she will no longer be white, since her skin color is changing. Lu, on the other hand, insists that she already *is* white, not brown, despite the fact that she would probably not be construed by others as white since her skin has an olive tone. She angrily denies having brown skin and draws another child in to support her evaluation. The conceptions of whiteness vary according to what each child understands and names as important. One significant aspect of Lu's denial is her anger at being assumed to have darker skin. She is annoyed that Mark would make such an error and appeals to another child to verify her skin color for him. Her indignation at his mistake is a clear indicator of the importance she is already attaching to her physical appearance and, more importantly, to valuing the category of whiteness. She seems to want to deny that she could possibly be dark or close to the category of Blackness.

Here we see an Asian child trying to find her place in a white-dominated society that implicitly and explicitly accents a racist continuum running from positive whiteness to undesirable Blackness. Once again, children's actions and understandings in their interactive settings reveal aspects of the larger society and its deep-lying historical roots. As they have entered and increased in number in the United States, each new group of color has usually been placed, principally by the dominant white group, somewhere on a white-to-Black status continuum, the common gauge of social acceptability. This racist continuum has long been embedded in white minds and practices, as well as in the consciousness of many Americans of color. First created in the 1600s and 1700s by dominant whites, this white-to-Black continuum runs from white to Black, from "civilized" whites to "uncivilized" Blacks, from privilege and desirability to lack of privilege and undesirability (Feagin 2000; Gordon 1997, 53). This long-standing continuum accents physical characteristics and color coding in which European-like features and cultural norms tend to be highly privileged. Not surprisingly, all children in this society learn at an early age that, generally speaking, whiteness is privileged and darkness is not—and thus their choices in this regard are usually not surprising. In particular, Asian and Latino American children, like their parents, may often find themselves placed by whites on the continuum without their active involvement, and thus they may struggle for a better placement, and definition, of themselves on that white-originated continuum.

In another situation, we see how white skin color and privilege are constructed and understood. It is summer, and a teacher asks Debi to supervise a popular activity. The children will construct an "international" handprint poster. The poster will function as a thank-you card for the director of an international organization that the children visited on a field trip. This project is set up to encourage the children to recognize that they are different from each other, with the goal of valuing these differences. A large sheet of paper is laid on a worktable, and poster paints, called "People Colors," are prepared for the children to use. In this classroom, white children invariably chose either white or pink paint to represent their color. Black, Latino, Asian, and Middle Eastern children selected a variety of colors.

The teacher tells Debi to encourage the children to pick a color that resembles them. "Tell them to choose a color that looks just like them. Ask, 'Which one matches your skin?' Then whatever color they pick is OK." Once again, the purpose of the activity is multiple: to draw the children's attention to the positive value of others, to have them identify themselves, to foster self-reliance in their appearance, and to share that identification with a wider audience. Debi will assist each child with painting the palms of their hands, pressing it on the paper, and writing the child's name next to the handprint. Several paint bottles are prepared, the paper is laid out, and the children line up to begin this favored activity.

As the painting proceeded, some children pointed out how closely the paint matched their skin or asked what Debi thought of their selections.

Not wishing to offer suggestions or encourage them to change their choice if the colors did not match, Debi accepted whatever they chose and painted it on their palms with a brush, no matter how distant from a physical match it might have been. She complimented their abilities and their choices. Most of the children made close matches.

One little girl, Corinne (4, African/white), approaches the table and takes a seat next to Debi. She eyes the bottles of paint critically. "Hmmmm," she says, handling first one bottle, then another. Debi says, "OK, Corinne, which color is the most like you? Which one matches your skin?" She looks over the bottles once again and chooses a pale brown, placing the bottle in front of Debi. "This one for one hand," she replies, continuing to scan the bottles, "and this one for the other hand." The second bottle contains dark brown paint. Debi smiles at her, feels a bit confused, and explains the assigned task: "No sweetie, you need to choose a color that matches your skin." Corinne gazes back evenly and explains, "I am. I have two colors in my skin." Debi assents to her selection immediately, and since she has met Corinne's parents she realizes that Corinne is representing herself very precisely. Debi tells the girl "OK," and proceeds to paint one of her palms pale brown and the other dark brown. She places first one, then the other, hand on the poster paper, making two prints. Then Debi writes Corinne's name between the two handprints. "Perfect!" the child says, smiling broadly and delighted with herself.

For Corinne the choice of two colors represents reality. She is blending the two color identities in her family. She is not laboring under any sense of confusion, fantasy, or inconsistency, as some conventional theories of racial awareness might suggest. Corinne's parents are white and African. Her choice of two colors is appropriate for her lived reality, where one parent is pale-skinned and the other dark-skinned. She stood her ground against the instructions to choose one color matching her skin. She chose instead to include both parents in her definition of her skin color, and thus of her self. The choice of two colors was not cognitively inconsistent but signaled her understanding of her biracial parentage and identity. This four-year-old clearly understands that the question of color is much more than a question of physical reality.

For the next child at the activity, color choice takes on a different but equally appropriate meaning. As Corinne leaves, Taleshia, a three-year-old African American girl approaches the activity table. Asked if she wants to make a handprint, she nods shyly. Her skin is deep brown. Told to pick a color that looks just like her skin, she scans the bottles and suddenly points to her choice. Debi picks up the bottle indicated and notices it is pale pink. "Is this the color you want?" she asks Taleshia. The child nods, holding out her hand, palm up. Asked again if she's sure, she quietly says yes. Debi puts a dab of pink paint on the back of her hand and asks again if she is sure. She nods vigorously. The contrast of the pink paint with her dark skin is dramatic, but she insists that her color is pink. Debi then complies with Taleshia's wishes and begins to paint the child's palm. The little girl is delighted.

There are several possible interpretations for Taleshia's choice of pink for her color. That choice might indicate nothing more than that she likes pink as a color. One might also see her choice as a sign of inner racial insecurity, a common conclusion in dozens of studies of Black children (see Clark and Clark 1939). What might she, or any other child, have chosen had a wider variety of colors (blue, green, purple) been available? If given a more extensive choice, what do kids choose? That experiment was not conducted in our research, and we are unaware of other research that explores this possibility. If the children's choices do not always reflect their "true" skin color, as an outsider might evaluate it, does it mean that they do not recognize the importance of accurate depiction of skin color? Or does it mean that their own or others' skin color has a different meaning for them?

While we did not conduct a formal experiment to test this speculation, one of the teachers set up an activity that touched on these questions. Jeanne has set up a mirror, several packages of colored paper, crayons, scissors, and pencils. The samples range in color from palest pinks to bright oranges, vivid greens, blues, deep browns, and electric reds. The object of her activity is to have the children create paper dolls that represent themselves. She has made a paper doll of her own, as an example. The children have watched her and are instructed to choose colored paper for their own doll that "matches what they look like." They are to "draw a person" on that color. This shape is then cut out and a face drawn on it with crayons or pencils. The dolls can then be dressed up in paper clothing cut from other media.

Jeanne's activity doesn't seem to turn out as she expected. The children take over immediately. For the most part, the children ignore the paper colors corresponding to physical skin colors and instead choose an interesting array of colors for their paper cutouts. Preferring reds and yellows, they create a rainbow of paper dolls. Nor do they limit themselves to drawing realistic faces on the dolls; they draw pictures of their families or depict friends and cartoon characters. Still, their selections are not arbitrary. One girl points to her work and declares, "That's me and that's my baby sister and that's my mom." A boy says excitedly, "Look, X-men in my head!" In short, the children made this activity into a highly creative exercise in experimental art. Swept up in their own interpretations of the moment, the children designed their paper compositions according to what they were thinking rather than exactly what the teacher requested. Because they did not adhere to her expectations, however, she concludes that her lesson is lost on the children. Later, Jeanne confides to Debi, "This activity is a complete failure. They just don't get the idea of what they look like, do they?"

This interesting experiment shows that children have their own lives and may adapt adult instructions, where possible, to their own goals and desires. Given the opportunity to be creative, the children do not limit themselves to realistic portrayals of their bodies as adults might see them. Does this mean that they do not understand the reality of their own bodies? That they are incapable of translating their thoughts into authentic depictions of themselves? Whatever else is the case, it likely means that connecting actual skin color to racial–ethnic identity is not always primary for them. The adult tendency is to deny that young children are capable of abstractions in their depictions of people, yet it was clear that some of these children were representing their ideas of themselves and their families abstractly and playfully. Adults generally expect children to be literal and adults to interpret and create meaning. Adults see young children as externally motivated in their behavior, driven by adult directives and disobedient if they fail to follow such directives, even in a fun activity such as drawing pictures. In this teacher's mind, her young charges are following her request, but they are doing so in a way that indicates, to her, their cognitive inconsistencies. This conclusion reflects and supports both commonsense and research judgments of preschoolers' abilities and as such is not challenged.

In the famous doll studies (see Clark and Clark 1947), Black children were asked to choose a dark- or light-skinned doll to represent themselves. A Black child who chose a white doll was deemed to be rejecting his or her racial identity. Using such criteria, Taleshia's choice of paint color could be interpreted as evidence of an identity crisis for her, as a problem. Black children are supposed to choose accurate color representation of themselves. Taleshia does not seem concerned, however. She is determined that her color is pink, and this determination continues across time and contexts.

In the continuation of this scene, the accuracy of Taleshia's color choice for her handprint becomes a matter of distress for another child. Robin (4, white) is watching from her place behind Taleshia in line, and she protests immediately, as soon as Debi begins to daub paint on Taleshia's hand. In an exasperated voice she exclaims, "She's not that color. She's brown. Look, Taleshia." She holds her arm next to Taleshia's arm and says, "See?" The contrast is striking. In the interest of adhering to the teacher's directives for proper completion of this activity, Debi tells Robin, "It's Taleshia's choice. She can choose any color she thinks is right." Robin snorts, insisting, "She's just not pink, can't you see that, she's Black." Robin shifts her attention to Taleshia, telling her, "Can't you see that you aren't pink?" and looking closely at Taleshia's face in amazement, mouth agape. She takes Taleshia's arm. "Look," she tells Taleshia, "you are *brown*! See? I am *pink*." Robin speaks slowly, emphasizing the colors, and looks over for confirmation of her definition. Taleshia roundly ignores Robin. Debi says, "Sure enough, Robin, you are pink." Robin looks relieved. "Now," she says, "Taleshia needs to be brown." Debi asks, "Do you want to be brown?" and Taleshia shakes her head vigorously, saying, "I want that color." She points at the pale pink bottle.

Peggy (3, white) joins the group. She also tells Taleshia that Taleshia is not pink and informs her, "You can't have that color." Taleshia frowns, shaking her head. "I want this color," she demands, touching the pink paint bottle. Peggy frowns at Debi, insisting, "I am pink, look, look at me, Debi, I am pink, she is brown, dark brown. You can't let her be pink 'cause she's not."

By now Robin is quite frustrated, so Debi interjects, "Taleshia can choose any color she thinks is right. It's her skin." Robin again offers an objection, but Debi continues, "It's up to Taleshia. It's her skin." The repetition finally proves effective, and Taleshia smiles, once again picks up the bottle of pink paint, and hands it to Debi. Her hand painted, she makes her print, triumphant at last. Robin sighs. As Taleshia leaves the table, and Robin takes her place, Robin remarks to Debi, "I just don't know what's the matter with you. Couldn't you see that she was brown?" Debi smiles and again reminds Robin that the choice is up to Taleshia. Robin finally gives up and chooses the same pale pink that Taleshia chose. She makes her handprint on the poster and, giving it one last valiant try, says, "See, I am *not* brown!"

Robin was determined to force the stereotyped identity of "Black child" on Taleshia, who clearly and emphatically resisted these racialized expectations. Utilizing her understanding of physical identifiers, Robin insists that Taleshia's choice was not an accurate reflection of reality as Robin saw it. The categorization of Black people into skin-color-linked identity–roles is an integral part of the operation of U.S. society. In this larger societal framework, Robin's evaluation of the situation might seem reasonable: Taleshia was not physically pink. Indeed, the contrast of the pale pink paint with her deep brownness was striking. Yet Taleshia stuck to her choice, despite Robin and Peggy's evaluations and the fact that much of her skin was deep brown. All three children demonstrate a strong awareness of the importance of skin color, and all three argued their convictions, a strong indicator that their awareness of both self and other was likely informed by the social significance of skin color.

Here, as elsewhere in our data, a child's self-definition relies heavily on the recognition and definition of others as "not" self. The idea and reality of the self is dependent on its interplay with others. People distinguish themselves by comparison to and in evaluation of others, and small children are no exception to this process. Robin's distress at Taleshia's selection is likely an indicator that she not only recognizes herself as not Black, but also sees herself as white. In this latter concept we see yet another example of a "sincere fiction" of the white self, for Robin apparently sees herself as superior and powerful in her own understandings. Her understanding of the power of whiteness seems to be linked to her orientation toward the actions of the racial "other."

A mainstream cognitive researcher, in evaluating Taleshia's choice of skin color as reflected by her paint choices, might conclude that she was confused about racial self-identity. If she had chosen pink in an experimental setting, eliminating the social context, she might have been considered by researchers to be racially confused or rejecting her own racial group. However, our association with the children over time enabled us to consider the context of each situation and couple it to the history of each child.

Taleshia had, on previous occasions, pointed out how pale Debi was and how dark her own skin was, as we note elsewhere. She had also explained that she was Black, that Debi was white, that Taleshia considered herself quite pretty, and that pink was her favorite color. Thus, we cannot conclude that Taleshia is racially ambiguous in thinking about herself or that she does not recognize her own skin color or its importance. We can surmise, however, that she has given the concept of her self and ideas about her skin color much thought and has incorporated these understandings into her operating procedures for daily living. Racial understandings are meaningful and socially significant in her world, whether they concern her definition of herself or her analysis of others' conceptions of her. That she distinguishes between the two is undeniable, especially given the vigor with which she rejects another's description of her and the enthusiasm displayed in her choice of pink as her color. She does not accept the imposed, white understanding that is periodically dictated to her.

A more thorough explanation is one that incorporates the nature of the present situation with Taleshia's personality, her family background, and the history of her previous interactions with others at the center. For example, if we include Taleshia's personality in an analysis of her behavior, we might conclude that she chose pink as her skin color because it is her favorite color. Her choice does not necessarily mean that she is unaware of her real skin color or that she is racially confused, but that she may be choosing a color that reflects her image of herself. If Taleshia's actual behavior is considered in isolation from the context of the hand painting activity, one could come to a very inadequate explanation of her choice. Instead, we can use our knowledge of her to interpret her selection, one that incorporates more of the child's personality and personal preferences. This interpretative understanding requires time with those being studied. Moreover, it requires that we acknowledge and accept children's abilities to create and negotiate the world in the same way that most adults do.

A second, simpler, explanation for Taleshia's choice presents itself when we incorporate another experience Debi had with her. Although her skin is very dark, making her selection of pink initially confusing to an outside observer, the palms of her hands *are* pale pink, as are those of many African American children and adults. Perhaps Taleshia was choosing a color to match the color of her palms. After all, the task involved the painting of the children's palms. Several weeks later, Debi sat with Taleshia on the floor at a story reading activity. As they listened to the teacher, Taleshia quietly held Debi's hands in hers, turning them slowly from palm to back. She repeated this activity with her own hands, placing them on top of Debi's and patting the hands to draw attention to her activity. She did this several times, contrasting her hands with Debi's and the tops of her hands with the palms, never saying a word, but smiling all the while.

This last explanation, that Taleshia was choosing a color to match the palms of her hands, would be elusive if not impossible if we had to rely solely on the original hand painting activity to analyze Taleshia's choice. If forced to rely on only one incident we might conclude that the child was racially confused. Instead, by including the child's social context and history we are able to explain her choices as appropriate and even creative. Her choice suggests that she was creating her own concepts of skin color and racial group as it is expressed in skin color, making decisions about which aspects of these concepts were important enough to include in the creation of her interactions with others. She knows who she is, and that view of herself is strong and positive. Clearly, children have much more sophisticated understandings of these matters than most adults are willing to concede.

TEACHER INTERVENTIONS IN SELF-DEFINITION

Adult definitions and reconstructions of children's activities have a strong influence on both children's lived realities and the research process investigating these realities. Taleshia's experiences are informative here. By the end of summer, Taleshia had changed her perspective and chosen dark brown paint for yet another handprint activity that Debi watched. This time, the poster activity was supervised by Lynne, a substitute teacher. The teacher led the activity using more aggressive steering, directing the children toward a "correct" choice of skin color. Of course the teacher's conceptions of race and color were the correct choices, and these conceptions were guided not by the children's experiences but by the teacher's decisions on appropriate racial designations. This time, Taleshia looked over the four colors carefully, her eyes going from pink to brown to pink. Lynne points out two of the darker brown bottles, suggesting that Taleshia pick one from these two. Taleshia hesitates, but finally, at Lynne's urging, she opted for brown. This is the first time in this type of activity that we saw her choose brown as her color, making it apparent that she considers that there is a choice. She is slow to choose, prompting Lynne to ask, "Do you want me to pick for you?" at which Taleshia shakes her head and picks up the brown bottle. "Good!" Lynne tells her, "That matches you perfectly!"

The teacher has not forced Taleshia to choose brown but has strongly guided the child to the selection, enthusiastically approving Taleshia's eventual choice of color. She was definitely shaping the child's behavior. But there is a third associate in this exchange. Charlynne, another three-year-old African American girl, is watching the interchange between Lynne and Taleshia. It is Charlynne's first time at the table, and she also chooses brown, the same color as Taleshia. The influence of the teacher's presence and her enthusiasm for the "correct" color choices are inescapable. Lynne's overt approval of Taleshia's choice is exuberant, and she praises Taleshia enthusiastically. Teacher praise is a prized commodity in preschool. Charlynne's place as the new child in the action encourages her to watch others' behaviors closely and emulate them in the expectation that she too will earn praise and attention. There is some recent evidence that teacher-led activities produce different behavior in children. One study demonstrated that the content, agenda, and structure of social interaction in a sharing circle changed when leadership of the circle was placed in children's hands (Danielewicz, Rogers, and Noblit 1996). When children controlled the sharing circle there was greater variety of interaction between them and more description. Humor was introduced to the circle, and time constraints on the sharer were longer. In contrast, when the teacher was in charge, the children's participation was constrained, limited mostly to responding to teacher questions. In another study dealing directly with racial issues, children were observed making racist remarks about pictures of Black people, but only when they felt assured that no adult was in close proximity (Jeffcoate 1977). Both studies support the idea that children's behaviors are radically different under child-led conditions. Our data so far provide evidence that children make sense of the world in very different ways when free of adult interference. Children typically refrain from a wide variety of activities when adults are present, a reaction that, on reflection, most adults should be able to remember from their own youth.

Mike (5, Black) uses a similar strategy to Taleshia's. In the hand painting activity, Mike had chosen brown paint to represent his skin color in the past, and he continues with this choice in this new activity. This time, however, he chooses dark brown for one hand and lighter brown for the other. The teacher asks him if he is sure, and he nods. She complies with his wishes and paints one hand dark and the other light brown. He seems pleased and writes his name between the two prints. Lynne makes no attempt to discourage him and does not insist that he chose only one color.

Later, Felippe, a teacher's aide, notices that Mike's contribution to the poster involves two different colors. As the children begin their lunch, Felippe teasingly comments to the child, "Hey, Mike, why did you do your hands in two different colors?" Mike regards him without a smile (usual for Mike) and holds up his hand, twisting it from palm to back to palm again. Felippe says, "Oh, I see, there are two colors on your hands." Mike shouts, "Yes!" and resumes eating his lunch.

Mike's selection of light and dark brown to represent the palm and back of his hands is not as dramatic a choice as Taleshia's, but it points to the similarities in the children's activity. Skin color is important enough to these African American children for them to incorporate it in everyday school activities in complex ways. They see color diversity where white outsiders might see uniformity. They are resisting outsiders' rigid expectations about their identities and understandings as Black children. It is the Black children who are insisting on describing reality. In our observations, none of the white children attempted to nuance their skin color selection in the same manner as the African and African American children did. They did sometimes protest when Black children tried to delineate themselves in a way that did not meet with their approval. Differences in skin color, not only between children of divergent groups but also in coloration within the group, are of recurring interest to the children we observed. Further, the salience and meanings of these differences seem to vary according to the children's own groups. African American children experiment with and call attention to actual variations in skin hue, while most white children tend to abstract the contrasts in Blackness and whiteness with less attention to the actual variability in skin color.

In another episode, where a teacher was involved, the children were not so eager to share their explanations of color. Here we see again that the presence of adults radically changes the nature of interaction between children. As we suggested above, children realize that adults disapprove of some of their activity. Their awareness of adults' opinions prompts them to avoid confrontations or arguments with grown people, choosing instead to merely acquiesce to adult demands.

Debi is sitting with the three children on the steps to the deck, playing Simon Says. Brittany (4, white) is Simon. While Debi stays in the background, Rita (3, white/Latina) and Joseph (3, Black) discuss what racial group they belong to. Keep in mind that this conversation is unprompted by adult influence and that the only adult on the scene so far is Debi, who is being thoroughly ignored. Joseph informs Rita, "I'm Black, and you're white." "No," she retorts angrily, "I'm not white, I'm mixed." The two debate back and forth for a few moments, their voices getting louder and angrier. Joseph maintains his definition of Rita, and she as vigorously denies it, reiterating and reinforcing her own conception. Debi listens and watches quietly, ready to intercede if the children get too upset. However, the noise attracts the attention of a teacher who enters the scene from inside the building and approaches as Rita shouts, "I'm mixed, you stupid!" into Joseph's face. He merely rolls his eyes at her, making her even angrier.

Patricia, an African American teacher, enters this scene from inside the classroom. She is joining the children on the playground. She listens to Rita's last declaration, quickly evaluates the situation, and intervenes. "You're not mixed, Rita, you're Spanish. What race am I?" Patricia is making an attempt to change the subject between the two, in hopes of calming the argument. Rita looks up at Patricia and reluctantly replies, "Mixed."

"Mixed!?" Patricia responds, laughing. "Mixed with what?" Rita ponders for a moment, looking uncomfortable. "Blue," she says finally. Patricia is wearing an entirely blue outfit today. "Oh," Patricia says, "I'm Black too, like Joseph; I'm not mixed. What an interesting conversation you guys are having." Patricia smiles ineffectively at the children, which prompts them to begin squirming and looking for a way out. Rita says nothing in response, and Joseph has remained silent throughout Patricia's exchange with Rita. The child leading Simon Says (Brittany) finally tells the kids to go to the playground, and Rita and Joseph run off in different directions. Patricia smiles at Debi, shaking her head, but offers no comments.

The research literature on children documents how interaction and collaboration in children's learning activities do not involve agreement on all issues (Rogoff 1998, 724). Indeed, the peer-group collaboration process often involves disagreements as part of the normal activities. Throughout the months of observations, Debi watched children engage in such arguments, about a wide variety of topics, and most of the time they managed to settle their debates peacefully and on their own. At worst, if the argument just would not resolve, one child might begin to cry in frustration. This invariably attracted a teacher's intervention. The episode described above again points up the interventionist stance that teachers take when children get loud in their disagreements with each other. The children's reaction to her interruption illustrates the power adults have to radically alter the content and direction of children's activities. Patricia entered the scene and immediately took over, guiding the interaction by drawing on her apparent belief that the children were confused. Further, that the two children took no notice of Debi, sitting a few feet from them, indicates that her status as "least-adult" was achieved.

Patricia did not make an attempt to get the two children to stop arguing but tried to join in, as though trying to lead them in their discussion. The majority of the time, teacher intervention took the form of peacemaking, with teachers actively instructing children to "be friends" or "work it out" when disagreements arose on the playground. That Patricia tried to involve herself in the children's conversation suggests that she was attempting to use the episode to teach tolerance. She had found what educators call a "teachable" moment. She is also instructing the children to categorize racial groups in an adult-centered manner.

Here, the teacher seems to allow no mixed category for a child's identity and self-conception. This is suggestive of a common adult tendency to limit children's understandings of the nuances of racial meaning. In Rita's case, her use of the term "mixed" probably referred to her knowledge of her parents' origins. Her mother and father were from different countries in Latin America. While she appeared white to outside observers, with pale skin and curly dark hair, her assessment of herself was that she was mixed. Joseph's insistence that she was white finally provoked her into an angry retort, complete with name-calling. Rita's racial–ethnic group status is very important to her. She reacts to the teacher's inquiry by becoming relatively uncommunicative. Clearly not wishing to engage in the argument with a teacher, Rita and Joseph abandon their interaction and address the more urgent need of responding to an adult. The lesson is not lost on them, however, given their behavior. It is better, in their world, to submit to the adults' definitions of racial matters than to attempt to enter an argument. Young children quickly learn that debates with adults are typically unproductive.

Crystal, a white teacher, made a more direct attempt to engage children in learning about color differences. In this instance, the teacher took advantage of a toy that a child had brought in from home to direct children's attention to skin color. When Taleshia (3, Black) brought a doll from home for show-and-tell, Crystal directed the other children's attention to how the doll's skin color was the same as Taleshia's. Crystal asked the child to hold her doll up next to her skin, so the other children could see. Taleshia complied with the directions, although she did so slowly and shyly. Crystal then asked the children if they saw anyone that also had skin color that matched Taleshia and her doll. The children immediately and unanimously responded, "Mike." Crystal then asked them if they knew anyone else who had skin the same color as Mike, Taleshia, and her doll, expanding the realm of inclusiveness. This time, the children hesitated. Eventually, one child called out, "Patricia." Crystal pushed further, asking the question again, but now the children fell silent, looking at each other. There are several other dark-skinned children in the group, but nobody offered any of their names. Crystal then asked them to look around the room and see if they could discover anyone's picture that fit the criterion of color. Finally, one white boy pointed to a picture of Martin Luther King Jr., and the lesson circle moved to another topic.

Viewed from a traditional cognitive or developmental framework, these children might be seen as confused, ignorant, or naive. Pressed to identify and connect skin color to people, the children often become reticent and need adult guidance to perform the task. Such silence may be taken to mean that they have no knowledge of what the adult asks. This is what observers who adhere to a certain cognitive focus might describe, especially those who limit their study to only teacher-led activities. Our alternative interpretation, however, draws from extensive contact with children as they interact with each other. We have seen them engage racial ideas in a variety of creative ways and under circumstances that were devoid of adult interference. Their activities in these situations encourage us to assert that they have far more capability with these ideas than the teachers, or many cognitive researchers, consider possible.

In the preceding example, the teacher had seized on another teachable moment, as all the teachers did if they could. She guided the children toward recognizing connections between people and skin color and attached some meaning to that recognition. Being intelligent, curious, and active human beings, the children have already accumulated substantial experience with the meanings of skin color and racial distinctions. As the teacher expands her teaching, they become aware of the objective she is pursuing and grow uncomfortable, not confused. Other Black and dark-skinned children are present in the group, but one child chose a Black teacher (Patricia) as an example instead, leading the focus away from the children and toward an adult figure. The children are acknowledging racial distinctions to the teacher, but they are avoiding attention to themselves. If we accept that racial talk is usually a forbidden topic for them, like sexual or other adult topics, then we can see that their maneuvers are often directed toward avoiding adult intrusions. In their view, the teacher is leading them down a path they do not wish to follow, and they turn the table on her and take her in a safer direction, one that reinforces her conception of them as innocent.

This might seem convoluted thinking, especially for small children, but consider that young children routinely engage in a wide variety of activities that they, more or less, successfully conceal from adults. During their times alone, with only other children present, they engage in considerable analysis of the ways of adults, if for no other reason than to learn how to incorporate those ways into their own lives. In the process, they acquire the ability to manipulate adults, since they soon become aware of the fact that adults view them as unsophisticated or helpless, and they take advantage of this. We know of no empirical research to support this contention, but as parents ourselves we can recall multitudes of occasions when our children informed us that they were "too little" to do some task. Often children themselves desire to maintain the ruse of childhood naivete and simplicity.

THE CHILDREN'S VIEWS

The complexity of what color means to children's evaluation of self, and what the self might look like, varies greatly. For some children participating

in a color exercise, the choice of a color that looks like them consists of simply choosing their favorite color. Whether or not that favorite is a physical
match to a human skin color seems irrelevant in some cases and highly relevant, usually in a distinctly individual way, in other cases. For some children, and for the Black children in our observations, the choice of color in
play exercises indicates a connection with deeper meanings around skin
color, with the color choice linked to an evaluation and understanding of
their own lives. For Taleshia, the colors she chose—at different times and
places—affirmed many things: skin color, favorite color, and her interest in
the contrast of her own skin with the skin colors of others around her. For
Corinne, color choice indicated the importance she attached to her diverse
family; she was very interested in explaining and displaying the dual nature
of her parentage. For Mike, the choice of skin color was more subtle: the
briefness of his interaction with Felippe suggests that Mike was at the least
aware of the subtleties attached to skin tones and their variations. That he
attached some significance to color was apparent in his choice to share his
thoughts with Felippe.

For some of the white children, such as Robin and Peggy, interest in
skin color was aroused by the seemingly strange and incongruous color
choices made by their African American peers. Taleshia's choices in particular caused some degree of consternation for the white girls. They were
adamant as they insisted that Taleshia was wrong in choosing pink as her skin
color and against advice continued to insist that Taleshia be corrected in her
choice. It is difficult to discern with certainty whether the girls' concern was
mainly for physical accuracy or if they attached some deeper meaning to
Taleshia's skin color. There is some evidence that the issue was much more
than a matter of physical accuracy. Significantly, the white children imposed
their understandings of color-choice accuracy on the Black children but not
on other white children. Strict insistence on a close match for white children
was not noted in any other observations of the children. It is important that
the two white girls felt not only the need to argue the point, but that they
chose to do so with Debi. When Patricia entered the discussion between Rita
and Joseph, the children fell silent and the discussion ended, in marked contrast to the heated discussion that Robin and Peggy involved Debi in.

Both teachers and children regularly seized upon the connections between skin color and other markers of differences between people, although
for different reasons. The celebration of ethnic and racially oriented holidays
precipitated considerable interaction among the children, and at times this
interest incorporated skin color and its salience to ethnic identity. Children
were keenly interested in any information about unfamiliar customs and

holidays. Non-Jewish children, regardless of race, delighted in activities oriented around Hanukkah, such as the making of challah and storytime books about the Festival of Lights. White children displayed intense interest in explanations of Kwanzaa, asking questions and listening quietly as teachers read books about this holiday. The history of Kwanzaa's origins was covered in the curriculum and was made a point of discussion by the teachers. That different holidays were connected to different racial and ethnic groups was not missed by the children. In the case of Kwanzaa, teachers explicitly connected the holiday to African Americans, as is appropriate. The children, however, refined and extended this meaning on their own. In this next situation, one child uses skin color as a determinant of what kind of ethnic activity another child can do.

Aaron (4, white) taunts Amy (4, Black/white). She is alone, playing quietly near the gazebo. He approaches her and sticks his tongue out, informing her, "You can't celebrate Kwanzaa, you're not Black." Amy retorts, "Oh yes I am. You don't know. You're stupid." "I am not," he replies, sniffing at her and adding, "and you're not Black." "I am too Black!" Amy responds hotly. "My Dad is Black and so is his parents, my granddad and grandma." "Stupid!" he shouts at her. "You're stupid!" she yells right back. "You don't know nothing about me." She rises and faces Aaron with an angry glare on her face. Aaron responds in kind, and they glare at each other until he finally backs down and leaves. Amy resumes her play.

It is immediately apparent that Aaron defined Amy's qualifications to participate in Kwanzaa celebrations according to her skin color. He has named and imposed his comprehension of what Black identity is and how it is to be measured and noted. Amy's skin was pale, and she had curly, dark blond hair. According to Aaron's interpretation, Kwanzaa was for "Black" people as he mentally defined them, and thus Amy was not to be included. She was, to all outward appearances, white. Amy, however, relied on her family history and her knowledge of Black and white ancestry and its meaning to define her capacity to be included in Kwanzaa. Each child was basing their interpretation of Amy's status on different criteria, each using a different model of explanation. For the white child, another's skin hue was decisive. For the Black child, skin color was but one gauge. Far more important were her ancestry and knowledge of her family. Her skin color was not a key factor for her. Note, too, that Aaron was asserting a certain white privilege in determining who is, or is not, white.

In yet another situation, skin color provides the opportunity for extensive comparison with the colors of other objects and the color of people. In this scene, Taleshia makes use of color to categorize other things and other people in order to draw a contrast with herself. Her under-standing of self, as an abstraction, is evident in this exchange.

Debi sits on the rug, cross-legged, with Taleshia leaning up against her. This is a common position for Debi, and children at times will vie for the use of her as a cushion. They are waiting for a teacher-led activity to begin. Taleshia snuggles up and says, "Your T-shirt is black." Debi agrees and adds, "I really like black. It's a pretty color." Taleshia nods, announcing, "Your hair is black." Again Debi agrees. The child continues, "And so is Mike's hair and Steven's hair and Mitchell's hair and Elizabeth's hair." She has named all the Asian and African American children currently in the room. Debi nods, "Black hair is prettier than T-shirts." Taleshia laughs, touches Debi's arm and remarks, smiling, "I'm Black too." Debi says, "Yes, and so is Mike." Taleshia nods again and says, "And Joseph." She holds her hand up, turns it from side to side. "See?" she asks. "I'm *Black!*" She shouts the last word, delighted; holds up her hands; and sings loudly, "I'm Black, Black, Black." By now she is in Debi's lap. She holds her arm up against Debi's legs. "I'm *real* Black," she notes, eyeing the contrast between the two skin tones. "And I'm *real* white," Debi replies, imitating her emphasis. Again Taleshia laughs and sings, "I'm Black, Black, Black!" The two remain in contact, with Taleshia singing and Debi serving as her perch, until the teacher-led activity begins.

The contrast between Debi's pale skin and Taleshia's dark skin is striking. The conversation she started was a device employed to engage Debi, first in a maneuver to gain possession of Debi's lap. Then Taleshia moved her comparisons from clothing to hair color to skin color. She made a game of it, moving with ease from one object to another, all the while proclaiming her awareness and delight in her own color. She also managed to get exclusive control over an adult's attention, quite an achievement for a preschool child.

Recall our discussion of Taleshia's choice for handprint color. This account is conclusive evidence that Taleshia knows that her skin color is dark and that she is aware of the meaning of skin color. Moreover, her sense of her Blackness has a strong positive accent. Recall that Taleshia is the child who wished to paint her own palm pink. As we see here, she does not see herself as white in her own mind or description of herself. She is not confused or upset with her Blackness. She sought out this compari-son, constructing it and drawing Debi's attention to the vivid contrasts. She is also providing confirmation that she is perfectly capable of distin-guishing between the nature of color for objects and the nature of color for people. She is using language about skin color issues. Her dialogue moves from a simple description of clothing to a more in-depth discussion of black as a color for people. She distinguishes between the colors of clothing and the colors of people, showing interest in the contrast between white and dark skin, and does not confuse the two. Additionally, she is not constructing her conception of herself in isolation, for she is engaged in conversation with another. Thought and language about racial and ethnic matters, as with many other issues, go hand in hand. Moreover, this activity is not the inner-directed fantasizing of a young child but rather an other-oriented behavior that shows Taleshia has given the matter of skin color some thought and has made social comparisons she wishes to share with an interested person.

For yet another young child, Charlynne (3, Black), color informs the creation of self-identity, except in this case the colors are not limited to shades of brown or white. This child compares her own color to the colors of children depicted in a picture book she and Debi are sharing. Once again, a child has managed to get the undivided attention of an adult. Debi's ability to devote herself to the attention of single children for long periods of time was productive in a number of ways, but in these cases the interactions produced data providing insight into the workings of two young children's thoughts about themselves.

Debi is sitting outside with Charlynne at her side. Since this little girl is physically disabled, she needs alternative activities to engage her. Debi's one-on-one availability was particularly useful for her. She and Debi are looking at a picture book featuring silhouettes of children, all executed in a rainbow of colors. The pictures show children engaged in a variety of activities: picking flowers, swinging, fishing, jumping rope, and the like. The two are slowly paging through the book, and Charlynne says little, smiling as each page is turned. Suddenly Charlynne points at the book and exclaims, "There's a girl like me!" The silhouette is of a seated girl, feet pointing straight out in front of her. "Except she's green, and I'm Black," Charlynne adds. Debi agrees and adds, "But I've never seen a green person. Have you ever seen a green person?" Charlynne giggles and says, "No, that's silly." Debi agrees, "You're right, it sure is." Charlynne begins to laugh in earnest. "She's green all over," the child chortles and begins to work through all the colors she knows, singing, "she's red all over, she's blue all over, she's yellow all over, she's . . . " Charlynne pauses, thinking hard. "Purple!" Debi offers, and the child shrieks with laughter. "Purple all over, she's orange all over." The singing continues, as Charlynne proposes outrageous colors and combinations of colors for the seated figure, culminating with, "She's *black* all over!"

By now, after all this considerable exertion, Charlynne is so excited that she can hardly breathe. Her attention to the book flags, and she switches to a game where she practices standing up without support, pretending to fall and flailing her arms around, crying out, "Oh, oh, look out, here I go!" Debi guards her against a fall, catching her as she wobbles. Charlynne is roaring with laughter the whole time, switching back and forth in her activity from her standing efforts to her recognition of the various colors that children might be. She and Debi carry on this way for a full half an hour. "Look at me!" Charlynne shouts to everyone who passes. "Look at *me*! I'm Black, not green." Children and teachers alike regard this announcement with baffled expressions. Charlynne is very excited, carrying on this activity until the time comes for the children to go inside.

Clearly, color is generating much meaning for her, with the grand finale of Black, her identity, given a heavy and very positive emphasis. She repeated the litany of colors again and again, always ending with black as she switched to the falling down portion of her game. She begins and ends the game by identifying her own color, despite the fact that color was not what originally caught her eye. Rather, the fact that the silhouette was of a child sitting with feet extended straight, the same posture Charlynne was forced into by her physical disability, was more compelling. In her attempt to distinguish between herself and the picture she ended up by comparing the color of the picture to the color of her skin. A succession of comparisons, to all the colors she could name, along with hauling herself up and standing unassisted, completed the process, with Charlynne announcing gleefully that she was not green but Black. The two characteristics, color and the ability to stand, were connected momentarily. Other children and teachers merely regarded her announcement that she was Black and not green with amused or puzzled looks, not realizing the events that had led up to this revelation. Again, a more casual or non-contextual assessment of the child's behavior could reach the conclusion that Charlynne was cognitively confused or maybe upset about her color. Someone who, in passing, heard her excitement about not being green would never have realized the extent of the effort that produced this conclusion. Knowledge of the content of the event leads to a different evaluation of her actions. She was drawing a contrasting mental picture of herself, using the green silhouette of a girl as the starting point and working forward to create a clear picture of herself. She tries out colors, all the while constructing a game and maintaining her interaction with Debi. This is a complicated and sophisticated endeavor for a three-year-old. In the end, it is clear that Charlynne has a strong and positive sense of her racial identity. We also see how a Black child works to assert a positive identity, thereby resisting the negative identity that the white-constructed image of Blackness often imposes.

More mental pictures are created in the next account, with color and skin again incorporating nonhuman objects. There are several rabbits in residence at this school. The two males are gray and white and black and white, and the solitary female is solid white. True to their nature, the rabbits have indulged in procreation, and the result was six bunnies: two solid black in color, three white, and one black and white spotted. Corinne (4, African/white) and Sarah (4, white) are playing with the bunnies, which are temporarily contained in a galvanized bucket while a teacher cleans out their cage. The bunnies are about a week old and are an object of great interest for the children. The two girls count the tiny rabbits and discuss their colors. Corinne announces, "The black ones are girls, and the white ones are boys." Sarah gazes into the bucket, then looks skeptical and asks, "How do you know?" Corinne instructs, "My mommy is Georgine and she is Black and she is a girl, so the black ones are girls. My daddy is David and he is white and he is a boy, so the white ones are boys." Sarah giggles. She picks up the lone black and white spotted bunny and asks Corinne, "Well, what's this one, then?" Corinne gets a huge smile on her face and yells, "That's *me!*" at the top of her lungs. Both girls dissolve into silliness, abandon the bunnies, and run off.

The dual nature of Corinne's origins is very important to her, and she makes great efforts to explain and clarify this to anyone needing educating, whether child or adult. Like all people, she experiments with what she knows to sharpen, deepen, and crystallize her understandings. She makes use of a variety of objects and situations to point out her skin color and its origin. Color matching seems to be one way of drawing out and explaining the relationship of skin color to self. For Corinne, the meaning of skin color and identity is complicated, and she does not try to simplify her explanation. She incorporates gender as well as color and family history to construct an explanation of each to another child. She is exploring the many meanings of racial group, gender, relationships, and color and experimenting with different definitions for each. Clearly, she is developing a strong sense of her multiracial identity and a positive sense of her self, in spite of the constant questioning she must endure from adults (see below) about these matters. Faced with the negative imagery that is generally imposed on Black children and biracial children like herself, Corinne presses forward with a very positive interpretation and delineation of her biracial identity.

Drawing on her awareness of her own racial group and her relationship to her parents, she supplies some of those meanings to her friend, extending her awareness of her family's characteristics and her biracial identity to another child. That she is incorrect in her system for assessing the bunnies' gender is inconsequential to the importance of her own self-definition. Her analogies make some experimental sense, to her and another child, affording each with an enhanced idea of the meaning of color differences.

In a separate episode, another child makes use of the center's animals to examine this relationship between color, gender, and self, again expanding and refining the base of personal knowledge. One day, a pregnant cat took up residence near the playground. For weeks, the mother cat evaded capture and cared for her babies, but eventually the animal control staff was successful in capturing her. Her kittens had become habituated to people, and the center's director decided that they would be placed in adoptive homes. Debi volunteered to take the kittens to her veterinarian and have them checked. On her return from this trip, the following exchange with a child took place.

Debi enters the classroom with the carrier full of kittens, and meets Mike (5, Black), who runs up and asks, "Whatcha got?" Debi responds, "These are the kittens that were under the deck." "Oh, I want one!" he replies loudly, snatching at the carrier. "They already have homes, honey," Debi tells him. He ignores her, stating, "I'll have that black one, because I'm Black and me and my mommy are Black." Told again that the kittens already have homes, he says, "Oh. You want to play a game?" He immediately loses interest in the kittens when Debi tells him she must wait for the parents to pick up their new pets and that she cannot play right now. Similar to the way in which Corinne explained her parentage, Mike determines that since one kitten is black it qualifies as a pet for him and his family. In this case, color matching takes on still another meaning. The variety of explanations and meanings offered by the children has begun to spread, providing some evidence that the children are sharing explanations and stories about color with each other. Several weeks after Corinne created her explanation for the gender of the rabbits, it becomes apparent that she has shared this explanation with at least one other child besides Sarah. Renee (4, white) is feeding the bunnies, which by now have become rather large rabbits, and announces that "the white one is a mommy." Lynne asks her how she knows this, and Renee responds, "Because she's white." Patricia, the African American teacher, is also present, and she questions Renee. "Are you sure, Renee?" "Yes," Renee responds, "the white one is a mommy, and the black one is a daddy." Lynne asks her, "Do you mean that the white one is a female, and the black one is a male?" "Yes," says Renee. "But how do you know that?" Lynne asks her. "Because she is white!" Renee says, with an exasperated look on her face. Clearly the distinction is apparent in Renee's mind, but she has difficulty explaining her rationale to the adults.

Renee and Corinne have probably discussed the matter of color and gender between themselves. Sharing conversations is a favored activity among the children, and they take every opportunity to indulge in this behavior. Private conversations, away from adults, are prized. Renee has absorbed the spirit of Corinne's analysis, but the details are altered. She has redefined the colors to reflect her own evaluation of color and gender. Since she is white, the variables may be altered to reflect whiteness as a female characteristic. There is some evidence that skin color, at least as it relates to determining gender, has become a topic of personal conversation among the children.

Racial markers and skin color are also used to point out differences between people. Once again, for Black children and for the children who are of mixed racial–ethnic heritages or from other countries these variables are compelling. One teacher, Jeanne, is reading a storybook to the kids. Afterward, the children respond eagerly to Jeanne's question, drawn from the story, "How are we the same and different at the same time?" The children mention hair, age, and skin color. No prompting or suggestions are needed to get them going. Taleshia sits next to Debi, with her hand on Debi's leg. She studies the contrast once again, then turns and says to Debi, "We're different colors." She continues to study the skin tones, turning her arm over and back several times. Other children make observations about height, hair, and other physical characteristics. Corinne offers, "My mommy and I have the same skin, but my daddy doesn't. But we're one family." For children in families where difference is a part of daily life the nature of racial group, skin color, and other differences may assume particular importance. The more differences are noticed, in any context, the more they become part of dialogue and behavior among the children.

On one occasion talk about racial group and color involved a group of four children. The dialogue begins with a discussion of clothing colors, which moves into a comparison of clothing, hair, and skin colors. Debi is pushing Taleshia (3, Black), Christine (3, Asian), and Amber (3, Asian) on the tire swing. Brittany (4, white) comes over and informs Debi, "You have on white shoes and black socks and then black shorts." "Sure do," Debi replies, "and you have on white socks and blue shorts and a blue shirt." This technique of simply repeating what the children told her has proven to be very effective in carrying on child-centered conversations. Brittany grins, looking down and regarding her clothing with some amusement. The similarity between her clothing and Debi's is apparent. Also apparent is Brittany's ultimate design: she seeks a spot on the tire swing. Taleshia then informs Debi that Debi has black hair. Debi replies, "Yes, but really I have black and white hair. See?" Debi bends toward the children and gestures to the gray streaks in her dark hair. Taleshia looks closely and then nods her head. Debi continues to push the swing, while the three girls chat.

"You," Taleshia says emphatically to Debi, "are white." "Yes," Debi agrees and continues, "and you are Black," once again imitating a child's remarks. Taleshia grins delightedly. "She's white too," Taleshia continues, pointing at Peggy, who has now joined the group. "Yes, she is white too," Debi agrees. Taleshia regards Elizabeth (3.5, Chinese) for a moment and then announces, "She's not white." "She's not white," Taleshia repeats. Debi agrees with the child's assessment and responds, "No, she's not white, she's Chinese." Debi extends Taleshia's remark to include nationality. "She's from China," Taleshia states, verifying Debi's remark and providing evidence that she realizes the connection between "Chinese" and China. "Yes, she is," Debi agrees, while Elizabeth laughs, apparently delighted that another person is bringing her into the conversation. "She's from China too," says Taleshia, pointing at Amber. "Yes, she is from China too," Debi tells her. "She's got black hair like you do," Taleshia continues. "She sure does," Debi notes. "So does Elizabeth. Very pretty black hair," Debi adds, making Elizabeth smile. "Taleshia throws her head back and laughs. "Everybody's got black hair," she says. "No," Debi disagrees, "not everybody. Who doesn't have black hair?" Debi asks her. "Robin," she replies. Taleshia thinks for a moment and adds, "Sarah." "Anybody else?" Debi asks. "Peggy!" Taleshia shouts. "Sure enough," Debi says, "but what color is it?" "Brown," Taleshia again shouts, delighted that she is getting the right answers to this game. "Right again. Is that the same as Robin's?" "No!" she shouts again. "What color is Robin's hair?" Debi asks. "Yellow."

Suddenly tired of the talk, Taleshia leans back and begins to sing, "Nanny, nanny, boo, boo, you can't get me!" to Sarah, who is passing by. "I want off now," she demands, and Debi lifts her down from the swing, replacing her with Peggy. Taleshia and Sarah enter a game of chase. Elizabeth and Amber begin to chant, "Ahhhh," starting low and rising up until it ends in screeching laughter as the tire swing moves from low to high.

The details of this scene are complex. Here the children are discussing and playing with various color and cultural issues, sometimes individually, sometimes all at once. They are quite excited by the game. A discussion of clothing quickly dissolved into an activity featuring categorization of different persons into racial and ethnic groups. The children begin their talk with a simple comparison of clothing, but the game soon evolves into a complex dialogue adding racial group, skin color, and national origins. Debi's responses to the children were primarily imitations of those addressed to her. Taleshia demonstrated a sophisticated ability to categorize the other children, recognizing that Elizabeth and Amber are not white. Yet she did not dichotomize color, reducing it to a matter of either Black or white. Instead, color, racial group, and nationality are combined. Taleshia extended her evaluation of the Asian girls' color to incorporate their national origin and racial group, noting that while they were not Black, they also certainly were not white. It became necessary to use yet another category: Chinese. This category was not a new one for the children. Taleshia knew immediately that being Chinese meant a person was from China. The complicated nature of difference is not lost on this child, who strives to keep a complex matter intact.

A word here on Debi's involvement in the conversation: All the while she was engaged with the children, it was on her mind that she not lead them to conclusions. When she offered a name for the "not white" category, she was drawing on her knowledge, shared by the children, that Chinese was a category of people. The ideas of nationality and ethnicity were well known to these children. They had been exposed to many different racial, ethnic, and national labels, through their experiences with each other and through structured lessons delivered by the teaching staff. Food, language, dress, and other markers had been widely shared. That Taleshia eagerly concurred with Debi indicates that this view was not novel. Much of what Debi did in this interaction was in imitation of the children, a practice that the children themselves engage in often. Further, the fact that Debi was not treated the same as other adults at the center is further evidence that the children routinely would not pay her much more heed than they would another child who made a similar suggestion. The children themselves were solidly in charge of the social comparisons and constructions underway at the school.

In the next scene the differences between the children become an occasion for mass comparisons. We are at the tire swing again, and Debi is pushing three children, Dao (4, Asian), Rita (3, white/Latina), and Trevor (3, white), and listening to their conversations. Joseph (3, Black) joins them. Rita remarks to Debi, "You know what? I like his hair." She points to Joseph's head. His hair is done in five or six rows of plaits that run from front to back and are gathered in a knot in the back. "It's curly," Rita continues, reaching out and patting Joseph on the head. Joseph smiles at Rita as she touches his head. He says nothing. "I like his hair too," Debi tells Rita. Trevor says to Rita, "That's because he's Black." Rita agrees, adding, "Yeah, and my hair is curly too. And it's getting long and pretty. But I'm not Black, I'm Spanish." Trevor says, "My hair is straight. Debi's hair is straight too, and really, really, really, long. Right?" He looks at Debi for confirmation. "Yup," Debi agrees with him, "my hair is straight and long and dark brown with lots of gray streaks." Trevor adds, "Because you're old." Debi nods. "Old as the hills, right Dao?" Debi addresses another child. Dao nods and says, in a low voice, "My hair is straight and short and dark." This remark is unusual for Dao, who is usually very quiet, rarely saying anything. During this exchange Joseph says nothing, although he has pointed out to Debi in the past that he is Black.

This is a child-initiated and child-directed interaction. Indeed, the research literature indicates that it is common for children to "initiate their involvement with adults, who may support children's learning by fitting their assistance into children's already occurring interests and efforts" (Rogoff 1998, 706). In this case, our children feel obliged to point out differences in coloring and hair type and are intrigued by these distinctions. Perhaps they suspect that other children would not notice or comment on differences unless attention is directed toward them. The exchange demonstrates the everyday nature of racial and ethnic comparisons within the center. At least eleven children were involved in the previous two dialogues, a figure that represents a substantial percentage of the center's classroom population. The children sought out differences and remarked on them in detail and at length, often with some sophistication. They are dealing with racial and ethnic identities, as well as racial–ethnic histories and cultural matters. They incorporated into their interactions many aspects of ethnicity and racial group that are not generally believed to be part of preschool children's repertoires of abilities. The extent of this sharing allows them to ask questions, support each other's conclusions, and contribute to the direction of discussion, skills developed to a significant degree outside the teacher-dominated spheres of center life. They are in charge here, acting on their thoughts and considerations. These scenes illustrate how peer relations become a critical aspect in learning about the meaning of racial and ethnic differences. No teacher initiated these conversations. Only one adult was involved, and that involvement was limited. The topic of discussion was both salient and spontaneous for the children.

The children here were wrestling with complicated and socially important ideas. These markers of racial and ethnic origin informed them about each other. They named, indicated, and discussed several aspects of racial group and ethnicity. These were frank and curious discussions of social markers useful in understanding the nature of the larger world and relationships within both that world and the more constrained and circumscribed world of the preschool.

SHARING IDEAS ABOUT RACIAL GROUP AND ETHNICITY

Since the center housed a racially and ethnically diverse population, there was plenty of opportunity for discussion about children's backgrounds. For individual children, skin color was not the only element in the creation of self-identity and self-concept. Nationality and ethnicity also occupied the center of recurring interactions in the classroom and on the playground. Sometimes this discussion arose from an activity or from an adult question to a child. On more than one occasion, however, the children themselves initiated dialogue with each other about their nationality or ethnic background.

In one situation, Kumar (6, Asian), who is visiting the classroom; Corinne (4, African/white); and Susan (4, Chinese) are discussing their origins. Susan says to Kumar, "You're not American. Where are you from?" Kumar replies, "Yes, I am American, I was born here." Susan shakes her head, "You don't look American." Kumar just looks at her, apparently waiting for further remarks, with some irritation on his face. Susan then informs him, "I'm from China. That makes me Chinese." Corinne adds, "Yes, see, she is from Chinese." "No, silly, not Chinese," says Susan, "China. China is the country. Chinese are the people." Corinne volunteers, "I'm from Africa." Susan nods, "Yes, you are from Africa, and now you are here." Corinne nods and smiles. Kumar says, "My brother is from Africa, and my mother and father are from Asia." "How can your brother be from Africa and your mother and father from Asia?" questions Susan. "That's silly. You can't be from different places." "Yes you can!" retorts Kumar. "I am from here and my brother is from Africa and my mommy and daddy are from Asia. We move around a lot," he offers in explanation. "So what *are* you?" Susan asks Kumar. "A person," he replies. He then leaves the group and goes to get a drink from the water fountain.

Kumar offered a detailed and precise explanation of his family's multiple ethnic origins. Not only was he able to describe the complexity of his family, but he offered a reasonable explanation for it. Though originally from Asia, his family had at one time lived in Africa, where a brother was born. He had been born in the United States. Susan questions him in detail, demanding explanations for what appear to her to be contradictions. Kumar was able to provide her with a detailed and accurate accounting of his family's complex national origins. Susan also observes that dark-skinned Kumar doesn't look like an American, a remark that causes him to fluff up in anger. We see that the discussion of nationality and ethnicity among children can arouse strong emotions. Kumar's response indicates that he is aware of what he looks like and that being born in the United States makes him an American. Yet Susan's categorization of what is an "American" does not seem to include dark-skinned, black-haired youngsters. She doesn't explicitly state what "American" looks like, but it is fairly clear that she is confounding a certain light-skinned appearance with American. Clearly, Kumar is uncomfortable with the entire dialogue. His final evaluation of himself is that he is a person, a status with little emotional baggage, but one with great dignity.

This example illustrates key aspects of our arguments about how children use and process ideas, understandings, and language about ethnic, racial, and nationality distinctions. A child has picked up an embedded feature of the surrounding white-dominated society and is experimenting with it in her everyday interactions. One issue here is the general understanding of what an "American" is. In most media reports, in the minds of most white Americans, and in the minds of many other people in the United States and around the globe, "American" is synonymous with native-born white American. Most recent newspapers have an article speaking of "American" public thinking in a certain way. These would include articles asserting that the "American public" has strong trust in local police officers, when in fact that public here does not include the majority of Black Americans (see Soteropoulos 1995). In the case above, even a four-year-old Asian child sees another child, whose parents have lived in Africa and southern Asia, as not looking "American." At the same time, she is clearly experimenting with the ideas and is willing to discuss the matter fully.

Experimentation with racial and ethnic concepts was part of most of the children's activities at the center. For the American-born children, trying out new concepts was enhanced by the ready availability of children from other countries. The diversity provided these children with opportunities to juxtapose their developing sense of self with their recognition

of others as different, contrasting a sense of self-identity with their growing awareness of others. Racial and ethnic markers became useful tools for
the task. The children from other lands often found that their origins became a source of conversation and interaction with others. Their racial,
ethnic, and nationality backgrounds afforded them opportunities to engage in personal interaction, thereby gaining attention and increasing
their knowledge of how these concepts functioned in social life.

The children of foreign-born parents afforded us with opportunities
to watch deep explorations of racial and ethnic meanings and understandings. For example, Corinne, the four-year-old child of a white American parent and a Black African parent, incorporated several social variables in her young life. She was a rich source of information about
racial–ethnic understandings among young children. Her biracial, dual-
continent origins were questioned on numerous occasions, yet this girl
successfully negotiated her biracial identity: not merely Black but also
white, not only American but also distinctively African. Her multiple identities confused many adults and other children, yet she easily accounted
for and understood her identities and was able to explain them and their
meanings to others. She had created an extraordinarily strong sense of her
self, one that she defended and explained with great dexterity.

One day, close to parent pickup time, Corinne, Mike (4, Black), and
Debi are sitting at a picnic table. The two children are coloring, ignoring
Debi and the other children around them. Corinne's father, David, arrives
to pick her up, and when she spots him she leaps up and runs to him.
They walk back to the table together, holding hands, and sit down again
with Mike and Debi. David greets Debi, remarking that he would like to
wait and meet his wife here.

"Who's that?" Mike demands, looking at Corinne's father. "That's my
daddy," she replies, beaming at her father. Mike regards the man unsmil-
ingly, then sniffs and shakes his head vigorously. "Uh, uh," he declares, indicating his disbelief. Corinne stares at Mike for a moment, then says, "Yes
he is!" David looks on in amusement, a smile on his face. "How come he
ain't Black?" Mike asks Corinne. "Because he's not," she retorts, glaring at
Mike and grabbing her father's hand. "Uh, uh, you can't have a white dad.
Black kids have Black dads," Mike states, smiling. "Yes I can. I do. We're
from Africa." Corinne's tone has now taken on a quieter quality, but she still
frowns at Mike. "Uh, uh," Mike insists, "nope." David sits smiling gently,
as though he cannot quite believe what is going on in front of him.

"Stop it!" Corinne is now yelling at Mike, which prompts David to
intercede. "Corinne's mommy is Black," he explains to Mike, retaining

his smile. Mike does not respond to him, instead staring at the man as though he does not exist. Corinne sticks her tongue out at Mike, who ignores her and continues to stare at David. "When Black people and white people fall in love and get married they have beautiful brown babies," David continues, hugging Corinne and smiling at Mike, who does not reply. At this point, Mike's mother also arrives to pick him up from school, distracting him and ending the episode.

Mike adamantly refused to acknowledge that Corinne's father was white, despite the facts that a white man was sitting right in front of him and that Corinne declared this man to be her father. Mike justified his disbelief by referring to a rule he had garnered from his own experience: Black children could not have white parents. Mike's denial of Corinne's origins, and by implication her multiracial identity, was met with opposition from her and an explanation from her father, but he persisted. As far as he was concerned, Corinne was a Black child, and Corinne's skin color and facial features confirmed his evaluation. Hence she could not have a white parent, since in his experience Black children invariably had Black parents. The contradiction of Corinne's parentage was too much for him to bear.

Mike was not the only person who challenged Corinne's explanation of her origins. Adults, too, questioned whether or not Corinne really knew who, and what, she was. One day, during a sharing circle, Corinne was invited to describe her family and her home. She eagerly launched into a description of her home in Africa, elaborating the story with a tale about riding elephants in the backyard. As Corinne spoke, Debi overheard Cindy and Lynne, two center employees, remarking on her story. "Isn't that cute!" Cindy said, "That little girl thinks she's from Africa." Lynne smiled and said, "Oh, she probably heard her parents say that she was African American and is just confused." Corinne continued with her story, blissfully unaware of the disbelief evident on the adults' faces.

Yet another adult directly confronted Corinne about her origins. Jody, a teacher who had not been acquainted with Corinne for very long, was reading a book with the child. The story concerned a mouse that built famous monuments (e.g., the Eiffel Tower) out of cheese and traveled the world to get his ideas. As Jody read the story, Corinne excitedly pointed to an illustration and interrupted, "Oh, those are pyramids, they're in Africa! I'm from Africa, you know," the girl shared with Jody, smiling and nodding her head. Corinne obviously expected agreement from the teacher, but what she got was surprising disagreement. "Oh no, honey, you're not from Africa," Jody smiled, shaking her head. "You're African American." Corinne looked at her and replied, "No, I am from Africa."

She named the country, then waited for Jody to continue. Clearly, Corinne had been through this before with other adults and was waiting patiently for the teacher to accept her explanation of her African origins. "Your mommy and daddy's ancestors came from Africa, but you are African American," Jody continued to insist. Frowning, Corinne retorts, "No, you don't get it, I'm from Africa. My daddy is from here."

By now, the teacher seems convinced that the child is confused and changes the subject, returning Corinne's attention to the story. Corinne, however, has either lost interest or is frustrated by the teacher's refusal to believe her story, and as soon as the book is closed she leaps down from Jody's lap and races to the playground. "Boy, that kid is confused!" Jody remarks to Debi, once Corinne is out of earshot. "Her parents must really be telling her some tales," she smiles. "Actually," Debi begins, "Corinne really is from Africa. Her mom and dad met there." Jody stares at Debi and reddens. "Oh," she finally replies, "how interesting."

Neither children nor adults had difficulty accepting that several of the children were born in Europe or Asia. Yet, whenever Corinne offered to a newcomer her story that she was from Africa, there was disbelief, especially on the part of adults. The task of explaining her origins became a recurring chore for Corinne. She was forced to continually defend herself, especially to adults, the authority figures in her life. They provided her with the most difficulties. Eventually, she acquiesced and no longer attempted to talk to adults about her origins or correct their mistaken beliefs. One day, when once again instructed by a well-meaning adult that she was African American, Corinne merely rolled her eyes and replied, "Whatever." She had learned a valuable lesson: Adults often do not believe what small children tell them, even if it is true.

In other settings, whites did acknowledge her African origins, but put a negative accent on that background. For instance, Corinne and Brittany (4, white) are playing in the dress-up area. When Brittany is finished putting on her costume, she remarks to Corinne, "Let's go. We've got to get our husbands from work." Corinne brightens and joins the game. They both get purses from a closet and begin to walk around in circles. When no husbands are forthcoming—the one boy in the immediate area studiously ignores them—they abandon that game and pretend to be mothers.

They choose dolls from the basket full of playthings, Brittany a white one and Corinne a Black one; place the dolls on the floor; and begin to undress them. Brittany then announces that she will get dinner ready and heads for the kitchen area. Corinne picks up Brittany's doll and calls after her, "I'll watch your baby for you." Brittany immediately returns to the dress-up area, snatches the doll from Corinne and says, "No, you can't take care of her. You're from Africa." Corinne frowns at her. Brittany refuses to give the doll to Corinne, who is still holding her own doll. "I don't want an African taking care of her. I want an American. You're not an American, anybody can see that," Brittany insists, frowning. Corinne frowns back, "I am too an American too. First from Africa, then America. Both." Brittany merely stalks away, leaving Corinne to stare at her. This play session is over.

It is evident from Brittany's remarks that she incorporates two important concepts into her system of socio-racial classification: Americans are synonymous with those who are visibly white, and Africans are invariably untrustworthy. "I don't want an *African* taking care of her," Brittany declares, emphasizing the word "African" and frowning deeply at Corinne. The status of "African" disqualifies Corinne from a position of responsibility, at least in Brittany's mind. The source of this understanding is less important than the way in which the children deal with it. What is critical in this exchange is the sharing of information between the two children. Brittany has delivered some vital information to Corinne, data about the centrality of whiteness that is well-known to most African Americans. It is now firmly a part of Corinne's life, despite her insistence that she is not African American. She has been told forcefully by another four-year-old child that Africans, and presumably by extension African Americans, are not worthy of trust. While she defends herself, and once again offers the explanation that she is both African and American, the pervasive specter of malignant stereotyping has again entered her world.

In numerous settings, whites, both children and adults, attribute characteristics to Corinne that are associated solely with the color of her skin. Her appearance as "Black" often overwhelms any attempt she makes to explain her complex racial–ethnic identity to others. Her knowledge is not accepted by other children and certainly almost never acknowledged by adults. The image of all Blacks being African American keeps non-Black minds and hearts captive. This problem, however, does not belong to the child, despite the fact that she must spend much time explaining her origins to others who are often skeptical of her ability. Corinne's dilemma is a result of her immersion in a society where whites highlight racial identity above almost any other social characteristic and are eager to force racial choices.

The belief held by most white adults that young children have little awareness of their racial–ethnic characteristics and identities acts to exacerbate a child's task of explaining herself to others. Teacher-led activities often did not lend themselves to encouraging children to explain and describe their own racial–ethnic understandings. These teacher–children activities were almost always designed around teacher questions and children's answers to those predetermined questions. This assertion is not an effort to blame teachers, or to suggest that they are somehow scheming to ignore or denigrate youngsters. This is merely the virtually universal nature of the schoolroom. Teachers ask questions; children answer. The nature of the teacher–child interaction in most cases of racial–ethnic sharing did not permit the children to engage in elaborate dialogue or provide detailed stories as they did in interaction with other children or with Debi. The children were usually limited to simple yes/no answers or an occasional explanation of an unusual custom or word. The following episode is illustrative of the pattern present when adults were in charge of self-description.

On a few occasions, especially when a new semester started or new children entered the facility, teachers led activities designed to introduce children to each other. These sharing circles were occasions for reporting all aspects of oneself, including racial group and ethnicity. Shortly after the center reopened from a holiday break, Dean, a teacher from another classroom, arranged to present new students from his room to our classroom. He begins the activity by announcing his name and that he is from the United States. The children then take turns sharing where they are from. "I'm from China," says Susan, predictably. "I'm from Korea," an Asian boy responds. "Where are you from?" Dean asks a boy, whose name tag reads "Emile." Before the child can reply, another teacher in the circle responds, "France." However, Emile vigorously shakes his head no on hearing this and points to the ground. "Are you from here, Emile?" Dean asks. Emile nods and continues to point at the ground, a smile on his face. "Are your parents from France?" Dean continues, smiling at the child. "I don't know," Emile shrugs. Dean turns his attention to the next child in the circle. "I'm from Sweden," a tall blond girl contributes. Most of the children seem to know where they or their parents are from but offer no detail. However, Kumar breaks from this pattern and tells a long, involved story about how he is from the United States, his brother is from Africa, and his parents are from Asia. "My dad is there now," he adds. "Where is your mom?" another boy asks. "She's here," replies Kumar.

Dean interrupts him, moving on to Corinne. She heaves a deep sigh and reports, "I'm from Africa." She waits, looking around her. "Really?" Dean replies, "Are you African American?" The look on Corinne's face is simply priceless. In a display of comical exaggeration, she rolls her eyes, shrugs her shoulders, and flops her hands into her lap in helpless resignation. "Nope, just plain old, stupid African," she sighs, obviously wishing this activity was over. Dean obliges her and moves on without remark. Given the question-and-answer format of these activities, the children learn that adults are not really interested in in-depth discussions with children, or in the racial–ethnic worlds in which they live and interact every day.

Teachers are too highly constrained by a lack of time and resources to allow children much more than superficial exploration of their identities. There simply isn't enough time available for each child to offer an in-depth story of his or her personal circumstances, no matter how much teachers would wish to encourage them. There are too many children and not enough adult listening ears. The teachers in this center expressed frustration with these limitations and often wished aloud that they had more time to simply sit and listen to the kids. But they were rushed by schedules and the children's need for care and pulled in many directions in each very active day.

CONCLUSION

Many African Americans have written about their early experiences with anti-Black racism, the lessons of the racial world, and survival techniques their experiences brought to them. Those lessons have stayed with them all of their lives. Only a few have written about the very earliest experiences, and these recollections provide our analysis with significant insight. Audre Lorde (1984, 147–48) describes one event that informed and guided her for the rest of her life. She was just five years old at the time.

> The A subway train to Harlem. I clutch my mother's sleeve, her arms full of shopping bags, Christmas-heavy. The wet smell of winter clothes, the train's lurching. My mother spots an almost seat, pushes my little snowsuited body down. On one side of me a man reading a paper. On the other, a woman in a fur hat staring at me. Her mouth twitches as she stares and then her gaze drops down, pulling mine with it. Her leather-gloved hand plucks at the line where my new blue snowpants and her sleek fur coat meet. She jerks her coat closer to her. I look. I do not see whatever terrible thing she is seeing on the seat between us—probably a roach. But she has communicated her horror to me. It must be something very bad from the way she's looking, so I pull my snowsuit closer to me away from it, too. When I look up the woman is still staring at me, her nose holes and eyes huge. And suddenly I realize there is nothing crawling up the seat

between us; it is me she doesn't want her coat to touch. The fur brushes past my face as she stands with a shudder and holds on to a strap in the speeding train. Born and bred a New York City child, I quickly slide over to make room for my mother to sit down. No word has been spoken. I'm afraid to say anything to my mother because I don't know what I've done. I look at the sides of my snowpants, secretly. Is there something on them? Something's going on here I do not understand, but I will never forget it. Her eyes. The flared nostrils. The hate.

Lorde's remembrance is a litany of hatred, recalled from her early childhood. This vivid memory of a silent exchange of hate has clung to her all her life, shaping her. It is searing. Even at five years old, she recognized the hate stare. This wordless communication of hatred and disdain was clear and life changing. Over time she has been racialized and sexualized from all sides, by multitudes of whites. Yet she survives by using tools that she says have no name or language to explain them. Only her family, teaching by living and quiet coping, equips her to understand the racism of her world. The toolbox metaphor is useful and powerful here. Living provides children with some tools that are used but that they may not be able to name. Regardless of whether or not a young child can name such social tools, they are still put to use. Recall Taleshia's use of Debi for comparison and reassurances when other children treated Taleshia with contempt. She was a steadfast battler, at three, standing her ground and identifying herself on her own terms. Although she may not have been fully cognizant of either the nature of the battle or the growing array of tools in her armory, she knew how to use most of them, where they were, when they were needed, and how long to persevere in their use. Such preparation is not always overt: Lorde reports that her mother supplied her with these weapons, too, without actively identifying the need for weapons. The need was felt, communicated indirectly, through example; learning to use the weapons came by living in a racist society and experiencing the daily acts of racism. Again, it is the process of living in the world that provides both the weapons and the need for them.

In this chapter we showed how white children and children of color use the racial–ethnic concepts widely found in the surrounding societal environment to interact and build and define the meaning of their own selves and the selves of others. We saw how they interact with each other and with adults—fine-grained data that are only available from extensive observations. Since the 1970s there has been recognition that we need more observational studies of children in the field (St. John 1975). Here we see the value of such studies. The episodes we observed in children's lives demonstrate how children obtain and organize ethnic and racial information from others and then use this information to construct their social lives. Racial and ethnic attitudes, group preferences, and self-identity are all parts of the same process: building a racial–ethnic reality.

In our study we see that the children are learning from cumulative experiences with racism, color coding, and racial–ethnic identities. Negative and positive experiences accumulate over time and in elaborate interaction, eventually, with a wide variety of different others. This makes such experiences longitudinal and significant as social phenomena. How children come to know themselves in racial–ethnic terms arises in part from their grounding in a racist society and in part from their own daily interaction with other children and with adults. Despite the fact that they might not be aware of the workings of the world in a refined, adult way, they have substantial abilities to employ self, color, and racial concepts by the time they are three. In general, the children we observed were able to use color coding consistently and in detailed comparisons, whether the color was of skin, clothing, hair, eyes, or inanimate objects. They routinely created complex explanations for themselves and each other based on skin color and offered descriptions and verification of physical characteristics in a variety of ways. Some, particularly children of color and those whose parents included someone from another country, were able to construct and maintain very complicated self-identities that incorporated aspects of racial group and ethnicity.

Our data are very much in line with the arguments of Lev Vygotsky (1978). Our children are indeed social actors actively involved in creating and thinking about their daily interactions with adults and other children. We see here just how critical interaction is to the development of the individual and the social group. While many of a child's activities may seem external and detached, they often become part of his or her internal makeup through the mental interpretation of the activities. How children manage their experiences does not arise from inside their minds alone but from their experiences with relevant others. Far from being limited to merely being aware of skin color differences and incapable of forming more than rudimentary concepts, as is proposed by much cognitively oriented research on children (see Porter 1971; Katz 1976), these preschoolers recognized the social importance of physical characteristics and incorporated their understanding into daily interactions with each other and with significant adults. In contrast to what some previous researchers have suggested (see Aboud 1977), they showed a strong curiosity about other racial and ethnic groups. They asked questions, formed distinctive groups, and discussed or explained such complex social concepts as national origins and racial–ethnic parentage. Racial and ethnic distinctions are highly salient for this group of children. The concepts of racial group and ethnicity—acquired through describing themselves to others and in the process of contrasting their self-assessments with those of others—assist them in building detailed images of themselves. This skill is essential for the acquisition of self-identification (Ramsey 1987). Accuracy in identification is viewed as critical in the traditional research literature, for if children cannot accurately define themselves they are considered to be egocentric and incapable of understanding the social meanings of critical concepts like these.

Since self-identification is understood in the conventional literature as children's development of the ability to accurately use labels that others would apply to them (Rotheram and Phinney 1987), it is reasonable to conclude that any sense of self must necessarily include a secure and accurate sense of others. Self is only created in a process of recognizing and defining oneself in relation to others. For our children in this diverse day care center, differences with others were apparent. The first episode described in this chapter shows that when racial distinctions are made available to young children, they soon note and experiment with those distinctions. They seize upon them to create games, playing with the idea of difference and incorporating it into daily activities. By focusing their attention on these differences, they solidified them and rendered them crucial for understanding the nature of social life around them.

It would seem that ethnographic field methods should be in common use in discovering the way in which children use racial, ethnic, and other important social concepts in their everyday lives. Unfortunately, this has not been the case, and most research has relied heavily on the administration of brief psychometric measures of racial–ethnic self-awareness. This research rarely recognizes the complexity and sophisticated understandings of children. In traditional studies it is rare for children to be allowed to blend racial and ethnic understandings, even when such blending is part of their lived experience. How they live their daily lives grappling with racial–ethnic descriptions has not been explored. Few qualitative studies of this self-identification have been conducted. When such studies are conducted, they generally combine ethnography or observation with some sort of quantitative attempt to measure self-identity (Erickson 1977; Light and Pillemer 1982; Spindler 1982). These latter studies use observational methods to obtain data on self-identification, but the data are mainly subjected to a narrowly conceived quantitative analysis in an attempt to describe racial–ethnic relationships in schools. Such methodological melding usually eliminates the richness of the field observational data and fails to capture the vitality of the interactive processes undergirding the development of children's identities (see Light and Pillemer 1982). The process is simply too complex and multilayered to capture adequately with conventional survey and psychometric methods.

As we have noted, developing a sense of self is inextricably linked to the concurrent development of a sense of the other. Yet a successful recognition of the existence of others is not enough. Children must be able to manipulate and negotiate their concepts and language about the other to accommodate their own growing and changing sense of self. This process of self–other creation is only possible in a social interaction. No individual child can create self-identity without the cooperation of a wide range of others, including peers, teachers, parents, and, most important, the broader social world. This social context has been most thoroughly ignored in most traditional research on the lives of children. Generally speaking, most researchers regard children as ingenuous or incompetent receptacles for adult information and instruction. However, as our data clearly show, children are competent, curious, and successful manipulators of the contextual information that comes their way. Most are no more disconnected from or unaware of the world than most adults, despite the sincerely held convictions of adults to the contrary. Some individuals' experiences may be somewhat less extensive or informed than others, but the impact and reality of experience are not dependent upon age or even of stage of cognitive functioning.

For most children, experience with racial–ethnic matters begins at birth. Indeed, it may begin before birth, due to stresses put on some mothers by racist beliefs and behaviors around them. Moreover, the formulations and beliefs about racial and ethnic origin are already in place in the social milieus into which children are born. We live in a society where race is central to social organization at all levels of life, and children are not invulnerable to these forces. Children enter the world equipped to make sense of these belief systems. Most soon recognize and accommodate the realities of social life. Those children who cannot recognize and manipulate their social realities are doomed to an uneasy existence, never really sure of what the world is and why it operates as it does. In a social world that is so thoroughly riddled with racial–ethnic discrimination and oppression, it is imperative that young children gain proficiency with key concepts early on, if for no other reason than that they must build a sound mental life. For Black children, and for children whose racial–ethnic origins are complex and invested with negative stereotypes, the need is for more than mere proficiency. Given the negative value that most whites continue to attach to darker-skinned peoples, the task for these affected children becomes one of constructing a versatile and effective set of coping and countering strategies. It is not enough that they merely recognize racial–ethnic markers or understand the history of racism in the United States. Even as young children, they must ready themselves for the constant bombardment of prejudice, stereotyping, and discrimination. They must construct a state of mind that prepares them for dealing with everyday racism and learning to survive or thrive in spite of that racism. Building a self is not a process of an isolated mind but of interaction with and evaluation of a social world. Every mind, in this sense, is a social mind.

3

PLAY GROUPS AND
RACIAL–ETHNIC MATTERS

A large portion of the time Debi observed the children was spent outdoors, either on the playground or the deck surrounding the building. The playground contained swings and slides, picnic tables, large concrete tubes lying on the ground, a sandbox, a rowboat, and a small,
shed-like building we nicknamed "the playhouse." Benches were placed
along the outskirts of the area, primarily to provide teachers with places
to sit and watch the children as they played. The following episode took
place near the playhouse, while Debi was sitting outside watching the children play.

Using the playhouse to bake pretend muffins, Rita (3.5,
white/Latina) and Sarah (4, white) monopolize all the muffin tins. Elizabeth (3.5, Chinese), attempting to join them, stands at the playhouse
door and asks the two girls if she can play. Rita shakes her head vigorously,
saying, "No, only people who can speak Spanish can come in." Elizabeth
frowns and says, "I can come in." Rita counters, "Can you speak Spanish?" Elizabeth shakes her head no, and Rita repeats, "Well, then you
aren't allowed in."

Elizabeth scowls and, hinting that Debi intercede, says, "Rita is being
mean to me." A plaintive statement like this is often used by children seeking adult intervention. Elizabeth didn't direct her remarks to Debi, or request that Debi intercede, but it was plain that she expected assistance with
this matter. After all, Rita was breaking one of the cardinal rules of the center: sharing was obligatory. Acting within the child-initiated framework,
Debi struggles to find a way to help Elizabeth without jeopardizing her status as a nonsanctioning observer. She has to be careful about how and to
what extent she interferes in this situation. She decides just to question Rita
and Sarah about the rules for play and asks Rita, "If only people who speak

95

Spanish are allowed, then how come Sarah can play? Can you speak Spanish, Sarah?" Sarah shakes her head no. "Sarah can't speak Spanish, and she is playing," Debi remarks to Rita, stating the obvious without suggesting she allow Elizabeth to enter. Rita frowns, amending her original rule. "OK, only people who speak either Spanish or English." "That's great!" Debi responds, "because Elizabeth speaks English, and she wants to play with you guys." Rita's frown deepens. "No," she says. Debi queries in surprise, "But you just said people who speak English can play. Can't you decide?" Rita gazes at Debi, thinking hard. "Well," Rita says triumphantly, "only people who speak two languages."

Elizabeth is waiting patiently to play, apparently hoping for aggressive adult intervention, which Debi does not offer. Debi asks Rita, "Well, Elizabeth speaks two languages, don't you Elizabeth?" Rita is stumped for a moment, then retorts, "She does not. She speaks only English." Debi smiles at Rita. "She does speak two languages: English and Chinese. Don't you?" Debi finally invites Elizabeth into the conversation with Rita, and Elizabeth nods vigorously in affirmation. At this point, Rita turns away and says to Sarah, "Let's go to the store and get more stuff." She and Sarah abandon the playhouse, leaving Elizabeth in sole possession of the area.

Young children often use racial and ethnic ideas and concepts to control interaction with others, maintain their individual space, or establish dominance in interactions with other people. For young children, who are almost always entirely under the direct supervision of adults, the opportunity to gain control over a social situation is rare. When such opportunities occur, the children may take advantage of the situation and sometimes organize their activities around racial or ethnic concepts. They may try out different strategies of interaction or employ the power of racial and ethnic concepts to exercise social control within their play, sometimes working toward including or excluding other children from an activity.

In this society we often use the term "child's play" to denote an activity that is simple, easy, and inconsequential. Child's play, in common usage, describes an activity that adults need not give much heed to, or even notice at all. It also denotes activity that reflects children's fantasy worlds, the assumed unreality of their inner lives. As we see it, these commonsense notions of play are wrongheaded. For most children, play is an essential component in human development, and its critical nature cannot be underestimated. Without play and experimentation with ideas, human beings of any age do not grow and thrive. What young children accomplish in their play helps to create their complex social worlds.

USING RACIAL AND ETHNIC IDEAS TO EXCLUDE

As we saw in the opening account, language is one of the ethnic markers young children can employ in their social lives. Four-year-old Rita clearly knows about languages and explicitly defines rules for entering the play group on the basis of language. She has experience with language as a social marker, since she has been raised in a bilingual household. She has spent her whole life immersed in a world where her first language, Spanish, is not dominant. The power accorded to English is familiar to her. She shows great awareness that each child not only does not look like the others but also speaks a different language. From a traditional child development perspective Rita might be seen as egocentric, strongly resistant to alternative suggestions, and bound to the structure of arbitrary rules. However, a closer look provides a *much* different analysis. Rita did not insist on adhering to rules; she changed the rules and developed new criteria for entry into the play site in response to each of Debi's questions about Rita's standards.

Here we see the crucial importance of the sociocultural context, particularly for the development of racial–ethnic concepts in a collaborative and interpersonal context. Rita creates rules for her social context and acts to defend them. The original rule, requiring the speaking of Spanish, fails. She realizes her preliminary attempts to exclude Elizabeth are not effective. Subsequently, this four-year-old then involves herself in a process of elaborating new rules, based on her significant and advanced understanding of ethnic markers. As challenges are presented, she adapts and extends her control, all the while maintaining her focus on excluding Elizabeth. The final "two languages" rule does not acknowledge the fact that Sarah only speaks English. Rita's choice of language as an exclusionary device is directed entirely at preventing Elizabeth from entering, not at creating or maintaining bilingual play space.

Exclusion of others can involve preventing association with unwanted others, as in the previous case, or removing oneself from the presence of unwanted others. We presented the next account preliminarily in the first chapter and will now recount the entire episode. Carla (3, white/Asian-white) is preparing herself for resting time. She picks up her cot and starts to move it. Karen, the teacher in charge, asks her what she is doing. "I need to move this," explains Carla, offering no more than a simple explanation. "Why?" asks Karen, gently. "Because I can't sleep next to a nigger," Carla says candidly, pointing to Nicole (4, Black), who is stretched out and sleeping on a cot nearby. "Niggers are stinky. I can't sleep next to one." Stunned, the teacher's eyes widen, and her mouth drops open. Karen then frowns in thought and tells Carla to move her cot back and not to use "hurting words." Carla looks amused and puzzled but complies with the teacher's directive and drags her cot back to its assigned place. Nothing more is said to either of the children, but the teacher shakes her head.

Three-year-old Carla made an evaluation of the racial status of another young child that is sophisticated and shows awareness not only of how to use racial epithets but also of one of the numerous negative stigmas attached to Black skin. This is an ancient stereotype. Like most children we observed, Carla is not the unsophisticated, preoperational child of the mainstream literature. She is using social material she has undoubtedly learned from other sources, probably in interaction with other children or adults. Here, Carla is applying this material to a particular interactive circumstance. We see once again the *active* aspect of racism as it operates in the United States. Everyday racism is not just about internalized views, attitudes, and understandings of identity; it is centrally about one person doing something to someone else. It is about action and role performance. The child is acting out her comprehension of what a white person does when they do not wish to be near a Black person—a reactive response common across many sectors of U.S. society. White adults often engage in this type of anti-Black behavior, so it is not surprising that their children should do the same. Adults are usually not quite so forthcoming in their explanations for that behavior, however.

Yet most of the center's adults expressed surprise and shock at the child's actions. Carla's brief action has become a major event. Later that same day, after the children have awakened and gone to the playground, the center's white director approaches Debi. Karen has called his attention to Carla's naptime behavior, and he decides to invite Debi into his plan to address the conduct: "I have called Carla's parents and asked them to come to a meeting with me and Karen about what happened." It is significant that the director felt no need to clarify exactly what he was referring to. He added, "If you want to attend I would really like to have you there. Karen will be there too." Debi then says she will be able to attend. "I suppose this is what you're looking for," he continued with a smile. "Well, no, not exactly," Debi replied, "but of course it is worth noting, and I am interested in anything that the kids do with race." "Well," he quickly replied, "I want you to know that Carla did not learn that here!"

Although the children in this study rarely used explicit racist slurs, the director's remark about the origins of Carla's epithet is typical of the responses adults gave in cases where children did use negative terms. The center's staff members were very interested in keeping children from being exposed to prejudice and discrimination, and they made use of a multicultural curriculum to teach children to value diversity. It often appeared that the center's adults were much more concerned with the origins of children's racialized behavior than with its nuanced content or child-initiated development. One of their goals was to foster in the children acceptance and value of differences. Another was to identify and eliminate the possibility of prejudice and discrimination. Both of these goals informed the process of helping Carla and her parents to deal with her incipient racism.

The meeting with Carla's parents was informative. Eight people were in attendance: the director, his secretary, Carla's parents, two teachers, a psychologist, and Debi. This encounter was clearly important to the people involved. At the beginning of the meeting, Carla's mother notes that she herself is biracial, with white and Asian parents. Carla's father is white. Both the parents were baffled when told about the incident. They feel that because of their own experiences as a mixed-race family they have done a lot to discourage prejudice in their children. They chose this day care center because of its diversity. They wished to foster the value of diversity in their family and were bewildered about their daughter's behavior.

On hearing what happened in the classroom, Carla's father remarked, "Well, she certainly did not learn that sort of crap from us!" Her teacher also insisted that Carla did not learn such words at the center. Carla's father offered this explanation: "I'll bet she got that ["nigger" comment] from Teresa. Her dad is really red." The room was silent for a moment. Puzzled about his remark, Debi asked what he meant. He responded, "You know, he's a real redneck." There is again uncomfortable silence, then the director stepped in: "It's amazing what kids will pick up in the neighborhood. It doesn't really matter where she learned it from. What we need to accomplish is unlearning it." Apparently relieved, the adults involved nod vigorously in agreement. They now have identified a problem that can be solved. The director ended the meeting by suggesting methods for teaching Carla about differences and offered her parents some multicultural storybooks about diversity for them to take home. The parents would be informed if she acted in such a manner again. The educational psychologist offered to help the center and the parents, perhaps with a workshop on diversity conducted with teachers and parents.

The reactions of these key adults illustrate the strength of their beliefs about the conceptual abilities of children. The focus is on child as imitator. A principal concern of the teachers, parents, and administrator was to assure one another that the child did not learn such behavior from *them*. Like the children, interestingly, they shape and reshape their conceptions collaboratively. Acting defensively, several of them exculpate themselves by suggesting another person is responsible. The director ends this blaming exercise by attributing the source of the child's behavior to the "neighborhood," a diffuse and acceptable enemy. From this perspective, once the source is identified, the task of unlearning prejudice can begin. Adult denial takes two forms, both revealed in this incident. Initially, the relevant adults seem to be shocked, and they refused to believe that a young child could know much about racial matters, much less use a racist epithet in a meaningful way. Once the fact of the child's behavior is accepted, all adults turn to denying that they are the source of racist behaviors. Also evident in this story is the lack of attention any of the adults paid to the possible impact of the incident on Black children at the center. Clearly, negative stereotypes are alive and well in the center's child culture. Somehow, racist thinking and action have gained a place there, and it becomes apparent in our next incident that it can spread rapidly to other children.

In another example, we see that Brittany (4, white) has discovered the negative power of racial insults and their ability to devastate other children. She uses this powerful language with several different children, across a period of time lasting at least six months. Many of these episodes were quite brief, but some were involved and complicated. We will describe only a few of the eleven separate incidents we observed where Brittany made use of racial ideas in a hurtful way.

In one encounter Brittany actively engages Mike (4, Black) in a long and drawn-out conversation, involving Debi as a mediator. Debi is sitting outside at one of the tables when Brittany and Mike come running up to her with a complaint. At first Debi is reluctant to get involved, but Mike is tearful and demands that Debi tell Brittany that he "has a white one." Mystified, Debi says nothing at first and looks first at Mike and then at Brittany, waiting for one of them to continue. Throughout her observations at the center Debi insisted to both children and teachers that she would not get involved in disputes. However, these two children were determined. Despite Debi's silence and knowing that she most likely would not offer sanction, they persisted.

Brittany solemnly and slowly shakes her head no. Mike whines loudly, in increasing frustration. "A white what?" Debi asks him. "Rabbit!" he exclaims, "at home, in a cage." Brittany continues her slow head-shaking, clearly infuriating Mike as she does so. He begins to cry in earnest, insisting several times, "I do too have a white one, I do too!" in a loud voice. No teacher's attention is forthcoming. So Debi decides to listen to the children, curious about what underlies this argument.

Debi asks Mike to calm down, offers him her lap, then turns to Brittany. "Why don't you think he has a white rabbit at home?" "He can't," the child replies calmly, gazing at Mike without blinking or smiling. He renews his howls. Debi hugs him and rubs his back as he sits with her, then tries again, asking Mike to describe his rabbit. "She's *white!*" he says indignantly, scowling at Brittany and ignoring Debi. His body stiffens. "Nope," she replies again, "you do not." Mike screams at her, stomping his feet for emphasis, "I do too!" Debi takes Brittany's hand, continuing to query her while Mike watches from the comfort of Debi's lap. Brittany informs her, "He can't have a white rabbit." Completely confused by now, Debi finally asks her why, and she calmly says, "Because he's Black."

Finally realizing Brittany's meaning, Debi smiles at her and replies, "I think he can have any color of rabbit that he wants." Mike nods his head vigorously in agreement, sticking his tongue out at Brittany, who ignores him and now concentrates on Debi. Mike informs the other child, "See. You just shut up. I can have any kind of rabbit I want." Brittany glances at him, sticks out her tongue at him, and says, "Can't." She again starts to shake her head no. She is very matter-of-fact about the issue. "You're Black." She seems to be baiting Mike, smiling every time she speaks to him. Mike is getting very angry, so Debi suggests he ignore Brittany and find another friend to play with. He follows this suggestion, but not before flipping Brittany the finger and sticking his tongue out at her one last time. She remains and moves close to Debi.

"Brittany," Debi asks her, "have you been to Mike's house to see his rabbit?" "No," she replies. "Then how do you know that his rabbit isn't white?" She looks at Debi in amazement. "Can't you see he's Black?" she asks, looking puzzled. "Of course I can see that he's Black, but I thought we were talking about his pet rabbit, not him." Debi is again confused, and Brittany leans toward her, explaining, "Mike is Black." She heaves a sigh, as though she is growing weary of explaining the obvious. Debi tries again. "Yes, Mike is Black, and his rabbit is white." Brittany again shakes her head no. Now weary herself, Debi inquires one more time, "Why not?" Brittany retorts again, "Because he is Black." She looks intensely at Debi, apparently regarding her as unbelievably ignorant. "Have you been to his house?" Debi asks one more time, trying now to get her to develop her understanding beyond the "He is Black" explanation. "No," she responds, "but I know that his rabbit is not white." "How do you know?" Debi says. The child replies, "Because Blacks can't have whites." Finally giving up, Debi says, "OK. But you might want to leave Mike alone for a while. You've made him really mad." Brittany smiles, continuing to sit next to Debi while watching the other children play. She shows no inclination to move away and instead tries to maintain her conversation with Debi.

Brittany insists that Mike cannot own a white rabbit *because* he is Black. Her explanation hinges on the rule that "Blacks can't have whites." She assails Mike with her point until he is driven to seek adult intervention. His plea for intercession is unusual, because he is a large boy who is normally in charge of interactions with peers. In this instance, however, he is driven to tears by Brittany's remarks. "Blacks cannot have whites" is her scheme. She appears to be operating with a separatist model in mind. Even the ownership of rabbits must be segregated by color—an apparently powerful image in her conceptual world. It is clear that she has a firm conceptualization of appropriate racial identities and role performances. As she understands and speaks about the social world, there are certain things that people holding a Black identity cannot do, and there are certain privileges that those who hold a white identity are permitted to do. Clearly, the latter is superior to the former. Recall again the idea of sincere fictions of the white self. Brittany has articulated her view not only of the racial other but also made it clear that she has a positive image of who whites are and what they can have and do. Here is yet another example of an individual racial construction that adapts societal mythologies.

Ideas of superiority and inferiority become a tool in Brittany's hands that she uses to dominate interaction with another child. She seems pleased with the level of control she has over Mike, because she persists even when adult intervention is sought. She extends her ideas in a similar confrontation with another child about a week later. In this case, Brittany and Martha (3.5, Black/white) are discussing who will get to take which rabbit home. Martha states that she will take the white one. Brittany again starts the "Blacks can't have whites" routine that she successfully used with Mike. Martha becomes upset, telling Brittany she is stupid. Debi watches this interaction, but this time does not intervene or attempt to conduct a conversation with either child. They have not requested her attention. This scene lasts about ten minutes until it escalates into shouting, and Jeanne, a teacher, breaks up the fight. "What's going on, you two?" Jeanne smiles at them and sits down on the floor in front of them. "What's the problem here?" They alternately stare at her, each other, and the floor. Neither girl offers to explain to Jeanne what the trouble is. They both look at her and say "I don't know" when Jeanne asks again what is going on. Jeanne finally shakes her head, smiles, and tells them that friends don't yell at each other. As soon as the teacher leaves and is at a safe distance, Martha takes a swing at Brittany, who runs away laughing and sticking out her tongue.

Brittany has successfully engaged two Black children in heated interactions with a foundation in matters of skin color. Even at age four she has a strong sense of whiteness and its power to control interracial interactions. According to much traditional child development analysis, Brittany is egocentric in her activity and thus resistant to other interpretations. When her interpretation was contested, she felt a necessity to resolve the cognitive dilemma she was confronted with. However, our interpretive approach underscores instead the social milieu, the interactive and negotiating context in which racial concepts become central. The salience of social power is driving her use of race as a qualifier for ownership of a desired resource (in this case, rabbits). Brittany's use of racial concepts first involves her in intimate interaction with other children and a nonsanctioning adult.

In the first episode Brittany was willing to engage Debi in a detailed discussion, taking valuable playtime to explain her reasoning. When confronted by a teacher, however, Brittany withdrew, refusing to disclose what was going on between her and the Black girl. Apparently, Brittany evaluated the different contexts and made decisions about her own conduct based on those varying situations. A teacher's involvement changed the situation by reducing Brittany to a powerless figure. No resistance was possible in this case, since the teacher's vested interest required her to instruct the girls to be friends. Despite the fact that the teacher asked what was happening, neither girl offered an explanation, in marked contrast to Brittany's intense interest in explicating her logic for Debi. Interestingly, Debi's involvement did not eliminate Brittany's power but instead provided her with the opportunity to explain her actions. Brittany has created a tool to dominate others, one based on a racial concept. In addition, all three children have developed the capacity to be highly selective about the adults with whom they share their racially oriented language, concepts, and behavior. This demonstrates their sophisticated knowledge, not only of their own thought processes, but also of the interpretations and understandings of others, especially adults.

Further evidence of this sophistication can be seen in another encounter, which we briefly traced out in chapter 1. Here, a white child is knowledgeable enough about broader racial relations to perceive the idea of racial–power inequalities. She employs this knowledge to exclude another child from play. During playtime in the afternoon, Debi watches Renee (4, white) pull Lingmai (3, Asian) and Jocelyn (4.5, white) across the playground in a wagon. Renee tugs away enthusiastically, but the task is difficult. Pulling this heavy load across loose dirt is more than Renee can handle. Suddenly, she drops the handle, which falls to the ground, and stands still, breathing heavily. Lingmai, eager to continue this game, jumps from the wagon and picks up the handle. As Lingmai begins to pull, Renee admonishes her, "No, No. You can't pull this wagon. Only white Americans can pull this wagon." Renee has her hands on her hips and frowns at Lingmai. The Asian girl tries again to lift the handle of the wagon, and Renee again insists that only "white Americans" are permitted to do this task. This is the breaking point, and adult intervention is now sought.

Lingmai sobs loudly and runs to a nearby teacher, complaining that "Renee hurt my feelings." Once again, we see the child's discretion at work. She offers no more than hurt feelings to explain her actions to the teacher. Since intervention is in order, the teacher approaches Renee. "Did you hurt Lingmai's feelings?" the teacher asks Renee, who glumly nods assent. This is a familiar ritual. "I think you should apologize," the teacher continues, "because we are all friends here, and friends don't hurt each others' feelings." "Sorry," mutters Renee, not looking at Lingmai, "I didn't do it on purpose." Lingmai stands silently. The teacher waits for a few moments, then finishes with, "OK, can you guys be good friends now?" Both girls nod without looking at each other and quickly move away. The teacher stands and waits for a moment or two, to assure herself that the conflict does not erupt again, then moves off.

There are several layers of meaning in this revealing interaction, a few of which we noted briefly in our first accounting in chapter 1. Here we see clearly the social identity–role of "white American" that Renee is enacting with some skill. We see the dimensions of superior identity, self-expectations, and active performance at the same time. This four-year-old understands that society is divided into categories in a racial hierarchy. She puts the concepts of "white" and "American" together and announces them loudly. It may be that she does not yet have a full understanding of what "white American" means, but she knows enough of its meaning to use it as an exclusionary tool in play. She is incorporating whiteness as part of her identity and knows that this identity gives her power over the racial others. And, most important, she acts on her understandings. She is an aggressive actor who goes beyond expressing a belief to actually enforcing that belief to exclude another child. With her hands on her hips and her frown, she is going well beyond words to have a nonverbal and active impact as an assertive white American.

The critical issue of group membership figures strongly in this incident. Racial understandings are used to assert the greater power of one group over another. Both Renee and Lingmai seem to have recognized the implications of Renee's harsh words and demands. Renee underscored the point that Lingmai, the child of Asian international students, was neither white nor American. Her failure to be included in these two groups, according to Renee's pronouncement, precluded her from being in charge of the wagon, a position of relative power in the day care milieu. Lingmai responded to Renee, but not by openly denying Renee's statements or identifying their content to the teacher. Instead, she merely complained that Renee had hurt her feelings. The adult in this conflict is left in the dark about what really happened, and Renee's experiment in race-based exclusion has succeeded. The lesson learned here might prepare Renee for future contacts with people of other racial and ethnic groups. As experience with social conceptualization increases, it begins to guide children in how they form and maintain relationships with others. Through her experience with Lingmai, Renee has discovered that the use of racial exclusion can be hidden from adult eyes, making it much more powerful as an interactional tool.

Although the incident probably left Lingmai with a painful memory, it provided her with critical information about racialized power relations. Both children now have more experience with racial exclusion. Both seem knowledgeable about the structure of the United States and the global racial hierarchy and seem to accept white American superiority. Renee exercised authority as a white American and maintained control of the play, not only with comments but also with her bodily stance and facial expressions. This finding extends previous research on young children's knowledge of status and power (Damon 1977; Corsaro 1979). It shows that children hold knowledge of the power and authority granted to whites and are not confused about the meanings of these harsh racial words and actions. Significantly, Renee continued to make use of the power of whiteness in several more interactions throughout the school year.

In another incident, whiteness is used by a Black child as an explanation for another child's remarks and actions. No adult is present in this episode except Debi, and the four girls completely ignored her. Lacey (5, white), Sarah (4, white), Claire (3.5, Black), and Brianna (3, white) are playing with dolls. Brianna has a white doll with black hair. Claire has a

Black doll with black hair. Brianna says, "You know what?" to Claire, who ignores her. "You know what?" Brianna repeats her question three more times to Claire, who finally looks up and appears annoyed. "My baby doesn't like you," Brianna announces. Claire gazes at her for a moment, then, without a word, returns to ignoring her. Undeterred, Brianna repeats her statement two more times. Claire finally responds, saying "Well, your baby's white. That's why." Brianna glares at Claire. They play in silence for a while longer. Then Claire leaves. Brianna turns her doll upside down inside a large bottle, announcing to nobody in particular, "She's having her hair washed." She jams the doll down into the bottle hard, scrubbing it up and down and frowning at it. She then turns and frowns deeply at Debi, who says nothing. Brianna's behavior is angry, and this anger attracts the attention of the two other girls. Lacey and Sarah watch Brianna, then glance at Debi, apparently anticipating that Debi will tell Brianna to "play nice," but Debi maintains her silence. Brianna finally abandons the doll on the ground and seeks other company. Her attempts to engage in interaction with other people have been unsuccessful. Shortly after her departure Claire quietly returns and resumes play.

Upon hearing Brianna announce that her baby did not like Claire, the Black child responded by pointing out that the doll was white, suggesting such dislike might be expected. Claire is probably operating out of her previous experience with whites targeting Black people negatively. Claire's matter-of-fact evaluation of the situation startled Brianna, who may have been anticipating that Claire would react to such statements by being upset. Claire, who seems to be a veteran of this type of interaction, merely left the scene, only returning when Brianna had departed. The Black child's departure seemed to anger Brianna, who then took out her anger on the hapless doll. That the other two girls waited for adult intervention suggests they, too, were experiencing some tension. Brianna's attempt to dominate the group had failed, but that she made the attempt demonstrates an expectation that a Black child would be upset by the statement.

POWER, CONFLICT, AND SKIN COLOR

Racial references have been used to increase the children's interactions. They employ racial language to control others. Language is about much more than words and communication; it plays a part in, and is embedded in, relations of power and influence. Exclusion happens in these power struggles when skin color is called into play and used to differentiate between who belongs and who does not belong. The results are racial rules of behavior.

In the next scenario a part-time employee at the center is pushing children on the tire swing. Felicia (3, white) refuses to let Joseph (3, Black) get on the tire swing. She informs him that "Black people are not allowed on the swing right now, especially Black boys." Joseph frowns, then begins to cry and goes to get Patricia, a teacher who is closest to the swing. It is noteworthy that Joseph chooses to seek the intervention of a teacher, rather than rely on either Debi or the part-time employee. Their adult status is obviously not enough for this. Patricia listens intently to Joseph and then takes him by the hand. She walks with him to the swing and points her finger at Felicia, saying, "I need to talk to you." Felicia begins to cry but makes no move to get off the swing. She clings to the chains suspending it as though her life depends upon her grasp. Patricia directs Felicia to get off, "Come on, I need to talk with you. You need to apologize to Joseph," framing her requests within a system of necessary behavior. Felicia still makes no move to get down, so Patricia removes her from the swing, tugging the child's hands off the chains. Felicia now begins to cry in earnest. Patricia tells Joseph to get on the swing and then picks Felicia up, walking over to a table and moving out of the range of Debi's hearing. Felicia is crying hard now, although it is difficult to tell if her tears are from remorse at her bad behavior or rage at Patricia's interference. Patricia places her on the picnic table seat and says something to the child. Apparently, Felicia is in "time-out," a common disciplinary technique at the center. Children who are upset or confrontational are sometimes removed from contact with others until they can control themselves and return to play. "Time-out" generally is limited to secluding a child for only a few minutes, with a standard time of one minute for each year of the child's age. Felicia continues to sob as she sits at the table. Patricia leaves the area, returning to the tire swing to push Joseph and ignoring Felicia's wails.

This incident is significant for a number of reasons. Here again racial ideas are used to assert a white status and identity with its privileges and a Black status and identity that is marked by lesser privileges. Note, too, Joseph's immediate response to the power of Felicia's words. He recognized immediately that she was engaging in a behavior that adults would probably sanction, indicating that he is already, at age three, aware of the power of racist language. However, he was also willing to confront this harsh use of language and bring strong authority to bear against Felicia, thus also displaying knowledge of the adult perspective on such racialized behavior. It is noteworthy that he sought out an official teacher, not just a lowly aide or the relatively powerless Debi.

In another example of a young child's perceptiveness on racial matters, Debi is sitting in the rocker, and Taleshia (3.5, Black) approaches her, asking to sit in her lap. Debi agrees, and Taleshia jumps up, settles herself in Debi's lap, and places her hands on Debi's arm. Debi yelps, as Taleshia's hands are icy cold. "You must be frozen!" Taleshia responds by placing her hands on Debi's face, and Debi pretends to shiver. Taleshia laughs. Peggy (3, white) is watching from the other side of the room with a frown on her face. Peggy comes over to the rocker and stands next to Taleshia. Taleshia looks at her and smiles, "Hi, Peggy." Peggy does not respond, except to deepen her frown. Peggy appears resentful, as she seems to think that Debi's lap is her personal property. She places her hands on her hips and glares at Taleshia, who merely stares back at her. Taleshia soon begins a conversation with Corinne (4, African/white), who is standing on the other side of the rocker. The girls begin to argue about who is the owner of the pictures on the floor next to us. Taleshia gets off Debi's lap to settle the debate with Corinne. Instantly Peggy climbs onto Debi's lap and settles in. Soon Taleshia returns and attempts to get back up on Debi's lap with Peggy. Debi welcomes her, but Peggy pushes Taleshia away and states, "I don't like her touching me." Taleshia frowns and places her hand on Peggy's forearm. Peggy whines, "Nooooo, I don't want her touching me." Debi informs Peggy, "That is not OK," and asks Taleshia to settle down. Taleshia nods her head vigorously, climbs into the lap immediately and lies back against Debi's chest. Peggy again complains emphatically, "*No*, make her stop touching me." Debi asks Peggy, "Why don't you want her to touch you?" Peggy replies, "She's cold and dirty." "I am not dirty," retorts Taleshia, "but I am cold!" She places both her hands on Peggy's face, a move Peggy greets with a shrill scream. "Stop it!" Peggy wails. "Get off me, you're dirty!" She seems to be quite upset. "Taleshia's not dirty, honey," Debi tells Peggy. "Why are you saying that?" Peggy does not respond to the question. The girls renew their struggle for control of the lap, jostling each other and frowning.

At this point Debi tells the girls that if they cannot listen and get along she will not sit with either of them. Smiling, Taleshia complies and sits down on the rug, in front of the rocker. Peggy, however, commences to argue with Debi about who was first on the lap. "If sitting with me is going to be a problem, then nobody will sit with me. I'll have to sit by myself," Debi tells her. Peggy looks distraught, refuses to sit down, and begins to complain to Mark, a teacher's aide, whose lap is occupied with Corinne. "Listen to Debi's words, Peggy," says Mark.

Peggy has acted possessively of Debi in the past, as have many of the children, but she has never used racial language in her attempts to reserve an adult's attention for herself. Peggy seems to equate Taleshia's dark skin color with dirtiness and has created a confrontation in an attempt to get sole possession of Debi's lap. The attempt is a powerful use of a racial stereotype and a strategy designed to diminish the Black child's control over a desired resource. The racial identities of the two children are immediately in the background of the events, though there is no specific use of racial terminology as such.

In the next situation, Taleshia's dark skin again precipitates a confrontation and a struggle for control of a different resource. Debi is watching the children play outside from a strategic place. There are two children at play with shovels and buckets in the sandbox a few feet away from her. As they both play in the sandbox, Brittany (3, white) informs Taleshia, "You're the same color as the rabbit poop." Taleshia stares at Brittany and frowns deeply. Brittany picks up a rabbit pellet from the sand, holds it up close to Taleshia's arm, and says, "See?" She smiles at Taleshia. "Your skin is shitty!" Brittany smiles triumphantly. "You have to leave. We don't allow shit in the sandbox." Taleshia stares at Brittany for a quiet moment, then slaps Brittany's hand away, retorting "Shut up!" and leaves the sandbox. She retreats to a bench about ten feet away and sits, glaring at Brittany, who continues to dig in the sand, supremely unconcerned with Taleshia.

The power of Brittany's comparison is not lost on Taleshia. She becomes immediately angry but does not seek out a teacher and complain. Taleshia is usually ready to seek help from a teacher when another child hurts her feelings, but this time the hurt must be deep indeed if all she feels able to do is retreat in helpless rage. The potential of racist constructions to wound is immense. Here the glorification of whiteness begins at a very early age.

The power of this racialized language to wound others is also illustrated in the following incident, again an interaction between Brittany and Taleshia. This situation occurred after naptime on another day. Debi is on the playground watching the children, when Taleshia arrives with a pained expression on her face. Debi inquires, "What's wrong, honey? Did you hurt yourself?" Taleshia looks distressed, and Debi imagines she has fallen and scraped herself. She cuddles up next to Debi and begins to mumble some inaudible words. Debi examines her for bleeding, as Taleshia is a tough little girl and not prone to cry. Taleshia continues to mutter softly to herself; Debi asks her to repeat what she is saying. "I can't hear you, honey. What are you saying?" Debi probes, placing her ear close to Taleshia's mouth. The child whispers, "Brittany told me that I can't go with Jeanne for swimming lessons anymore." By now she is firmly in Debi's lap, not just perched on the edge. Curious and finding no evidence of physical injury, Debi says, "Well, I don't think that's true. How would Brittany know what Jeanne is going to do?" Taleshia took a deep breath and continued, "My mommy says that I'm going with Jeanne." Debi agrees with her, encouraging her to believe what her mommy says. "Brittany says I can't go in the swimming pool because I'll get the water all dirty." Debi gazes into Taleshia's face and tries to gauge her mental state. She looks back at Debi and states, "I won't do that to the water." "No, honey, you won't make the water dirty. You don't behave like that, do you?" Debi said reassuringly, aware now of how the little girl is interpreting Brittany's allegation. Taleshia shakes her head solemnly. "You listen to what Jeanne and your mommy say, OK?" Debi tells her, putting her down on the ground. "OK," she says.

Taleshia believes that Brittany is suggesting Taleshia will pee in the pool. This is apparently Taleshia's evaluation of her latest encounter with Brittany. However, it seems to us that Brittany is once again targeting Taleshia's dark skin color. When Debi mentioned the incident to Anne, another classroom teacher, Anne is alarmed and says she will speak to Brittany. She adds, "Well, I'm not surprised. Brittany's parents are sort of, well, you know, the typical redneck. You know, they . . . are rather derogatory of other cultures. And the mum's always all la-de-dah, you know, dressed." Debi nods. Anne attributed Brittany's remark to imitation of parental behavior. This is again suggestive of the tendency many adults have to assign blame to parents or other influential adults when young children use racial language. Parental input and home environment figure strongly, in both research and public commentaries, when adults are trying to analyze children's use of racial language. Apparently, adults rarely consider that children are creating such events on their own, drawing from ample cultural material in their own interactive situations.

We do not know what Taleshia concluded about Brittany's remarks. Debi reassured the child that she was not dirty and encouraged her to trust others around her. However, Taleshia was upset enough to seek out adult intervention, and she temporarily lost her playful nature, becoming uncharacteristically quiet. The accumulation of such events was beginning to make her wary. Taleshia knew that Brittany was implying something offensive. The recurring nature of these incidents could reinforce Taleshia in assuming the worst. By the age of three this Black child had become vigilant for racial language directed at her and reacted strongly to negative remarks about her skin color, especially if those remarks came from white children. She understood at some level that whites were forcing on her a certain negatively constructed status and identity that she was unwilling to accept. She would not play the part they wished her to play. Yet the pressures were incessant. The beginnings of what whites allege to be Black "paranoia" are located in a child's continuing experiences with whites acting in racist ways. One is not paranoid, as many African Americans have said, if many whites really are out to hurt you. These roots of racism in U.S. society go deeply into the beginnings of childhood learning and behavior. Black wariness for instances of racism is not extreme, mistaken, or misdirected attention to imagined slights. It is a reasonable and accurate response to a barrage of daily insults, precisely grounded in the earliest experiences with white society.

The following incident describes how Black vigilance is put to use. April (3.5, white) and Taleshia are both on the tire swing, a favorite attraction for the preschool children. Nicholas (4, white) is seeking a place on the swing, and he pushes Taleshia to one side. As he pushes, he attempts to place Taleshia's hands over April's, making room for his own hands on the chain. Taleshia allows him to manipulate her hands, making no attempt to move them off April's hands. However, April now yells "*No*," and strikes out, not at Nicholas but at Taleshia. Taleshia frowns but continues to keep her hands placed firmly on April's. By now, Nicholas has released Taleshia's hands. April again yells, "*No*, stop it! Get *off* of me! Don't touch my hands!" April screams at Taleshia and begins to kick at her, frowning deeply. The kicks become harder and harder, and Taleshia shuts her eyes and begins to cry, although she does not relinquish her grip on April's hands. April kicks at Taleshia with all her might, but still Taleshia, eyes shut tight, lips compressed, and crying softly, will not let go. Nicholas stands by and watches this scene with a smile.

Crystal, a classroom teacher, approaches the trio and tells them to get down. Crystal instructs April to go to time-out. April refuses to move. Crystal repeats her instructions, but April is obdurate. Crystal is apparently frustrated and relents, helping Nicholas to get on and allowing April to remain on the swing. The three children eye each other and remain silent. Crystal stays near the swing, maintaining a watch on the children. Taleshia, who had stopped her crying when Crystal approached, watches the intervention with interest. Taleshia begins to sing, which appears to annoy April anew. "Those are not the right words, you stupid," April says to Taleshia. Taleshia ignores her and continues her singing, now louder. Crystal moves away, thereby freeing the children on the swing from her direct supervision.

Taleshia continues to sing what sounds to Debi like a nonsense song. The three appear to have reconciled, but suddenly April grabs the sides of Taleshia's head in both of her hands, getting right up in Taleshia's face. "Those are not the right words, you stupid nigger," April growls under her breath, apparently anxious to avoid further teacher intervention. Taleshia, however, ignores April, singing louder and smiling, apparently pleased with the irritation she is creating for April. April and Nicholas both grab at Taleshia's face now, trying to cover her mouth. Taleshia pulls away and keeps up with her singing. April and Nicholas persist, and Taleshia stops, frowning at them and saying, "Stop it!" as the other two try to cover her mouth. "Stop that singing, stupid nigger!" April hollers loudly. A nearby teacher's aide, hearing the shouting, intervenes and removes both April and Nicholas from the swing. April starts to cry in protest, but the aide instructs the child to sit in time-out for three minutes. April sits with a scowl on her face; Nicholas leaves to chase another boy; and Taleshia retains her place on the swing, smiling and continuing her song.

Interestingly, this time Taleshia did not seek the intervention of an adult, although she most likely saw Debi nearby. She chose instead to respond to the harassment on her own, sticking to her place. More important, she increased her retaliatory aggravation of the other two children, seemingly daring them to annoy her. She worked hard at maintaining her place on the swing, apparently seeking teacher attention for the actions of the other children through the device of singing loudly. As it developed, Taleshia took over this situation, quickly moving from victim to victor. None of the children mentioned the racist comments to the adults who intervened in this episode. It remained unknown to them, as they heard none of the racist names. Such missing information can reinforce adult beliefs that children do not notice racial markers and are not capable of using epithets in an accurate or meaningful way.

While racial denigration at the center usually targeted children of color, occasionally a white child suffered from name-calling. Children of color occasionally manipulated an interaction by introducing skin color as a factor, as this episode illustrates. Jill, a teacher's assistant, pushes the swing. Robin (4, white) is next in line for a place on the swing, which holds only three children at a time. Taleshia (3.5, Black), Corinne (4, African/white), and April (3.5, white) are already on the swing when Jill stops it and asks, "Who will get off to give someone else a turn?" Mike (4, Black) rushes up and says, "I want April to get off." April, who was the last one to get a turn retorts, "No, I just got on." Mike leans toward her and shouts, "Yes!" April insists, "*No!*" This exchange continues for several rounds, until Mike finally yells, "Get off, white girl! Only Black folks on the swing, you see?" Mike has articulated a racial rule to create his own Black play group. April, not to be intimidated, yells a final *"No!"* at the top of her lungs.

Now Mike, who is frustrated that his demands are not met, turns his attention to Taleshia, telling her, "You're ugly, and your mama plaits your hair funny." Taleshia scowls at him. Jill, who appears to be confused and upset by the scene, finally says, "Mike, stop it. I don't like the things you're saying." Mike ignores her, turns to Taleshia and repeats, "Get off, ugly! Get off, Black ugly girl!" In response to Mike's gendered comments, Taleshia does get off, apparently deciding to appeal to higher authority. She stalks off and approaches Anne, a classroom teacher, to complain. Jill does not resume pushing the swing but waits for the official judgment from the teacher. Jill does ask Mike to get off and sit in time-out. He remains seated on the swing. She repeats her request, and again he does not budge. Robin now joins in and begins to repeat the center's rules for the swing. Mike sticks his tongue out at Robin and says, "Shut up, white girl. Get off this tire!" He continues to grip the swing.

Becoming increasingly distraught, Jill tries one more time to get Mike to sit out, telling all three kids that she will no longer push them if they are going to act ugly. Mike finally goes, but as he sits on a bench he puts his face in his hands and pretends to cry. Anne and Taleshia approach him, Anne looking concerned and Taleshia with a triumphant look on her face. Jill goes over to the bench and sits down next to Mike, talking to him about turns and his crying. Anne asks Jill, "What happened?" Jill replies, "Mike didn't want to share." Now Mike begins to cry in earnest. Anne says, "Well, Taleshia and I need to talk with him about hurting feelings." Anne gathers Mike and Taleshia up and takes them to a quiet corner to talk. April is left out of the intervention but has abandoned the swing for other pursuits.

Taleshia apparently reported to Anne only that Mike had "hurt her feelings," which, as we have seen, is a common complaint on the playground and one for which there was a standard response from adults. Jill, in fact, employed that response when she informed Mike that she "didn't like" what he was saying. Children were usually encouraged to be "friends" and to "work out" their difficulties without name-calling and anger, but details of their conflicts were rarely offered to teachers, nor did teachers seem to expect such particulars. The teachers' task lay in resolving the children's conflicts quickly and administering the standard "friends get along" routine. The plaintive, "He hurt my feelings!" was usually sufficient to engage adults in some type of sanctioning intervention. In this interaction both skin color and gender played a significant part. At one point, Mike seems to be suggesting the negative imagery (ugliness) of Black girls and women that is circulated in the larger white-dominated society. Here is an example of the way in which children of color themselves participate in the perpetuation of a racist society. Noteworthy, too, is April's reaction. She did not report that Mike had hurt her feelings, leaving that to Taleshia, who apparently only made a general complaint. April maintained her own power, not succumbing to Mike's demands even when he resorted to the hurtful racial remarks. Moreover, the white teacher reinforced this power by leaving April out of the later dialogue and discipline, which involved only two of the Black children.

In another situation, Del (4, Black) wrestles Travis (4, white) to the ground. Del is large for his age, closer to the size of a six-year-old. He sits on Travis's chest, loudly announcing, "Stay down there, you. I'm Black; I'm powerful. I'm Black. I'm strong." Travis's face screws up, ready to cry. He struggles, and Debi begins to rise from her seat, ready to stop this situation. However, Del dramatically switches his demeanor when he notices Debi, saying, "Travis, you OK?" He looks closely into Travis's face. Travis says, "Get off me!" Del rolls off and begins to mimic Travis's crying. Travis rises quickly and, frowning at Del, runs off. Del begins to laugh loudly, rolling around on the ground for a moment in glee.

There are several layers of meaning in the words and actions of this episode. Del seems to have accepted an image of Blacks, especially Black men, as being strong and powerful. This could mean that he is expressing some positive consciousness suggested by his parents, perhaps as part of their teaching about strategies for dealing with everyday racism in the child's life. The Black identity–role pressed on Black Americans by white Americans often generates resistance. One type of resistance historically is the Black power movement, with its strong accent on "Black is beautiful." Blacks have sometimes appropriated the negative stereotypes, turning them into positive affirmations of their humanity. In this manner, what whites take to be negative was rejected and replaced with a strong positive interpretation of Black history and tradition. Today, this view remains an important source of resistance to racism by Black adults and children. In this case, Del has a moment of feeling strong and superior, an uncommon moment in the trajectory of a typical Black boy's life. Still, the strong assertion of this positive sense can have negative consequences. Del uses what is positive for him in a way that might create a negative and racialized reaction in another child. The most critical aspect of this interaction, however, is that both are trapped in the structures of a racist society.

Among the majority of white adults there is a stereotyped image of Black men as being physically strong if not athletic (see Feagin 2000). Thus, Del's actions have the potential to reinforce an old stereotype in the eyes of a white child and perhaps in his parents and friends. Del's performance is setting up the potential for Travis to draw on this experience and use it as support for later open use of such a stereotype. If Travis later does become consciously aware of the image of the Black male as physically strong and threatening, he may recall this early experience with a very young Black male. This process illustrates how societal stereotypes can be reinforced in individuals. Old racist images, strengthened by even one negative experience with a Black child, can acquire a dominant place in a white mind that is inundated by racist images and predispositions. It would be a mistake to assume that a single experience could have little influence on an individual's mindset. Most adults can recall some single moment of trauma that unduly influenced the rest of their lives, such as a scare from an insect, a fall from a bicycle, or confrontation with a bully. Had Del and Travis both been white, an incident like this would have no potential for a racialized conclusion, then or later in time. The key variable in this interaction seems to be Del's assertion of strength associated with Blackness. Both boys, like most adults of all racial and ethnic backgrounds, are caught in the racial history of the United States, one whose long arm constantly reaches from the distant past into the present.

The dispiriting nature of the previous examples should not lead us to conclude that all the children's interaction that centered on race was exclusionary. Much attention was also devoted to including others in play and creating inclusive opportunities for play. The desire to keep another child's company was sometimes predicated on race or ethnicity, especially when it came to the use of language differences.

USING RACIAL–ETHNIC CONCEPTS TO INCLUDE AND INVOLVE OTHERS

Young children can use racial and ethnic understandings and concepts to include others—to engage in play or teach about racial or ethnic identities.

The next examples show children incorporating interpretations of racial or ethnic status in more positive ways, again in interactive and collaborative settings. As we will see, certain cultural tools, particularly language, are important in such settings.

One day several children from another classroom come to our classroom to visit. Elizabeth (3, Chinese) and Amber (3, Asian) spot another Asian girl in the new group of children and run over to her. They speak several sentences, all in Chinese, to the other child, who gives no sign that she knows what they are saying. After watching and listening to Elizabeth and Amber carefully, the other child finally shrugs her shoulders, obviously puzzled, and leaves to rejoin her group. Elizabeth and Amber always speak English with Debi, the teachers, and with any of the other children who are not visibly Asian. They usually speak Chinese only with each other, their parents, and other Asian kids. It was interesting to watch them try to speak to another child who is obviously Asian, but who does not seem to understand Chinese. We discovered later that the little girl they were trying to talk to was Japanese. Here racial–ethnic group, as defined by physical appearance, encourages the two girls to try to engage a stranger in conversation.

In another situation the cultural tool of language is used to foster interaction. Ling (5, Chinese) has a book that teaches the Chinese language. She announces that her grandmother has given her the book and that she is learning Chinese. Debi asks if she is making progress. "Oh yes," she says happily, "I have already learned many characters. They're called characters, you know." She points out several. "What does that say?" Debi asks, pointing to one. "Cat!" Ling beams. They spend some time reading from her book, and then Ling leaves to show off her reading prowess to another child.

Over the next several weeks Ling underscores for the observer how cultural understandings gradually develop in social contexts, for she engages numerous others in reading Chinese with her. Carrying the book everywhere, she tries earnestly to teach others to read and write Chinese characters. It matters little to Ling if her audience is adult or child; she is heavily invested in her newfound position as teacher of those around her and revels in her power over language. For their part, the other children rapidly embrace Ling's instruction. Chinese characters soon appear on other children's drawings and on the playground. Children actively embrace these new characters and concepts and incorporate them into their activities, a clear suggestion of how children learn racial–ethnic ideas from each other. Yet there is more to this than mere imitation. The children indicate that they know the characters are a different language from the dominant classroom language and are delighted with their new secret code. They take great delight in explaining the characters to interested others, offering to "read" to those who do not understand Chinese. Ling's efforts also demonstrate she is aware that non-Chinese people, including adults, do not know how to read Chinese. Her assumptions about others' inability to communicate reflect a cognizance that the Chinese language is distinct from the linguistic experience of most people around her. She recognizes this even though she herself is just learning to read Chinese.

In another episode, Jewel (4, Middle Eastern/Asian) uses her knowledge of different languages to draw an adult into a child-initiated game. Jewel, Cathie (4, white), and Renee (4.5, white) are trying to swing on a tire swing. Rob, a college student, had been pushing them but left, leaving the swing without a motor. Jewel starts to chant loudly and says something that sounds to Debi like "Unchee eye. Unchee eye." The other girls join in and succeed in attracting Rob's attention. He returns and begins to push the girls again. With a smile, he asks, "What are you saying?" Jewel replies, "It means 'pants on fire'!" The girls roar with laughter. Rob smiles and urges Jewel to "say that again." She begins to chant it again, now drawing Rob into the play. Rob asks, "Tell me some more." Jewel shakes her head, continuing to chant "Unchee eye" and laughing uproariously. Rob persists, asking Jewel to teach him how to talk that way. Jewel obliges, making up new chants and repeating them until the others get it, then changing the words and repeating the behavior again. Cathie and Renee are delighted. The playing continues for a long while, with the girls chanting and Rob pushing them on the swing.

Initially we thought that Jewel might be translating the phrase "pants on fire" into one of her two home languages, one of which was Arabic. Jewel's parents made a special effort to see that their daughter was proficient in both her parents' languages. So it seemed likely that Jewel was translating the English phrase into one of her home languages.

Later, however, we learned by chance that Jewel was developing sophisticated ethnic play around her language skills. When asked what "Unchee eye" meant, she translated it for Rob as "Pants on fire." Rob accepted this, and the game continued. Several weeks later, however, Debi heard Jewel's mother greet her at the door with the same phrase: "Unchee eye!" the woman exclaimed with a smile, picking up her daughter and giving her a hug. It seemed strange that a mother would use the words "pants on fire" to greet her child. Interestingly, about two months later when Debi presented this account to some graduate students in a seminar, one student burst out laughing. When Debi asked him what was funny, he informed her that the words Jewel had used translated to "Jewel" in Arabic. The mystery was solved. Jewel had simply employed her own name to engage significant others in her play.

Jewel's use of her name illustrates Willis's (1990) concept of symbolic creativity among children. Jewel was able to facilitate and increase interaction with an adult of another cultural background by choosing word symbols that intrigued the adult's curiosity. As the interaction continued, she elaborated on that symbol, creating a new realm of ethnic meanings that worked to accomplish her goal. She successfully shaped an adult's participation for some time by catching his attention with language she realized he did not understand. This required that Jewel not only understand Rob's perspective, but also evaluate the extent of his knowledge of language. Both these mental activities require a strong sense of self, in this case an ethnically shaped self, a solid understanding of other, and considerable interpretive capability. In this way Jewel is quite similar to adults, who must juggle language and culture to accommodate interaction, especially if they are not native to U.S. culture.

In this day care center, some children came from cultures other than that of mainstream America. In several cases, such as Jewel's, a child lived with two cultures at home and entered a third culture when at the center. Jewel's case was not unique. Some children spoke English and at least one other language, and in a few cases these three-, four-, and five-year-olds were capable of using three languages. The adults in the center were fascinated by the ability of such small children to exercise such command over language. This fascination afforded the children with many opportunities to engage adults in word games, providing the children with individual attention and adult time. The following situations demonstrate the power of language and how it can be used by young children to create friendly social interaction with others, gently manipulate other people, and create and maintain control over social situations.

Freda (4, white) spends some time in Europe with her mother's family. She and her mother have returned to enroll for the school year. The two of them sit at a table with two teachers and Debi. Freda's mother chats with her daughter in their home language, which is not English. Freda listens to her mother, then replies, but begins shaking her finger, apparently scolding her mother. Freda's mom laughs, then tells Crystal, a classroom teacher, about what her daughter just said. The child had been expressing a desire to begin to practice English long before the family returned to the United States. "Just now," the child's mother says, "she told me that I had better start speaking English, too, so that I won't forget." This family speaks their own language at home, while Freda speaks English at school.

Little Freda has reminded her mother that now that the family is back in the United States they must all begin to speak English instead of their home language. This four-year-old is very aware that two languages are in use and that the choice of language depends on place and audience. She has shared this concern with her mother, reminding her to speak English also. For Freda, social context is perceived and important, for she distinctly separates the places she can use either of the two languages she speaks.

Recognizing that languages are different and that this difference is important for interaction is analytically important in the next account of a child and a group of adults. Here a child is once again in charge, attempting to use her knowledge of more than one language to engage adults in conversation. Corinne (4, African/white) arrives at a table where two teachers, a teacher's aide, and Debi are having a chat. Lorene, the teacher's aide, asks Corinne if she will sing "London Bridge" in her home language. Corinne begins, and although she knows the tune very well, the words do not sound like "London Bridge" to Debi, who is conversant in that language. As Corinne carries on with her song, her parents arrive to fetch her. Lorene tells Corinne's dad that Corinne has been singing in her home language. "Really?" he says, "What song?" "London Bridge," Lorene replies. "Sing it again, Corinne," she asks. Corinne starts again, eyeing her father and getting a huge smile on her face as she sings. He listens and then remarks, "Well, I didn't think she knew that song. We'll have to teach it to her." Corinne continues to smile, and she tugs on her mother's hand, wanting to go. When her parents make no move to leave she darts away, laughing. Corinne has been trying to fool the adults, pretending to know the words. Lorene asks, "Was that 'London Bridge'?" and Corinne's father replies, "The tune was right, but I think she's making up the words." Debi joins the conversation, remarking, "All I could get was 'everybody sit down'." Corinne finally returns to the table, and she and her family depart.

As we have seen, this use of language to encourage others to play or to maintain control over a situation is fairly common among the children. Corinne seemed to take special delight in languages, but she was not alone in her use of language to create opportunities for interaction. The Asian children spoke to each other in their home languages and to teachers, other adults, and non-Asian children in English. They knew that teachers, for the most part, spoke only English. If a child wanted attention or company and was not receiving it, beginning a performance in another language was often a way to accomplish this goal. This strategy worked especially well if the child was from another country, and the adults expected that a second language might be used. The following incident illustrates the power of language and how it can be employed to retain control over an adult's time and attention.

Language is used in other settings for getting attention or for creating interaction. Mitchell (4, Asian) and Michael (3, Asian), two brothers whose parents are from two different Asian countries, are talking to Debi, inventing language as they go. They are having a wonderful time. They ask, one after the other, if Debi knows what a certain nonsense phrase means. For example, Mitchell says, "Mago agoo dado!" then asks Debi, "What did that mean?" When Debi replies that she doesn't know, he states, "It means 'yes'!" He repeats his questioning, using other words that have no meaning to Debi, and then translates the meaning. He and his brother seem to be delighted with themselves and take turns making up words and quizzing Debi on them. Soon Heather, a teacher's aide, joins us. Intrigued, she asks Mitchell what language they speak at home. He turns to her and very seriously replies, "Florida language." She stares at him for a moment, trying to discern if he is teasing her. She decides he is not. She asks him if he speaks Chinese at home. He says, "No, just Florida." She repeats her question about language to him, trying several other Asian languages, Korean, Japanese, but to each query he responds the same way, "No, just Florida." Heather finally gives up and tells Debi, "Somebody is being really silly today, don't you think?" Debi laughs, and the kids laugh, too, pleased with themselves. Heather, however, does not seem amused.

These two young boys, ages three and four, have successfully engaged two adults in a long conversation. They have done this by recognizing that the adults had little or no understanding of other languages and use this knowledge to maintain their attention. Debi treated their actions as a game, responding to them as though they were teasing. Heather, however, seemed to be convinced that the boys were really speaking another language but could not get them to admit it. For the boys' part, by turning this interaction into a game they managed to keep adult attention for a full thirty minutes, no small accomplishment for children in a day care center setting, where one-on-one adult attention is often rare and fleeting.

In another situation, language is again used in play to create and maintain leadership for one child. Ling (5, Chinese) manages to attain leadership of a play group through the use of her home language. Ling and Erin (4, white) are playing follow-the-leader with April (3.5, white) and Nicholas (3.5, white). The younger children are in the lead. As they run across the playground, Ling suddenly takes the lead and shouts out something in Chinese that sounds like a command. April and Nicholas stop dead in their tracks, scream, and run for the playhouse. Erin erupts in delighted giggles, doubling over with laughter. Though Debi could not hear what Ling has said, her actions appear deliberate. She and Erin consult with each other for a moment or two, then go to fetch April and Nicholas from the playhouse. Ling issued another command, again in Chinese, and the three other children race off. This was repeated several times, and in several different formats, until the game was interrupted by the call to go inside for naptime.

It is likely that Erin, April, and Nicholas had no command of Chinese. It appears that Ling was using Chinese to create a game where she is in command. This is similar to the game invented by Michael and Mitchell to keep Debi occupied in the previous situation and to the gaming atmosphere that Jewel created with Rob on the tire swing. This time, however, the interaction occurred only between children. Some children recognize that adults are not the only people who are limited to one language; children too, in particular white American children, are limited to a single language. In such cases bilingual children have realized that others do not share their facility with a second language and use that awareness to generate associations with others. For them, the language knowledge holds power to create and maintain important social interaction.

The next account features interaction only among children, and the power of language as an organizer for friendship takes center stage. This account points out the ease with which adults misinterpret children's behavior. As we have seen previously, adults tend to try to control children's use of racial and ethnic concepts and often interpret children's use of these ideas—and their associated language—by depending on their own conventional understandings of children's social abilities or their knowledge of cognitively focused perspectives on children.

This episode dramatically and clearly demonstrates the way in which children's sophisticated employment of social abstractions is developed creatively and independently without adult collaboration or supervision. Jason (3, Middle Eastern) and Dao (4, Chinese) have developed a friendship over a period of several weeks, despite the fact that Dao speaks almost no English and Jason speaks no Chinese. However, the two are inseparable buddies, spending every available moment in each other's company and imitating each other's activities. The adults at the center often commented on the boys' relationship, at times wondering aloud about how they communicated. Yet the boys experienced little trouble in getting along and spent hours engaged in play and conversation.

As this friendship develops, Jason's mother, who was pregnant at the time, comes to the head teacher with a problem. "Jason has begun to talk baby talk," she informs Jeanne. "Oh, I wouldn't worry about it," the teacher reassures her. "Kids often do that when their mom is expecting another baby. It's a way to get attention." Jason's mother seems unconvinced and asks the teachers to watch for Jason's "gibberish" and to let her know about it. Apparently, she sees this as a developmental problem for her young child and is justifiably concerned.

In the meantime, Jason and Dao continue their friendship. Teachers remark on their closeness despite Dao's severely limited command of English. One afternoon, Dao and Jason are playing with blocks near Debi as she sits in a rocker holding another child. Deeply involved, the two boys chatter with each other, ignoring Debi. However, the talk is unintelligible to Debi. She listens for signs of baby talk on Jason's part but does not understand a word either of them say. Still, they appear to have no difficulty cooperating in constructing block towers, and laugh together each time a tower collapses. Soon Jason's mother arrives to take him home. He steadfastly ignores her and continues to play with his friend Dao. She tolerates his disregard of her and waits for him to finish, appearing to be in no great hurry. A teacher joins the scene and begins a conversation with Jason's mother. When Jason finally acknowledges his mother's presence, he does so by addressing her with a stream of words that make no sense to any of the nearby adults.

"See, see? That's what I mean," Jason's mother says excitedly to the teacher. "He talks baby talk. It's really getting bad." The teacher remarks that perhaps after the baby's arrival this will disappear. Jason ignores the exchange. After a moment's thought, Debi gets an insight and says to Jason, "Honey, would you say that again in English?" Jason nods quickly and responds, "I want to check out a book from the library before we go home." Both Jeanne and Jason's mother look at him and then at Debi, astonished. "Oh, my goodness!" the teacher exclaims, "How did you know to ask him that?" Debi gestures toward the boys and says, "It just now occurred to me. It seems reasonable. They talk all the time." Debi watches the two women. "That's amazing," Jason's mother responds, shaking her head. "What language do you think they are speaking?" she asks Debi. "I don't know," Debi responds. "I don't understand a word of it. Maybe it's invented."

With the cooperation of Dao's father, who listened in on the boys on another occasion, Debi finally determined that Jason had learned enough Chinese from Dao and Dao had learned enough English from Jason to form a blended language sufficient for their private communication. What adults thought was baby talk—and what was thought by the teacher to be a child's jealousy expressed toward a new sibling—was an innovative synthesis of two languages formed by young children maintaining a cross-ethnic friendship. This is a normal human phenomenon and, if the boys were adults, would likely have been interpreted as an innovative pidgin language—the simplified language that develops between peoples with different languages living in a common territory. One revealing aspect of this account is that the powerful adults in the boys' lives had not even thought of this possibility. Their status as children prevented even the adults who were closest to them from considering this alternative explanation.

One of the ethnocultural definers of Dao's social life was his inability to speak English, which caused him grief because it kept him from following teachers' directions promptly. He experienced difficulty in creating friendships, for most other children were not patient enough to accommodate him, and the teachers usually could not take the time to sit and explain things slowly to him. Thus Dao was a quiet and cautious child, particularly when teachers were nearby. Jason's ability to develop a language in interaction with Dao was empowering for the Asian boy: the language was the cement that bonded the boys together. The boys' collaborative actions were not only creative but were directed toward bridging their ethnic and cultural differences. The boys were natural multiculturalists. In this case their humanity united them.

Yet another child's interaction with adults was characterized by her refusal to use English in the presence of adults, even when prompted and encouraged. Angela (3, white) is the daughter of bilingual parents. With other children, her use of English was adequate. Her bilingual parents were skilled in English and reported that they spoke it and their own language (another European language) at home, in part to encourage Angela in the acquisition of bilingual skill. Angela, however, refused to speak English to the adults at the center. One afternoon, Angela approaches Crystal, a teacher, holding one shoe in her hand. Crystal asks her, "Do you want me to fix your shoes for you?" Angela nods yes, clearly understanding Crystal's question. Crystal invites Angela to sit down, then asks the child, "Can you say 'shoe' for me?" Angela shakes her head no, not uttering a word. The teacher finishes the task, and Angela leaves. Debi remarks to Crystal, "Maybe if you tried to get her to tell you in her own language you would have more luck." Crystal nods and laughs, "That might be worth a try. That kid just never says a word."

Meanwhile, Angela has found Sarah (4, white) and Robin (4, white) to play with at a nearby table. The girls are chattering away, and Debi moves nearby to listen. Robin says, pointing to a puzzle piece in front of Sarah, "Hand me that piece." Sarah complies. Angela then says, "I need that one" to Robin, who hands her a puzzle piece. Angela's English is accented, but clear. "Look, look," Angela says excitedly, "it works!"

Although it was clear that Angela was able to understand English, spoke it with other children, and was encouraged by the teachers to learn the language, Angela steadfastly refused to speak anything, either English or her home language, when in the presence of sanctioning adults. With other children, however, her command of English seemed adequate. Context and companions are critical for this child, who does not cooperate with adults but speaks easily with other children. Angela is substantially in control over when and with whom she speaks English.

Language use varies considerably among the children, and contextual variables clearly influence how and with whom languages other than English are employed. For some children, using another language is a way to engage adults, capturing personalized attention and placing children in control of interaction. For others, it provides an opportunity to prevent adults from getting too close, such as in Crystal and Angela's interaction. Still others, like Michael and Mitchell, use language to create a game, playing with the sounds of words. A clear cultural differentiator, language enables children to select with whom they will play and what the content and direction of that play will be—both critical social choices for preschool children.

The creation of friendships is important for children, as it is for most adults. One day, Debi is sitting at the lunch tables with the children, listening to a conversation among Mike (4, Black), Brendan (4, white), and Joseph (4, Black). Joseph remarks, "I'm best friends with Brendan." They are sharing their food. Mike tells Joseph, "Uh uh, you can't," shaking his head solemnly. Joseph looks puzzled and then nods his head yes and says, "Yes, I can." Mike insists, "You can't be best friends with Brendan." "Why?" asks Joseph, who is beginning to smile. Brendan sits silently, listening to the exchange between Joseph and Mike. "'Cause he's white," Mike explains candidly, glancing over toward Brendan as he speaks. Mike continues by adding, "Black folks is best." Joseph just looks at Mike blankly, and Brendan frowns at the final remark. The conversation ends with Mike laughing loudly.

Brendan appears to be perturbed. A Black boy has just announced that Brendan cannot be friends with another Black boy because he is white. This incident occurred in spite of the center's consistent message that all children can be friends and must try to get along. The power of the message that Mike has just delivered is certainly as salient to Brendan as the messages that teachers deliver to the children, especially since the boys are age peers, and Mike and Joseph are both Black. Once again, Mike has apparently determined that Black children should stick together. His proclamation gives little information about its origins, but again it may reflect some parental teachings about Black solidarity in the face of discrimination. As we suggested earlier, this may be part of a defensive strategy that many Black Americans use against the exclusionary environment of racism. Whatever its provenance, once again this early experience for a white child might eventually be used to reinforce racist views of Black boys or men that are learned from important adults in his own life experience. The long-term consequences of a racist society are inescapable for all involved.

CONCLUSION

In *The Collective Memory* (1950, 38) Maurice Halbwachs notes, "A 'current of social thought' is ordinarily as invisible as the atmosphere we breathe. In normal life its existence is recognized only when it is resisted." These words hold significance for our analysis in this book. We contend that the deeper strata in children's lives are important to study if we are to discover workable solutions to the racial–ethnic discrimination and oppression that still pervade this country. Halbwachs's insight is that our connections with the collective mind, embedded in our associations with others, ordinarily do not occupy our conscious minds. This hidden character does not diminish the importance of our connection to the collective experience. The subtle traces of social thoughts are both compelling and shaping our lives. Our understanding of and responses to the world, including the world of racial and ethnic markers, occur within the framework created by our collective attachment. Halbwachs (1950, 40) further suggests adult life casts a shadow over children's experiences, in that much of what children encounter in daily life is in preparation for the adult life they will eventually lead. However, like most scholars Halbwachs, too, quickly dismisses childhood experiences, referring to them as the inchoate functioning of future adults.

Yet our own data, as well as the commentaries of many Black writers (see Lorde 1984), provide convincing evidence that the experiences of childhood create the foundation of adults' individual and social lives. Children must move into and adjust to the adult world, but that world often does not adjust to them. Indeed, children who are frequently faced with hostile adult situations, such as many Black children are, have much of their childhood taken from them. For Black children, inclusion in a tough adult world begins at birth. In a racist society, Black children encounter social strife and inconsistency almost immediately. Much of childhood is removed from them, since they have known that type of suffering reserved for adults. They have had to confront it on the same level as adults (Halbwachs 1950, 40). As a rule, the first whites they encounter make sure that Black children cannot evade the suffering of contemporary racism. They are challenged with it in most of their daily activities with friends, classmates, and significant adults.

Audre Lorde's words, which we cited in the last chapter, point to how the experiences of childhood undergird adults' lives. Lorde (1984, 146) declares, "When I started to write about the intensity of the angers between Black women, I found I had only begun to touch one tip of a three-pronged iceberg, the deepest understructure of which was Hatred, that societal deathwish directed against us from the moment we were born Black and female in America." Black children are stereotyped or hated by many white Americans—a depreciation routinely revealed to every Black child. This social reality is solidly located in the children's earliest experiences in a society that continues to deny the power of systemic racism.

The friendship and peer relationships that children develop in their earliest years can generate or reinforce stereotyping or intolerance based on racial or ethnic origins. It can also facilitate and encourage friendship and mutual social esteem. In the children's accounts throughout this book we see how and where friendships and other peer relationships are critical to the lives of small children. These early social relationships supply them with fundamental skills, assist in their developing a solid sense of self, and help to provide them with understandings of social structures. These peer relationships allow children to try out their social skills at multiple levels and learn how to be a child or adult, to be male or female, or to be white or not white. As we have demonstrated, peer relationships among young children are not monolithic. Some are tension-riddled and reflect attempts at exclusion. Other interactions are centered on attempts at inclusion and group-building. Friendships motivate children to think about and treat friends in a different way from mere classmates (Matsumoto, Haan, Yabrove, Theodorou, and Carney 1986). Children's close friendships outside their family, such as their associations in the day care center, tend to be somewhat different from their relations with family members (Dunn 1993). Indeed, because friendships and other peer relationships necessarily involve more than one individual, they should be investigated in terms of their social contexts. As we see it, research on children should move away from the assessment of individual attitudes and toward studies of interpersonal and intergroup relations if we are to gain a deep understanding of children's lives.

Early friendships are often precursors of relationships formed later in children's lives. How and with whom children form relationships at this stage can influence how and with whom they will choose to affiliate with as they grow up. Early friendships inform children on what social groups are suitable for them and what groups they can expect to be included in over time. Some recent research suggests that these early relationships are the foundation for social understanding, intelligence, self-evaluation, social comparisons, and social competence. The quality of children's early relationships is central to their overall development (Dunn 1993).

Including a study of racial–ethnic matters in investigations of early peer relationships is essential for understanding the nature of racial–ethnic relations among adults. Racial and ethnic tensions and oppression are factors in the social worlds of children, as are the intriguing differences that compel children to explore and include dissimilar people in their worlds. As our accounts demonstrate, these aspects of life are routinely important in children's interactions and interpersonal relations. The connections between racial–ethnic relationships and understandings and a general life orientation are not simple. They depend on the individuals involved, the contexts within which the relationships evolve, and the structure of the larger social world that provides the standards, rules, and opportunities for relationship formation.

Still, in the contemporary United States the social standards and interactive frameworks imposed by the dominant white group continue to create and reinforce de facto racial separation and oppression. Many white adults still harbor deeply racist images and stereotypes and practice racial discrimination in settings they traverse in their daily lives. Not surprisingly, children are not protected from the reality and pain of this racist context, and their activities often reproduce and experiment with what they observe and understand about that racist society.

In the United States neither young children nor adults experience "race" in the abstract; rather, they do so in concrete and recurring relationships with one another. Despite the fact that "race" has no scientific meaning, its reality in the world of interaction is indisputable. In these situations individuals, whether they are the perpetrators of discrimination or the recipients of discrimination, are caught in a complex web of separating and alienating relationships. What could be egalitarian relationships, for children or for adults, are too often turned by the racial schisms of the larger society into alienated relationships. The tragedy of racial–ethnic conflict is that it divides human beings from each other and severely impedes the development of common consciousness.

4

USING RACIAL–ETHNIC CONCEPTS
TO DEFINE OTHER PEOPLE

When the children became rowdy in the afternoons, teachers would often initiate a story circle, to calm them while they waited to be picked up by parents. Early one week, Mindy (4, white) and Debi were sitting in a story circle, waiting for a teacher to begin reading aloud. Mindy occupied Debi's lap and was engaging Debi in a conversation about the latter's ethnic heritage. "You are an Indian," Mindy said emphatically, looking Debi in the eye. "Why do you think that?" Debi replied, rather puzzled. She could recall no recent stories at the center about Native Americans, or "Indians" as the children persisted in naming them. Mindy replied, "You have a braid." Debi, suddenly enlightened, explained, "I'm not an Indian, sweetie." The child then remarked, "Well, your mother must be an Indian, then." "No, my mother isn't an Indian either," Debi replied, and then told Mindy, "My hair is braided because it's too hot in the summer to wear it loose." Mindy reflected on this information for a moment, then responded, "Of course. All Indians braid their hair." She had decided the matter; no explanation from Debi was going to change her evaluation: Debi was an Indian.

As we have already seen, the children at the day care center often explored the complex language and concepts delineating skin color, hair differences, and facial characteristics in order to establish individual identities, define themselves and others, and create relationships. We have already touched on how they use these ideas to define others, but in this chapter we dig more deeply into this matter. The children recurrently use racial or ethnic concepts in their interpretations of differences perceived in others. Further, they offer explanations of others in terms of these concepts. Providing meaning for the "other" in con-

129

trast to "self" is inextricably linked to the developing definition of one's own self and identity. As we have shown in the previous chapter, we simply cannot conceptualize our selves without reference to others. This separation of self and other is essential for understanding both the individual's own mind and the social world. Children's explorations and investigations are recurring and commonplace, as they tune in on these concepts in relationships with playmates, teachers, and other people who are significant to their daily lives. Experimentation with racial and ethnic concepts is not an isolated activity of a single mind, however, for either children or adults. Rather, it is interpersonal and interwoven with an array of social situations and activities. Mindy's interpretation of Debi's hairstyle was grounded in a racial–ethnic image, and her analysis was not unintentional or naive. She attached braided hair to the image and concept of "Indian," to the point of insisting that an ancestor of Debi's must have been Indian, extending her ethnically grounded explanation for Debi's appearance to incorporate Debi's ancestors. This shows an awareness of relatedness, a skill generally not accepted as possible for four-year-olds to possess.

Viewing or researching children in an individualistic way usually does not provide the information necessary for a full understanding of their racial–ethnic thinking and actions. The differences between child and adult behavior are not really remarkable. Just as in adult thought and action, children's social knowledge and related behaviors can be organized and consistent, or disorganized and inconsistent. Further, this state of affairs changes over time and with each child and may vary from situation to situation. Most of our accounts show that children form their ideas about others in situations with constantly varying dimensions and changeable sets of actors. Children's thinking about racial and ethnic matters does not necessarily require cognitively consistent internal processes. Certainly we can demonstrate that adults also do not exhibit consistent thinking about race and ethnicity. Rather, the process of acquiring skills with racial and ethnic concepts usually consists of learning rules—and exceptions to rules—about racial group and ethnicity on a situational and episodic basis. These rules and exceptions are not static, model representations of an objective and invariable reality. Instead, the rules are innovative and dynamic, with children adapting and cultivating them to suit their current situations. For children, just as for adults, the process of learning about racial and ethnic distinctions involves an exploration of a broad realm of human differences, not merely a "one size fits all" technique for mirroring adult behavior.

IDEAS ABOUT OTHERS' RACIAL AND ETHNIC ORIGINS

As we saw in the opening account, at times children draw on their stock of ethnic and racial knowledge to offer explanations for others' appearance, particularly if those others are perceived as looking very different from the child. Debi's hair was quite fascinating for the children, since it reached the back of her knees, and it often provided them with an occasion for comments. The incident between Mindy and Debi was intriguing and analytically challenging. Why did she judge Debi to be a Native American? Initially, we were puzzled. Mindy had been looking at picture books to fill the time spent waiting for her ride home, so Debi investigated the possibility that she had been reading about Indians. While there were many books available in the classroom featuring Native Americans, Mindy had not been reading such a book prior to her announcement about Debi's hair. All those books were still on the shelves, and the books the children had been using were scattered across the floor. After Mindy left for the day, however, Debi examined all the books featuring Native Americans more closely and saw no illustrations that might have contributed to Mindy's evaluation of Debi's ethnic origins. The Native women featured in the available books were shown with their hair worn loosely, not braided or tied back. Debi recalled no stories about Native Americans being read to the children, at least not within the past few weeks, nor were there any posters or other activity materials that could have compelled Mindy's construction of Debi's racial or ethnic origins.

The mystery was finally resolved through later events. One rainy afternoon, a few days after Mindy's remarks, Felicia (3, white) was sitting in Debi's lap while watching the cartoon video *Peter Pan*. As they watch, the movie gets to the scene where Princess Tiger Lily and the Indians are featured. The princess wears her hair in a long braid. Suddenly, Felicia jumps from Debi's lap, races around to the back of the rocking chair, grabs Debi's hair, and announces, "Debi is an Indian!" at the top of her lungs. Startled, Debi turns around and asks, "What makes you say that?" "You have Indian hair," Felicia replies, reaching around and tugging on the braid. Debi assures the girl that she is not Native American. "Oh yes you are, see?" she says, delighted, lifting up Debi's braid and swinging it around. "You are an Indian!" Felicia announces triumphantly. She is delighted, and by this time several other children are watching the interaction. Debi smiles and tells Felicia, "No, I'm not an Indian. It's just too hot out to wear my hair loose." But Felicia would have none of this explanation and responded, "Your mommy and daddy are Indians too!"

Felicia had seen this movie before, as had all the children at the center. Maybe she had viewed it with Mindy and has subsequently made a connection between dark, long, and braided hair and the status of "Indian." For Felicia and Mindy there is little doubt that Debi's hair signals her racial–ethnic background, despite the fact that they are technically wrong in their evaluation. The marker of dark hair in long braids is firmly entrenched in the children's way of reckoning the world. They are in the process of establishing racial identities, both their own and those of others. Debi's assurances that she is not "an Indian" do not dissuade either of the girls from their interpretations.

These two children show an awareness not only of what makes up the visible characteristics of a racial group but also insight into how visible markers are passed from generation to generation. They demonstrate a child's ability to grasp salient characteristics of a racial–ethnic category not their own and apply those characteristics to categorize others in a collaborative and evolving way. The consistency in their explanations for Debi's hairstyle suggests that they probably communicated with each other about the mystery of Debi's hair, striving to place her in a category appropriate to her physical appearance. That Debi says she is not Native American does not end their experimentation. The children's excitement about their newfound knowledge is contagious. These two little girls expressed a need for a racial category for Debi, and when a reasonable marker presented itself in the movie it was seized upon and put to use. Of course, their assessment of Debi's category was incorrect. However, it does reflect an accurate representation of "Indians" as they are depicted in the media that children are routinely exposed to, and it extends the power of this representation throughout the center. Now the children have a living, breathing "Indian" right in their midst. Over the course of the next week, moreover, at least two other children shared in this racial evaluation process, both picking up on the intriguing symbol of hair type. It is likely that this new interpretation was absorbed by yet other children, who were until then only onlookers. Conceivably, they might also have put it to use at a later point in time.

A considerable amount of time had elapsed between Mindy's original pronouncement and Felicia's identical verdict. Both conventional wisdom and much cognitive research strongly suggest that children this young are incapable of retaining complex social information for very long. They need constant reinforcement and heavy repetition of conceptual information before it can even be retained, much less put to use. Most adults insist that the only way for children to receive such information is through direct teaching, carefully structured in an age-appropriate manner, and delivered from adults. However, the two episodes recounted here demonstrate that the children themselves are at least as efficient in interpersonal teaching as are their adult teachers. They often practice exciting new ideas with other children.

Also evident in this series of events is the likely source of Native American imagery—a Hollywood movie. In the process of making sense out of their social worlds, children, like adults, draw their raw materials from their surroundings. Since movies are such a constant condition of the environments of the majority of Americans—on television as well as in theaters—it is not surprising that they are one source of many stereotypes children work with in their own interactions. Here, too, we see that children not only draw certain adult stereotypes from their surroundings but also use them for their own creative and original purposes, in this case to play with and categorize Debi. Notice, too, that their use of ethnicity does not demean or diminish the status of "Indian." It simply attaches a marker to Debi, connecting her to a group of others and thus making sense of her rather dramatic physical difference.

Hairstyle is only one among dozens of meaningful ethnic and racial emblems in our society. It is commonly used by children to delineate others and seems especially important to girls. As we noted above, Debi's hair provided the children with countless opportunities for play, and most of the time it was girls who were the most interested. Another criterion for defining others is facial features. At the beginning of this study, when Debi had been on the observation site for two days, Roger (3, Latino) provided her with a succinct example of the process. Roger was playing with Robin (4, white) and Michael (3, Asian). The three children were settled on the outside patio, building an enclosure with wooden blocks. Robin and Roger eagerly piled up the blocks into a wall as Michael watched, making no effort to contribute to the labor. He seemed content to merely watch the other two. Suddenly, Roger glared at Michael and announced, "I don't like you." He then turned his attention to Debi to gauge her response and determine if she would put a stop to this situation. He glared at her, and she merely looked back at him, waiting to see what would happen next. When no interference was forthcoming, he returned his gaze to Robin and cooed, "I like you, you look pretty." Turning back to Michael, Roger continued, "You look funny. You look ugly." Michael also just looked back at Roger, saying nothing. Roger continued to build, and when Michael attempted to assist the two of them by handing them blocks, Roger pushed him away, declaring, "You look funny.

You go away." Michael departed, outwardly indifferent to the other child's remarks.

At first, we thought this exchange was only about gender. Roger found a little girl to be "pretty" and another little boy to be "ugly." Roger deemed Robin "pretty," an adjective often applied by boys to girls. After some reflection, which was stimulated by later observations at the center, we decided that this episode was probably focused more on Michael's obvious facial differences from Roger than on gender. Michael was not only declared to be "ugly" but was evaluated by Roger as "looking funny." Perhaps Roger's only issue was gender: we cannot be certain in this individual instance. Still, Roger's choice of words did not reflect the common gendered terminology that young children often use (see Thorne 1993). Young boys generally acknowledge that girls are pretty but would rather associate with other boys. Girls are useful for games of chase and for teasing. Roger chose to associate with Robin and seemed to differentiate based on the physical differences between Robin and Michael rather than the difference in gender. His declaration of likes and dislikes puts an emotional loading on his racial choice. Once again, we see children using racial–ethnic markers to define others for purposes of exclusion.

In another example, two of the center's children use eye shape to delineate otherness. Robin (4, white) and Nicholas (3.5, white) run up to Debi on the playground, holding the outer corners of their eyes upward. They are giggling furiously. Debi asks them, "What on earth are you guys?" They both laugh, and Robin says, "We're different people. Like Lu." Lu is a four-year-old Chinese classmate. Lu's Asian ancestry and a perceived physical characteristic, the shape of her eyes, provide the white children with a method for delineating differences and defining both themselves and another simultaneously. Debi smiles at them and says, "Oh, I see." They both run off, still laughing and holding their fingers to their eyes in imitation of Lu's features.

As in the opening example of Robin and Trevor in chapter 2, there is no overt animosity here, nor is there an indication that Nicholas or Robin is intentionally trying to belittle another child. Indeed, Lu herself is nowhere to be seen. The two white children have seized on a physical characteristic often identified by adults in the larger society as a *racial* marker, and they are employing it to present Lu as the "other" and themselves as obviously distinct from other. These young children are playing a game, drawing upon their growing knowledge of difference to reconstruct a racial concept in play. Apparently they have seen other children do this imitation of Asian eye shape. Their active portrayal of Lu as "different people" is a solid indicator that they are aware of themselves and others as distinctly different. More important, they have also concluded that this knowledge must be shared with Debi. This shows that the children are not merely toying with racial understandings but have decided that it is important enough that they must share their interpretations with an adult. They sought out Debi to demonstrate their language and cognizance of difference, without pausing to gather either her approval or disapproval. They were teaching *her*.

As we have seen previously, the recognition that languages differ provided the children with numerous opportunities to create social groupings and categories. In the next account, the children engage one another in learning about each other. Late one afternoon, Corinne (4, African/white) has positioned herself at the pick-up door, as a sort of child sentinel. She greets each parent as they arrive to pick up their children, calling out to the appropriate child to alert him or her that his or her parents are there. She never misses, correctly matching parents with children, except when the people involved are Asian. As each Asian parent arrives, Corinne calls out to the wrong Asian child. For instance, when Ling's father appears at the door, Corinne cries out, "Lu, your daddy is here!" After each misidentification she giggles and announces loudly, "Oh, I'm so sorry!" She then calls the right child. Her exaggerated behavior indicates that she knows she is misidentifying. Her actions are a game that occupies her for a full forty-five minutes. Soon, Lu's dad arrives, prompting Corinne to look at Lu with a smile on her face, then announce, "Dao, your dad is here!" She laughs aloud between each announcement, laughing even harder when the incorrectly identified child frowns at her. She does not play this game with the non-Asian kids.

Clearly, Corinne has identified these children as members of a distinct racial–ethnic group, and she plays with this idea, actively creating a situation that accents the children's Asian ancestry. That she ignores other racial groups, at least for the time being, indicates that she is working on her interpretation of what constitutes Asian people. She is developing her ability to differentiate between individuals using their racial-group characteristics as a marker. She works on this idea over an extended period of time, indicating that this matter is not of fleeting interest. Most important, her play has a teasing quality to it. She is quite deliberately misidentifying the children and is taking great pleasure in her activity. Play is a serious learning experiment for young children. Without play, they will not become functioning members of the social world. This play centers on racial identification and again demonstrates our contention that race is a compelling factor.

FOOD AS A TOOL OF IDENTIFICATION

Distinctive ethnic cooking, and the names of ethnic foods, provided some of the children with important tools for defining each other. Food was always a hit at the center, and both children and adults brought in dishes to introduce to the center's population. Differences between what some children ate at home and what was served at the day care center became an opportunity for several children to demonstrate their knowledge of ethnicity as revealed in food choices. In the following example, a child's knowledge of food transforms an interaction between her and several others into an opportunity to share language differences and cultural understandings.

One day, Lu (4, Chinese) brought Chinese food from home for lunch and showed it to all who demonstrated any interest. The dish was reddish in color, consisting of shredded meat that had been cooked in some sort of sauce. Crystal, a classroom teacher, asked her, "What do you have for lunch today, Lu?" inviting the child to share the name of the dish. Lu replied, "I don't know." She pauses, then announces, "It's Chinese food." Crystal smiles at her, chuckling slightly, and says, "No honey, I know it's Chinese food. I was wondering what the name of the food is. Do you know its name?" Crystal obviously thinks that Lu has misunderstood her question.

"I know what it is!" William (5, Middle Eastern) joins in, excited. "I had it at Cheng-Li's house." Crystal turns and asks him, "Do you know the name?" "No," he replies, looking a bit dismayed. Then he offers, "But it's good." Again Crystal laughs, returning her attention to Lu, who offers a name we can only approximate here. "It's yoo soo." Crystal tries to repeat the words, struggling to remain respectful. "Yoo soo," she says, looking at Lu. The child laughs, then says, "No, it's yoo soo." Lu accents the words differently and has a different quality to her voice. Crystal's approximation is flatter and sounds heavy, but she tries again, and fails, then tries four more times, each time eliciting a laugh from Lu. The food naming has become a learning game, with Lu in charge of instructing the teacher. This is a position that all the children relish. Finally, Lu says, "That's OK, Crystal, you don't speak very good Chinese because you're American." Crystal agrees, then becomes distracted by another child's request for help at the table.

Lu smiles at Debi, holds up her plate and invites, "Try it. It's wonderful." Debi says, "OK," then goes to the kitchen to get a spoon. When she returns, Lu again offers her plate but first says, "Say the name." Debi responds with, "Yoo soo," trying to imitate the tone Lu is using, and she gets a broad smile in return. "You speak Chinese!" she marvels. "Oh goodness no," Debi says with a laugh, wondering what it was that she was saying in Chinese, "but I really like Chinese food." Debi takes a tiny portion and tastes it. The dish resembles barbecue, but is very sweet. "Yummy! Tastes very good. Did you make it?" Debi gently teases Lu. "No," she says, giggling. "My Mommy cooks it." Debi offers, "It tastes like American barbecue." "Yes," she agrees, "but it isn't American. It's Chinese."

This distinction appears to be quite important for Lu. She took the initiative and pointed out the ethnic origins of her lunch, first to other children, then to a teacher, and finally to Debi. She worked carefully and thoughtfully with Crystal, encouraging her to pronounce the dish's name and responding kindly when the teacher proved to be a somewhat less than adequate student. Lu then turned her attention to Debi, offering a taste of the dish, but with a stipulation. Debi must demonstrate her skill with Chinese first. The exchange between this child and her grown-up students is captivating, centering on Lu's determination that they learn to pronounce words in a language that she knows is not their own. That she knows neither Crystal nor Debi speak Chinese is evidenced both by her patience with Crystal and her surprise at Debi's attempt. It was clearly startling to Lu that Debi was able to pronounce the words, showing that perhaps Lu had tried to introduce her language to other non-Chinese speakers in the past. It is obvious that she discerns the complexity of language, race, and ethnic differences between herself and the adults, a cognitive task that is beyond the abilities of many adults. It is also clear that these differences are a source of authority for her, allowing her to demonstrate her superior knowledge of these matters. For young children, opportunities to take charge are few and far between, and Lu relishes her social power in this situation. Moreover, she uses her comprehension to take control of the interaction, modeling and adopting the teacher position in an appropriate way. All of this shows her strong capability with the ideas of self, other, language, and ethnicity.

Other children quickly pick up on this exchange between Lu, Crystal, and Debi and begin to offer their food, explaining what nationality of food they have brought that day. "Try this!" Joshua (4, white) exclaims loudly. "It's peanut butter. That's American food," he explains gravely, regarding his sandwich. "What about French fries?" William (5, Middle Eastern) demands. "Are French fries from France?" he wonders aloud, addressing nobody in particular.

One consequence of this new interest in ethnic dishes is that food has now become a topic for much serious discussion among the children at the center. Periodically, foods are labeled according to their ethnic origins, and sophisticated questions are asked about where food comes from and why some food is Chinese and some food is American. The discussion continues among the children for the entire lunch period and persists until after naptime as a playground conversation topic, suggesting that this matter is of more than ephemeral interest to the children. The rapidity with which this food discussion spread throughout the center indicates how fascinated young children can be with cultural differences. The children attach ethnicity to all manner of foods, from peas to bagels, and make up names if an appropriate ethnicity is not readily apparent. More important, this episode provides us with further means for understanding how children use ethnicity to identify others. We can examine Lu's analysis of Crystal's inability to identify or pronounce Chinese words. The Asian child defined this failure as a function of Crystal's nationality. Lu reassures Crystal, pointing out that it is okay that she cannot mimic the Chinese name because Crystal is American. Lu has accurately identified her own abilities in comparison with another's limitations and framed her understanding in comparative cultural terms. This level of understanding on the part of a four-year-old girl is deep and sophisticated—one more example underscoring the weaknesses in Piagetian stage theories of child development (discussed in chapter 1) in regard to ethnic distinctions.

THE MANIPULATION OF OTHERS' BEHAVIOR

Definition of others is often a prelude to efforts to control or manipulate others or in justification for the need to influence the behavior of people. As we demonstrated in previous chapters, this control sometimes necessitates bringing others into line, forcing them to accept a definition for themselves that may not correspond with the meaning they have developed on their own. This process of redefinition can allow children to dictate the behavior of others, affording the controlling individual more power to create or influence relationships. Keep in mind that for young children social power of this sort is extraordinarily rare. This next episode demonstrates the way in which one child can influence the subsequent activities of another and facilitate the spread of racially based knowledge.

Renee (4, white) uses the power of racial control to direct her relationship with another child, Corinne (4, African/white). Much as she did in her attempts to control play with a wagon (see chapter 3), Renee again uses the power of whiteness to justify her control of Corinne's play. However, Corinne's responses to Renee's bid to manipulate and define her indicates that Corinne is unwilling to accept Renee's definition, despite the power of whiteness that Renee evokes. The two girls are playing in the dress-up area. Renee is putting on a long dress and a coat, obviously preparing herself for a trip. Corinne is not involved yet and sits quietly, watching Renee get dressed. As Renee finishes, she approaches Corinne and says, "Let's go. We've got to get our babies from school." Corinne brightens at this invitation, joining Renee in the game. They both walk briskly around the dress-up area, simulating a long trip to school.

The girls cease their walk and retrieve dolls from a nearby toy box, Renee choosing a white doll and Corinne a dark-skinned one. Renee puts her doll down on a small ironing board and announces that she will get the baby's dinner ready. She heads for the play kitchen area adjacent to dress-up. Corinne picks up Renee's doll and cradles it, announcing, "I'll watch her for you." Renee immediately returns to the area, frowning. She retrieves the doll from Corinne and says, "No. You're from Africa." Apparently startled at this exclusionary definition, Corinne is silent for a moment and then frowns back at Renee and says, "So? I'm from America too." Renee refuses to return the white doll to Corinne, who is still holding her own doll. The girls regard each other with frowns. Renee repeats, "I don't want any Africans taking care of her. I want an American. You're not an American, anybody can see that." Renee eyes Corinne with disdain. Corinne retorts, "Well, I'm an American too. First from Africa and then America," she says, glaring at Renee. "So I can take care of her." Renee merely frowns more deeply and walks away, carrying the white doll with her. Corinne puts her own doll down with a slam.

This episode is reminiscent of the encounter between Corinne and another white child, Brittany, which we examined in chapter 2. At this point, Corinne begins to talk aloud, to herself. Although Debi is within five feet of the child, Corinne does not address her, seeking neither Debi's intervention or her attention. Corinne fumes, in a clearly audible voice, "I am *too* an American, and an African. I know French and I can speak English and I know African," she announces to the world. Renee, who is now in the kitchen play area, gives no outward indication that she is listening to Corinne. She cannot escape the diatribe, however, as Corinne's voice is loud and firm. Corinne continues to discuss her dual identity with herself and finally picks her doll up and declares, "We are going back to Africa!" At this point Renee returns to the dress-up area. "My daddy is going to get a job in Africa," Corinne tells Renee. "So?" Renee retorts. "My mommy's going to be a lawyer, and she can sue your daddy and she'll get a job in America. And that's better because it's in America." Corinne replies, "Uh uh," and shakes her head. "Africa is first, then America." Renee shakes her head no, whereupon Corinne tells her, "I won't be your friend anymore." Renee pretends to ignore her and continues to play with her doll. She sniffs, and says, "I don't care." Corinne repeats her threat, but Renee ignores her. Corinne waits a moment for a further response, and when none is forthcoming she departs, proclaiming, "I am *not* Renee's friend!"

This is a long and involved interaction, incorporating racial group, place of origin, language differences, and perhaps social class. As she has before, Renee insists not only that America is best, but that Corinne can't be American. "Anybody can see that," she declares, apparently relying on both her knowledge of Corinne's biracial background and Corinne's darker skin color to support her contention. Renee accepts Corinne's African origins but works hard to negate them, implying through her rejection of Corinne's ability to care for the doll that there is something about being African that diminishes one's caring abilities. Renee is redefining Corinne as a less-than-worthy other and relies on denigration of her origins to accomplish this task.

Reacting as she has a number of times previously, Corinne refuses to accept this new signification of herself and works hard to deny Renee's meaning. Corinne invests great energy in identifying herself as dual, both African and American, not only Black but also white, and capable of speaking at least two languages. All this holds importance in her life. Her insistence underscores the important place language use has, in both child-centered and adult worlds, as well as the prominence of Corinne's birthplace and family history. She locates her identity firmly within her knowledge of her own origins, placing emphasis on her father's occupation. Not only is she not confused, she includes considerable detail in her account of her own identity. Finally, to top the whole incident off, Corinne publicly rejects Renee's friendship. Both children are adamant: Renee makes her point by ignoring Corinne, who steadfastly refuses to be ignored. The interpersonal relationship is imperiled, but at the same time it is redefined as each child considers the nature of the other's racial–ethnic background and its importance.

A considerable knowledge of personal and group history is apparent in both girls' behavior. Corinne and Renee both recognize that Corinne's origins are different from, and might conceivably be defined as inferior to, Renee's origins. There is no argument there. Corinne's vehement rejection of Renee's evaluation indicates that she is perfectly aware of the threat contained in that definition. What appears to matter most to

Corinne, however, is the element of ability that is connected to those origins. Renee insists that ability to care for the baby is limited to Americans only, presumably to *white* Americans, and that Africans are not suitable for such tasks. Her words indicate that she considers incompetence to be intrinsic to African origins. There is no doubt that Renee is highly aware of Corinne's racial ancestry. She defines it with a glance at Corinne, and Corinne confirms it with her lengthy and boisterous tirade. Renee also takes action to implement her understandings, removing the doll from Corinne and leaving the play area.

For her part, Corinne recognizes that her dignity has been assaulted, and she vehemently denies that she is inferior, not only to Renee but also to whomever is within earshot. She relies on her dual African and American identities to support her contention. The argument dissolves into a debate about whose social origins are best, a discourse that, at least for Corinne, takes place both internally and interactively. A social hierarchy emerges, based in part on racial and national origins and in part on language. Each child is wrestling not only with the idea of other in contrast to self, but with the added complexity of the self and other relationship between Africa and America. The abstractions here are extraordinarily intricate and sophisticated. Most important, Renee's logic is thoroughly grounded in racism, not of her own devising, but obtained from a society where racial and ethnic origins are crucial for defining the power of social interaction.

Identification of racial or ethnic others is not always so complicated, however. In another situation the use of racial and ethnic matters initially seemed to function as a way to identify other children. The idea of racial or ethnic identity is also dominant in this next episode. Mike (5, Black) and Lacey (4, white) are sitting at an outside table, coloring and cutting out paper. Crystal, a classroom teacher, is sitting with them, and Debi is on a bench a few feet away. Mike pats Lacey on her arm and, pointing to Michael (4, Asian), remarks, "Do you know him? Are you his friend?" Lacey regards Mike briefly, then looks to where he is pointing. Michael is on top of the slide. "Who?" she asks Mike. "Him," Mike repeats, "that China kid." Lacey spots Michael and says to Mike, "Of course, silly, I'm everybody's friend." Mike gazes at Lacey without smiling and says, "Even Brendan?" Mike seems very serious and regards Lacey intently. "Who?" Lacey asks. "Brendan," Mike says again, then further clarifies, "the white Brendan." It is rather odd that Mike feels compelled to identify Brendan as white, since there is only one child named Brendan at the center.

Lacey now appears to be annoyed and says to Mike, "Of course. Why are you asking silly questions?" He does not reply, but continues to look at her. A few moments later, Mike picks up a pair of scissors and pinches Lacey's arm with them. "Stop that!" Lacey commands. Crystal interrupts the children immediately, saying, "Michael! Scissors are for cutting paper, not people." Mike looks at Crystal and tells her, "I wanted to see what she looked like underneath." Crystal's mouth falls open, and she looks over at Debi, obviously alarmed at this declaration. She regains her composure and tells Mike, "Lacey looks the same underneath as you do. All children look the same underneath." Crystal laughs, and Mike finally smiles. Lacey, however, is not amused with Mike's attempt to operate on her arm, and she leaves the table.

Adult involvement in this incident began with Crystal preventing Mike from hurting Lacey but evolved into a brief, informal lesson on the similarity of people underneath the skin. Significantly, Mike framed his description of the other children to Lacey, and drew her attention to them, by describing them in racial and ethnic terms. Finally, Mike ended the discourse by focusing on Lacey's skin color. Skin color distinctions seem to be a critical component of the world for Mike.

In another episode, racial group characteristics are used as part of a marriage game. The children at this center, like children in other research (Thorne 1993; Holmes 1995), frequently discussed marriage and potential mates, often dressing up as brides and grooms; conducting weddings; and creating pretend households complete with husbands, wives, and children. In one of these encounters, we observed that skin color comparisons were central and significant.

Karen (5, white) and Pete (5, Black) are sitting next to each other at lunch. She is holding her arm next to his, intentionally contrasting her pale color with his dark skin. Karen announces to him, "I'll marry you when we grow up, Pete. I want to marry a Black man." She then giggles. Fondly, she strokes his arm and smiles at him, and he smiles back at her. Neither child is bothering to touch their lunch. Instead they sit and gaze at each other, starry-eyed. Their expressions are so goofy that they make it difficult for Debi to maintain her composure, but she remains quiet so as not to distract their attention from each other.

Karen soon switches her approach, changing from arm comparison to hair stroking. She pats the side and top of his head, stroking it gently while continuing to smile. Pete shuts his eyes and continues to smile. He resembles a happy puppy. Soon he begins to hum loudly, getting an even sillier look on his face. Pete finally opens his eyes, tilts his head, and looks at Karen fondly, whereupon she gushes, "I like your hair, Pete." He just smiles. Yung-Feng (4, Asian) is sitting at Pete's other side, watching

Karen's activity. He, too, begins to stroke Pete's head. Apparently this is amusing to Yung-Feng, and he begins to laugh. Their head-patting quickly becomes boisterous.

Karen leans forward and frowns at Yung-Feng, instructing him to "Stop it!" He obeys her but then begins to push Pete's head from side to side, watching Pete intently. Yung-Feng then places his hands on Pete's cheeks. For his part, Pete allows these bodily manipulations. Yung-Feng maintains his grasp on Pete's face, gazing intently at the Black child's closed eyes. It is unclear whether he is waiting for Pete to open his eyes or for Karen to interfere. Perhaps he is merely intensely interested in the contrast between his hands and Pete's dark skin color. Pete finally ends the interaction by bursting into laughter and collapsing onto Karen. Yung-Feng also erupts in laughter, and all three children dissolve into silliness.

Despite the almost comical nature of this interaction, all three children seem to be working with complex ideas. Racial membership and identity are meaningful for both Karen and Pete, who are using marital concepts as well. Not content with merely professing love for another individual and saying that she wants to marry Pete, Karen instead stresses that she wants to "marry a Black man." This is an explicit and directed recognition of both her own racial group and Pete's. At least in this case, her attitudes toward interracial relationships do not yet mirror those of the majority of whites in the larger society (see Feagin 2000). Here racial identities are positively influencing the choice of a pretend husband. As the event proceeds, Yung-Feng joins in and appears to compare his own skin color with Pete's. The language and concept of racial–ethnic group membership—and the differences constituting this membership—are again matters of serious reflection, musing, and experimentation in children's interactions, grounded in play.

ADULTS IN THE PRESCHOOL WORLD

According to conventional wisdom, adult intervention is deemed essential for young children to gain explicit knowledge of racial and ethnic distinctions and meanings. In the case of this day care center, adult involvement with the children was limited in scope and nature. When the adults did engage with children, they usually did so as parent, caretaker, or teacher. Generally, teachers maintained social distance from the children, especially during free-play periods, unless the children got loud or sounded angry. Then teachers intervened, primarily to stop arguments.

As we have observed previously, Debi rarely took such action, relying instead on the teachers' ability to head off difficulties before they got out of control. Only if a child was in danger of physical injury would Debi intercede. Generally, the children did not seek out adults unless they needed something in particular, such as help with toilets, or to push a swing, or to stop another child from hurting them. Still, children at the center could not avoid adult contact at all times, and they did little to actively avoid contact with adults unless their behavior was prohibited (as it often was!).

At times, the children sought out individual adults for personal attention. Direct adult connection with an individual child was a prized commodity, especially when the child was able to assume control of the interaction. Since teachers were generally unable to provide any prolonged, individual attention, the more peripheral adults at the center were commonly put to use for such interaction. Hence, Debi's lap became a valuable resource since she had no other official duties to force her away from contact with individual children. Because times when teachers were able to be engaged with an individual child were rare, a child who was able to keep a teacher involved in an interaction—other than discipline, of course—was accomplishing a feat.

For one teacher, contact occasionally involved a discussion of her ethnicity. Anne, a classroom teacher, is from Europe and speaks with a distinct accent. One rainy afternoon she and several children are inside, watching a video called *The Great Mouse Detective*. The characters in this movie are European and speak English with clipped, exaggerated accents. As Anne and the children watch, Joshua (4, white) turns to Anne and says, "Hey! They talk like you." Other children immediately join in, proclaiming, "Yeah, they all talk like Anne," who responds, "Of course they do." She deepens her accent, exaggerating her speech to accent that of the cartoon characters. "They have style." The children burst into laughter. Here a child inaugurated the discussion of ethnic differentials among whites. Then other children participate in this use of nationality and ethnicity as markers to distinguish people. The teacher, perhaps unwittingly, reinforced this newly discovered ethnic distinction.

Children frequently involved other adults in interaction, if possible, and sometimes used teacher's aides as playmates. Aides were more approachable than teachers, since they had fewer classroom duties and less overall authority. Further, aides provided children with enhanced opportunity for control of a social situation. Aides were far more likely to encourage the child to direct activity. In this next interesting situation, a three-and-a-half-year-old is in charge. Use of a language other than English also takes on interactive importance for this little girl, and she is extending her knowledge of Spanish to include an adult. Rita (3.5, white/Latina) is busily translating a storybook for Heather, a teacher's aide. She sits next to Heather on the rug. Heather's job is turning the pages, at Rita's direction. The focus of attention is a picture book of baby animals. After Heather reads each page in English, Rita points to the pictures of the various animals and says the animal's name in Spanish. She is engaging, attentive, and patient, reciting the name in Spanish until Heather repeats it to Rita's satisfaction. Heather cooperates willingly, becoming the student to Rita's teaching. Here, a three-year-old instructs an adult on how to speak Spanish properly. Rita insists that Heather say the Spanish name after her, repeating it until she is satisfied that Heather has mastered the word. Rita is guiding the interaction because she holds an advantaged understanding of Heather's language capabilities. Rita is imitating the actions of adults, but also enhancing that imitation, accommodating the adult's inexperience with a foreign language.

As in the definition of one's self, racial group and skin color figure strongly in children's identification of adult others. One morning, Felicia (3, white) and Debi are seated at a table, waiting for teachers to begin the day's activities. Felicia observes Claire's mother as she drops Claire (5, Black) off at school. Felicia tugs on Debi's arm and comments, "Well. Her mom certainly is Black too. And she's wearing boots." Startled, Debi regards the girl with a smile. "Sure is," Debi replies. Felicia gazes after Claire's mother for a moment. "You know," she continues informatively, "Joseph's mom is Black, and she has really weird hair." (Joseph's mother wears her hair in dreadlocks.) Debi, not sure of what to make of this, merely nods and says nothing, allowing the child to retain control of the conversation's direction. "Well, gotta go!" Felicia announces, running off.

While this incident took only a few moments, it shows how one young child is using racial understanding to build a social category. Felicia associates skin color with family membership and ancestry, noticing that Black children match their parents and that these parents are unlike the ones she is familiar with, in dress or hairstyle. Felicia is laying the foundations of racial categories through her accumulating observations of these differences. She is engaged in an evolving process of constant comparison designed to solidify her understanding of other peoples.

How they look physically provides the children at the day care center with frequent opportunities for such comparisons, which they sometimes linked to their interpretations of racial or ethnic group membership. One day, Yung-Feng's father, Mr. Yu, arrives early to pick up his son and sits with a group of teachers and aides at a table outside. Some parents made a regular practice of spending time conversing with the teachers and watching their children at play with others. Yung-Feng (3, Asian) is playing with Jason (3, Middle Eastern). When he spots his father, he abandons Jason and comes over to the table. Jason follows, and both boys sit close to Yung-Feng's father. Jason then asks Mr. Yu, "Who does Yung-Feng look like?" The man thinks for a moment, then tells the child, "He looks like his mommy." Mr. Yu looks at Debi and smiles. Jason continues, "Who does Yung-Feng's mommy look like?" Mr. Yu appears puzzled for a moment, then smiles and says, "She looks like Yung-Feng." Jason smiles, and Yung-Feng begins to laugh. Mr. Yu then asks Jason, "What does your mommy look like?" The boy thinks for a moment, then says, "She looks like me!"

This discourse involves an investigation of the differences between Yung-Feng's and Jason's appearance. The two boys are similar in height, weight, and skin tone. They are best friends and rarely apart. Physical differences that a racially oriented adult might accent are eye shape and hair color, with Yung-Feng's accented and imperfect English providing further contrast. Jason involves Mr. Yu in a discussion of who Yung-Feng resembles, which eventually leads back to reflections on Jason's own appearance. Like much of the conceptual development among children, there is a game-like quality to the interaction. Perhaps Jason is extending a conversation he had earlier with Yung-Feng and draws in Mr. Yu to resolve his questions. Just as Felicia displayed earlier, Jason shows some interest in and knowledge about the continuity in physical appearance between parents and children. Both children are interacting with an adult in order to confirm their own thinking about racial and ethnic characteristics. They are trying out concepts for categorizing family membership and creating criteria for inclusion in a group category. We suspect that such thinking and experimentation with ideas is commonplace in children's society, despite the fact that it is revealed to adults only sporadically.

ACTIVELY TEACHING ABOUT
RACIAL AND ETHNIC OTHERS

From time to time the adults we observed would incorporate racial or ethnic commentaries into their interactions with the children. For the most part, this consisted of drawing the children's attention to racial or ethnic differences, with the goal of encouraging children to recognize and value the variety of people in the world. This is in keeping with the antibias curriculum the center used and with one goal of the center, which was the promotion of positive relations among diverse children. The director and staff embraced these principles and worked hard to incorporate positive teaching about difference into the children's daily activities.

At other times, adult involvement moves beyond just teaching about the positive value of differences. Marcie, a volunteer at the center, is holding Jeremy (3, white/Asian) on her lap. He is visiting from another classroom and is waiting to be picked up. They are sitting in one of the rockers in the play area, and Debi is in another rocker, holding Elizabeth (3.5, Chinese) as she reads a book. Marcie comments aloud on how much she adores Jeremy's facial features. "I just love those Oriental eyes and that blond hair," she says, making conversation with Debi and speaking over Jeremy's head. "He is just so adorable." Debi smiles and nods, watching Jeremy, but saying nothing. The child seems uninterested in Marcie's remarks. "I think his father is half-Asian," Marcie continues. "Isn't it strange how the boy got that blond hair? I thought that if you were biracial you would be sure to have black or brown hair." Debi replies to Jeremy rather than to Marcie, complimenting his appearance. "You've got beautiful hair, sweetie." He merely looks at Debi, then looks at the door. Marcie continues her comments about him but still does not address him directly.

Outwardly, Jeremy appears to ignore the adults' remarks. He is watching for his ride home and seems to be unconcerned with Marcie's comments and Debi's responses. However, this episode suggests that Marcie may believe Jeremy to be incapable of significantly attending to racial and ethnic distinctions or meanings. Indeed, from her action it seems likely that she considers Jeremy to be deaf to her words. Her comments suggest two beliefs. First, she seems to be of the opinion that biracial children have certain characteristics in common and that racial groups are physically distinctive in quite traditional ways. Racialized identities are implicit in the references to physical characteristics. Second, she appears to feel safe in discussing such racial characteristics within the hearing of two small children. This suggests that Marcie might consider them incapable of understanding her remarks. Neither Jeremy nor Elizabeth commented at the time, but the experience of hearing one adult's remarks about racial–ethnic characteristics certainly provided both children with another piece of information about how adults make racial–ethnic distinctions in the larger society. The exchange at least illustrates the casual inculcation to race that happens in children's everyday lives.

On one occasion Patricia, a classroom teacher, made use of overt ethnic (cultural) differences within the context of a game with several children. Patricia draws the children into a game of follow-the-leader and uses ethnicity to distinguish between the children. The technique is in keeping with the curriculum, encouraging the positive valuation of difference. Eight children, Corinne (4, African/white), John (5, white/Middle Eastern), William (4.5, Middle Eastern), Nicholas (3.5, white), Michael (3, Asian), Renee (4, white), Martha (4, Black/white), and Aaron (5, white) follow Patricia around the playground. Patricia leads the group single file, going through a variety of motions (e.g., under the slide, around the boat), and the children imitate her movements. This is active, creative play, and everyone, teacher and children alike, is having a good time.

Patricia soon announces to the line of children that they have become a "dragon." She fetches a sheet from the playground equipment box and returns to the line of waiting children. Patricia plays the dragon's head, draping the sheet behind her from her shoulders, and the children all cluster under it. Patricia steps out, and they march around the playground like a float in a New Year's parade. "Just like in China!" Patricia declares. The children seem to think this game is just hysterical, and they scream with laughter. They parade a little longer, and then the dragon game changes to a game on the slide. Patricia leads the children to the set of large playground equipment. The children climb the ladder to the slide. Patricia positions herself at the bottom of the slide with a teacher's aide and tells the children that they are now slices of bread. "We'll slice you off the loaf as you come down!" she announces, smiling. When they slide down, Patricia catches them in the sheet, which has now become the "toaster." The children are having a great time, again shrieking with laughter and rushing to re-climb the slide and get sliced anew.

First down the slide is a young blond boy. He plops onto the sheet and Patricia announces, "Here's a slice of German brown bread!" The child smiles at her and rushes to get back in line for another turn. A little girl is next. "French bread!" Patricia calls out. The child erupts into giggles and races around to the ladder again. As each child lands on the sheet, Patricia makes up another ethnic bread name for them. One boy is "Italian" bread, a girl is a dumpling, and two boys are pita bread. Patricia's knowledge of bread is formidable, because she rarely repeats a name. The game is hilarious, and everyone involved is roaring with laughter.

Patricia has used this spontaneous activity to incorporate some ethnic and nationality concepts into her interaction with the children. She makes ethnicity into a game, associating it with various foods. The children love this activity, and the breads that they were named during the game become part of their interactions with each other for several weeks afterward. The children frequently identified themselves as an "ethnic bread" name as they played with each other, and on later occasions they attempted to re-create this game. It was not only a resounding hit with the children, but a solid learning experience in regard to ethnic and nationality categorization. By accenting the children's differences, she is encouraging them to explore their own ethnic identity and that of others in a positive and interactive way. The children later incorporated this learning into their daily lives without Patricia's prompting, re-creating the activity without adult encouragement. Their accommodation of the activity highlights the importance these concepts hold for them.

Patricia periodically made use of her time with the children to introduce positive racial and ethnic understandings to them. On another occasion, she gives "high fives" to two brothers, Michael (3, Asian) and Mitchell (4, Asian), and a third boy who is standing nearby, Elijah (3, Middle Eastern). Patricia shows the three boys how to give high fives, slapping their palms with hers while they have their hands raised in the air. She then teaches them to "give me some skin," softly running her palm over the boys' outstretched hands. Next she tells them, "Give me some on the brown side." This time instead of running her palm across theirs she uses the back of her hand and runs it quickly across all three boys' palms. When they look a little confused, she shows them the difference between the palm and back of her hand. "See?" she tells them, "the top is brown and the bottom is pink." The boys view her hand, then look at their own hands, turning them over and back to compare. There is little difference for them to see. The children are pale-skinned, and the palms of their hands are almost identical to the backs. Patricia, seeing their puzzlement, says, "Never mind!" in a happy voice and leaves to deal with another child's request for help. Michael, Mitchell, and Elijah stay where they are. They continue to compare the backs and palms of their own hands and then expand this activity to a comparison of each other's hands. After a few moments they lose interest, and the group breaks up.

Patricia engaged children in interactions that incorporated some aspect of racial or ethnic concepts numerous times. She used books, games, and playtime with the children to encourage them to note difference and assign meanings to these differences. Such active conceptual teaching seems to have influenced the children. Some of Patricia's activities took on lives of their own and continued among the children without her involvement. She made racial and ethnic concepts a compelling and important part of the children's experiences, in accordance with the center's emphasis on valuing diversity positively and incorporating the multicultural curriculum's recommendations.

Other teachers also tried to include racial or ethnic concepts in lessons and interactions. In one situation, Jeanne is reading to a group of children, using a book featuring children of many colors and racial–ethnic groups who are dressed in distinctive costumes. It is a beautiful volume, with detailed illustrations of a wide variety of ethnic groups. She invites the children to look at the book, then choose those on the pages who look the most like them. Respect of other people is at the center of this group activity. Jeanne is in charge; one by one, she asks each of the ten children in her group, "Do you see your color here?" First is Joseph (4, Black), who immediately says, "I see black." Jeanne asks him to show everyone else. He gets up and comes to her, then points perfunctorily to the two Black people on the page. Next, Brendan (5, white) takes a turn, pointing to a picture of a red-haired man with pale skin. Each child takes a turn, and each accurately identifies a figure in the book that looks like them. They don't always match on gender, however. Brianna (3, white) selects a blond-haired, blue-eyed little boy as the one who most resembles her.

When the activity is concluded, Jeanne goes to answer a telephone call. When she leaves, the children begin their own activity. Nobody leaves the rug. They cluster closer together and center the book between them. Now they seem eager to compare their own skin colors with each other. The white children busily compare their arms to those of the Asian children, then they all compare to each other. But nobody compares their skin color to Joseph, the only Black child, who sits on his own. There are multiple analyses possible for understanding Joseph's behavior. Perhaps the difference in color is so apparent and dramatic, that nobody, Joseph included, feels compelled to elaborate those differences. Perhaps Joseph, anticipating being the focus of an unwelcome comparison, deliberately removes himself from contact. Or perhaps the children have excluded Joseph in the past and are merely continuing what has become a custom. Maybe Joseph is simply tired and wishes to discontinue activity for a while. We can only speculate, but each scenario holds potential. Joseph's position at the center bears watching.

What began as a teacher-led activity evolved into an impromptu comparison of skin color among the members of this small group. Once the teacher left the area, however, the nature of the activity changed. As soon as the children were in charge, the focus moved from an artificial comparison to children in a book to a real-life comparison of each other's skin. This scene points out the potential for researchers and teachers alike to underestimate children's abilities with racial and ethnic concepts. The original intent of the activity, to identify self, was transformed into an activity focused on comparing self to others. The children took the racial tools used by the teacher and in her absence transformed them for an interactive purpose. The children were able to see that others were different and sought to categorize the differences, a skill that mainstream theory suggests "egocentric" preschoolers cannot achieve.

In another activity, ethnicity enters the scene as a child shares her experiences with a sharing circle. Ten children, the teacher, Crystal, Debi, and two teacher's aides are present for this activity. Crystal is reading aloud from a book that encourages children to think about themselves. She reads the entire book, then closes it and asks, "What are you thinking about?" The children share their thoughts, mostly telling stories about themselves. As each child speaks, the others listen quietly. When Crystal comes to Corinne (4, African/white) and asks, "What are you thinking about?" the girl replies, "Elephants." Crystal raises her eyebrows and smiles. "Elephants?" Crystal repeats, waiting for Corinne to continue. "Yes, elephants. When I was in Africa, I saw elephants by my house. The man who had them told me when I was bigger I could ride them." Cindy, an aide who is holding Corinne in her lap, smiles in disbelief, shaking her head. Crystal notices Cindy's reaction to Corinne's anecdote, then reminds the group, "Corinne is from Africa, remember?" All the children indicate that they remember, and one offers the name of Corinne's birth country.

We have noted before the reluctance of adults to believe that Corinne is from Africa. On several other occasions adults who were new to the center remarked that Corinne was confused when she told them about her origins. In one case, when Corinne informed another child's parent that she was from Africa, the woman replied, "No, honey, you're African American." Neither Corinne's parents nor Corinne identified in this way, but to the stranger unacquainted with the possibility that Corinne was indeed African, her explanation of her own origins was impossible to accept. This disbelief was limited to Corinne alone. When white children who were from European countries, or Asian children, announced their ethnic origins to white adult newcomers, not one ever expressed doubt during our observation period. It appears that Corinne's skin color so firmly signaled her African American identity to adults in this racist society that they could never conceive there might be an alternative explanation. Nor did they ever believe the child. Instead, they either sought verification from another adult, or they insisted to Corinne that she was mistaken about her own history. This illustrates two predominant themes in children's lives. First, they are assumed to be incompetent and in need of correction or guidance about their personal lives. Certainly, this mindset asserts, little children can have no knowledge of racial origins or their meanings, even their own. Second, and more important, adults display a uniformity of thought about race. There is only one explanation for Black skin in the United States: its possessor is African American. The power of this conviction is a strong indicator of how much we rely on the very limiting characteristic of skin color to define others' group affiliation. Whites can afford to be indifferent to the nuances and multiple possibilities of race. This unconcern is exacerbated if that dark-skinned person is a child.

CONCLUSION

The data presented in this chapter show that children's use of racial and ethnic concepts incorporates many aspects of socially distinguished variations, including hair color, eye shape, skin color, and language. Each factor is used separately and in combination, depending on the nature of the children's interactions. Who they are with is as important as what they are actually doing, with adult presence alternately shaping and interfering with children's developing racial mindsets. The number and variety of factors used to identify other children and adults are commonly complex and intricate. In some cases identifying others by ethnic or racial group involved the use of several racial–ethnic characteristics at once, resulting in the creation of complex categories of people. Among young children categorization by racial and ethnic characteristics is usually not naive or simplistic. It is not limited to comparing and matching skin colors or engaging in racial naming. As we see it, research relying on apparently one simple racial–ethnic identifier as the way to tap racial–ethnic attitudes is clearly too restricted in scope.

Jason could have limited his investigation of differences and similarities to just himself and Yung-Feng. There were enough differences between the two boys to provide ample information for comparisons. However, he chose to involve an adult in his conceptualizations, drawing the father into the discussion by requesting information on which family member his child resembled. This example and similar accounts show that the children have a sense of the continuity of racial–ethnic differentials between family generations and a realization that this continuity extends to groups other than their own particular circle.

In some cases, children identify the racial group or ethnicity of others in order to create an opportunity for discourse. They are involved in pioneering group formation, with groups delineated according to racial characteristics, whether physical or behavioral. Karen's attention to Pete, promising to marry him when they were grown up, involves an active recognition of his membership in the Black group. Here, interestingly, Karen is employing racial distinctions to facilitate social interaction, to keep Pete close to her.

In interactions with adults, children both create and receive multiple, complex messages about the meaning of racial group and ethnicity. Teachers and other adults involved in education consider these to be important concepts. Teachers often incorporate them into lessons and formal discourse. While the overt goal is usually to teach tolerance, there is nothing to stop children from taking these lessons and reshaping their content for interactions in other contexts. The concepts are dynamic and infinitely adaptable, and children take advantage of this to construct complex social meaning. Social tools provided by the adults at a day care center are rapidly transformed, thereby increasing their usefulness for children's goals. Critically important is the fact that the children do not just imitate adult behavior, as is evidenced in the many interactions described in this and previous chapters. Couple the children's creativity and originality with the ubiquitous presence of racial and ethnic meanings from the larger society, and one sees how the developing social worlds of children quickly become pervaded by racial and ethnic understandings and behaviors. These children have moved past mere curiosity about racial and ethnic distinctions. At the same time, they are also discovering the social meanings attached to other categories such as gender and class. Since children are creative and adaptive, we can expect that their accumulation of this knowledge and experience will be put to imaginative use when appropriate opportunities arise.

At this day care center, the children's abilities to define others based on racial and ethnic differences showed great sophistication and depth of experience. This is not surprising given the diversity of the population, and that children and teachers often created opportunities to incorporate racial and ethnic concepts into their daily dealings with each other. Repeatedly, our accounts reveal that young children can and do make extensive use of racial and ethnic concepts and understandings. All they need is the opportunity to experiment, which school settings provide in abundance.

Like the children studied in multiethnic elementary schools in England (Troyna and Hatcher 1992; see also Connolly 1998), the children at our day care center explored a broad range of racial and ethnic understandings and behaviors. As in the Troyna and Hatcher (1992) study, the creation of racial and ethnic meanings was conditional on the extent and character of contact with racial–ethnic others. However, unlike those elementary school children in England, our children have had more extensive experiences with children from a variety of backgrounds. In our center, this contact was intense, mutable, and continual. This interaction generated many opportunities to recognize differences and to compare and contrast selves with others. The meanings of interactions between children can best be understood by viewing them in context and accounting for the social processes that underlie the interactions. Most of these children were able to embrace and value the perspectives of others, no small feat for children who have often been considered incapable of even recognizing their own racial or ethnic group.

5

HOW ADULTS VIEW CHILDREN

One would expect that all adults are "experts" on childhood, especially if the criterion for expert is lengthy personal experience as children. Of course, every adult has years of experience being a child and living as such in an adult-dominated world. Yet, once adults reach adulthood and are confronted with children—their own or those belonging to others—they often admit that they are dumbfounded by the activities of children. Despite adults' long years of expertise *as* children, they often seem ignorant or baffled in dealing *with* children. Adults usually resort to strong assertions of the many mythologies—such as the innocence, ignorance, or naivete of childhood—in order to explain children's behavior, thereby disregarding their own complex histories and sophisticated understandings and succumbing to commonsense rationales. They cling to the conviction that children are cute, guileless, and incapable of thinking or feeling in ways that adults do. These are highly effective stereotypes that depict children as more or less blank tablets. Children are thus extremely subjected to contradictory social expectations.

Teachers, parents, and researchers often hold to the traditional ideologies of childhood. However, these convictions about the nature of children and childhood are sincere fictions, not stubborn denials of otherwise apparent facts. In general, adults do not observe children behaving in ways that are out of accord with adult images of children and then change their appraisals of children. Instead, when adults observe children doing things that are not "age appropriate," they label them as disturbed, precocious, or confused. This fixation on the dichotomy of children's innocence/deviance blinds adults to accepting the reality that children often engage in quite mature and sometimes very sophisticated behavior. As we have demonstrated in the previous chapters, young children are capable of handling complex social ideas and putting those ideas to use in contextually appropriate ways. The adults around them, however, seem determinedly unaware of how adept the children are, particularly when it comes to racial and ethnic knowledge and interaction.

In this first incident, we see the strength of the adultcentric conviction that children possess either no racial knowledge or extremely limited information. Debi had a discussion with a parent, Mrs. Johnson. Her daughter, Amy (4, white), was enrolled in the classroom, and one day Mrs. Johnson stopped Debi to inquire about the progress of the research. The director had notified parents about the project at the center and invited them to stop by and ask questions at any time. Mrs. Johnson had read the statement announcing the study and was interested in its progress.

Amy had a physical disability, and her mother was concerned that Amy remain independent, hence she had spent a lot of time talking with her daughter about handicaps, differences between children, and what Amy might expect in the larger world. Amy's needs had been discussed with the teachers, and Mrs. Johnson had assured them that Amy's disability would not slow her down. Amy, her mother informed the staff, had been thoroughly grounded in the idea of difference, what that could mean for her relationships with other children, and how they might respond to her. Hence, Debi anticipated that her meeting with Mrs. Johnson would be straightforward and informative.

"So, tell me about what you're doing here," Mrs. Johnson began. "I'm curious, you know, because little kids don't really understand race." Debi replied that the social science knowledge of how children dealt with racial matters was quite limited and began to explain that this study was designed to investigate some gaps in existing research. Debi began: "There's not much work done on what children do when they are away from teachers and parents. How they begin to use race and racial concepts has just not been looked at in the way we are conducting this study." Mrs. Johnson interjected, "Well, Amy didn't even notice race until they started teaching it to her here. She thought that Black kids were just kids." Her rejoinder to Debi's explanation was a common response from numerous white adults to whom we explained our research. Debi was about to clarify when Mrs. Johnson added, "There's too much attention to differences. We are all alike, and we shouldn't highlight difference. It gives them the wrong idea," smiling at Debi.

"I'm a good liberal," she continued, "but there's just too much emphasis on this diversity thing. We should concentrate on teaching them how similar they are, not how different." Mrs. Johnson then strongly suggested,

"That's why we have so much tension nowadays, you know." She was giving her perspective on the state of U.S. society. Debi replied by referring to the center's official curriculum. "One of the goals of a diversity curriculum is to teach the children to value differences and appreciate each group's unique history and contribution to our society," Debi offered. "Our curriculum is designed to counter traditional education's historical tendency to ignore differences. This tendency has resulted in most minority groups being ignored in traditional curricula. This creates consequences for minority children, such as loss of culture, feelings of exclusion, and feelings of deprivation." Since Mrs. Johnson seemed interested, and did not interrupt, Debi continued, "The antibias focus is an attempt to correct decades of neglect and help children to know and appreciate the great variety in our society." Mrs. Johnson acknowledged that these were valid points but added that diversity was a more appropriate topic for older children. "Little ones like Amy just don't understand race. They have to have it pointed out to them. Like Amy. I have to teach her about difference."

"And Amy knows about difference, that's for sure." Mrs. Johnson was alluding to the child's disability. Then she noted, "But that's because I teach her. She has to know, with her disability, that the other kids might tease her or hurt her feelings. But she would never have noticed on her own that the other children were different colors." Debi was puzzled by this assertion but said nothing. "Amy does not notice such things unless somebody points it out to her," Mrs. Johnson continued, "and I think it is unethical to teach little kids about . . . this." Debi then invited her to look at what the center did actually teach: "Would you like to read the curriculum we use here? There are copies available to check out, and I could make an appointment for you with the director or head teacher. I'm not sure I'm the one [who] is best able to discuss the curriculum's goals, I'm not a teacher." Mrs. Johnson replied, "No, I already know what the curriculum is; that's why I enrolled Amy here. But this race stuff, that's just not right." Debi reassured her that the center did not teach "race stuff" and again invited her to meet with the teachers or the director. "Well, perhaps," Mrs. Johnson finally agreed, "I'll talk to Jeanne. But you're just wasting your time, you know. Children this age cannot be racists." Then Mrs. Johnson left with Amy in tow. The child had stood quietly and listened to the entire conversation. Debi reported the discussion to Jeanne. "Some parents just don't get the idea of the curriculum," Jeanne reassured Debi, "but we can clear up any misconceptions she has."

This parent seemed to be suggesting that her child noticed only one type of difference, and only that which pertained to her own personal experience with a disability. This is one way that the notion of egocentricity reveals itself in everyday life. Not limited to scholars and researchers, it is entrenched in commonsense understandings of children's abilities. Mrs. Johnson seems to epitomize the average adult's working knowledge of cognitive development: children are generally incapable of knowing about complicated social issues such as race. Like numerous other adults, especially whites, she emphasized that small children are generally incapable of seriously understanding racial–ethnic differentiation. She stressed that she taught her child to anticipate other children's cruelty and noted that her child was an expert in perceiving difference, but only one type of difference. This account illustrates the recurring adult perception that children are mostly egocentric— that is, generally incapable of attending to or understanding anything but their own experiences.

The exchange between Debi and Amy's mother is a study in the contradictory nature of adult attitudes toward children and toward racial–ethnic matters. This mother seems convinced that her analysis of the situation is the correct one, to the point that she feels compelled to save Debi from "wasting time." Evidently, she does not conceptualize children as "racists." However, at no time did we ever present our research as an attempt to identify "racism" in children or to suggest that we believed children to be "racist." We always indicated that our interest was in discovering how children managed to recognize and manage racial and ethnic concepts. Yet some adults transmuted our project into one that centers mainly on the most negative aspect of our work. Many white adults experience distress when they become aware of children's interest in and abilities with racial and ethnic concepts. This mother argues that it is wrong to encourage any young child to attend to racial matters because, otherwise, they would not be aware of such things.

Debi's conversation with her indicates the denial that many parents and other adults, especially those who are white, engage in when they are confronted with children's racial comments and behavior. Little kids are not supposed to understand serious racial matters. When most adults are confronted with evidence that three-year-olds are masters at managing racial–ethnic relations, they often become disturbed, try to rationalize the evidence away, or dismiss our evidence as unique. Much of this interpretation process is facilitated by the belief that little children are confused by social complexity and possess no significant comprehension of even their own personal and social experiences. Indeed, throughout this project we have been continually confronted with adults' strong disposition to view children as nonracial. However, our evidence indicates that once racial–ethnic issues become a component of children's lives, they quickly accommodate the complexity inherent in racial–ethnic relations.

In this next account, we see a small part of one child's effort to explain her racial–ethnic background in the face of constant and predictable adult disbelief. Recall from previous chapters that Corinne—with one Black parent and one white parent—experienced constant pressure to explain her national origins to interested, but usually dismissive, adults. Periodically, adults would discount her knowledge of her own origins.

Debi is outside and engaged in retrieving toys from under the deck. Vicky, a teacher, is collecting the toys as Debi hands them out to her, placing them in a box after the dirt is cleaned from them. Four-year-old Corinne is a few feet away, occupied at the play table. A volunteer, new to the center and trying to get to know the children, approaches Corinne with a smile on her face. "Hi!" the young woman says brightly. "My name is Cheryl." "I'm Corinne," the child replies, looking up from her play. "Want to play with me?" Corinne asks, pleased that an adult is taking an interest in her. "Sure," replies Cheryl. "What are you doing?" "I'm doing chemistry," Corinne replies. "You can watch." Cheryl smiles and settles down next to Corinne. "Where are you from?" Cheryl asks Corinne. "Africa," Corinne responds, glancing warily at the woman, and asks in return, "Where are you from?" The woman responds, "Oh, I'm from here—here in this state, that is." Debi has paused in her toy collection efforts and is watching and listening carefully to this exchange. Cheryl seems to regard Corinne with some amusement. "Africa, huh. That's really interesting." Corinne eyes her, waiting. Her experience is that most grown-ups do not believe her when she tells them where she is from, but this particular adult just lets the information go and asks, "What kind of chemistry are you doing? Tell me about it." Corinne launches into an explanation of how the colors change when you mix them together, and the woman listens intently. Mike (5, Black) joins them at the table, disrupting Corinne's play, and she leaves to run to the tire swing. The young woman retires to the picnic table to watch the children at play.

Debi has completed her task and found all the toys. She extricates herself from under the deck and moves to sit at the picnic table. "Boy, is that little girl confused," the volunteer offers, beginning to talk as Debi approaches the table. "She just told me she's from Africa." Debi smiles and begins to verify Corinne's assertion, but the young woman does not allow her to speak and continues, "Isn't that cute? They get so mixed up. It's amazing how they twist things around, you know, mix up what they hear at home. She probably heard that she's African American." By now Vicky has joined the group, and she interjects, "Oh, no, Corinne's really from Africa." Vicky names the country and adds, "She speaks two languages too." The volunteer, looking sheepish, replies, "Oh, that's just so cute!" She gets up and heads for the tire swing, where she begins pushing the children.

The volunteer's assumptions about Corinne's identity illustrate how adults anticipate the extent of children's knowledge. They interpret what children do according to what the adults expect children to be able to do at particular ages and stages. The expression "that's so cute" was frequently used by all the adults at the center. When children's behavior does not match adults' expectations, the adults adjust their evaluations to suit their preconceptions. It was simply inconceivable, for most of the adults, for this young child to be from Africa. In their perspective, Corinne suffers from childish confusion, and this confusion must arise from some other adult's misguided attempts to teach her about her heritage. Incongruity is thus satisfactorily explained in the adults' minds. Interestingly, in this particular incident the misconception is cleared up. Corinne, for once, is vindicated by another key adult. However, for the most part adults are never challenged in such evaluations of children. Adultcentrism prevails.

Corinne was routinely disbelieved and corrected by newcomers who were not aware of her heritage. Teachers usually explained to newcomers that Corinne knew what she was talking about, but we never observed any of them apologize to the little girl or attempt to engage her in conversation about her origins. In this regard, it is significant that Corinne was the only child at the center who we observed being routinely dismissed and challenged when she discussed her origins with other people. Several other children enrolled at the school were also from foreign countries, but we never witnessed an adult challenging their knowledge of national origin. Apparently, adults had no difficulty in accepting that one child is from Europe and another is from China. Adults routinely expressed interest upon learning that a young child was from another country, asking them about their families and experiences, except when that child was Corinne. Corinne's accurate and detailed stories of Africa were dismissed as confusion or fantasy. Corinne was an adept storyteller, and her stories were confirmed by her parents. Indeed, they reported that she had a sharp memory of details that even her mother and father did not recall until she reminded them. Apparently, there was an interesting interaction going on for this particular child. Her dark skin and facility with words prompted adults to dismiss her stories with much more ease.

Although other children's stories about themselves and their origins were not disregarded with the same dismissiveness as Corinne's, the children were often deemed to be unable to think seriously about racial–ethnic distinctions and concepts. On one occasion, Michael (3, Asian) was playing with an assortment of cardboard cutout dolls that he had brought from home. He had shared them with the other children during the morning's activities and was now involved in disassembling them. But they are giving him some measure of difficulty, and he struggles in his work with them.

Michael approaches Debi and makes a request for help. "Read this to me," he says shyly, holding out one handful of the cardboard figures and another of instruction sheets. Debi looks at what he is holding. "Goodness," Debi says to herself, "The instructions are in Chinese. Now what do I do? Think fast." Debi regards the child and asks, "Did you get these from home, Michael?" searching for a way to tell him that she cannot read the instructions without encouraging him to think she is simply refusing to help. He nods and says, "Help me to put them together. The instructions tell you how. You read them to me." Debi smiles ruefully and tells him, "I'm sorry, Michael, I can't read Chinese." She shows him the instructions. "See," she points out, "the words are in Chinese." He regards the sheets of paper and shrugs his shoulders, his face reddening in sudden embarrassment. He gazes thoughtfully at Debi for a moment, then tells her, "Well, you must go to China then. You will read Chinese there." Debi agrees with him and says, "I'll bet I would learn to read Chinese very quickly if I were in China." He smiles at her and nods in agreement, then turns to find someone who is not illiterate.

Anne, a teacher who is sitting with Debi and Michael at the table, starts to chuckle as Michael departs. "Isn't that cute?" she remarks. "He doesn't understand that you don't speak Chinese. Well, I guess that's something to show that children don't recognize racial differences, don't you think?" She regarded Debi with a quizzical look on her face.

In fact, Michael's initial mistake does verify what developmental psychologists propose: Young children overgeneralize their own knowledge to others. Yet while Michael did not immediately recognize that many adults, regardless of their authority, could not read Chinese, he did not insist that Debi read to him when she pointed out that she could not recognize the language. He seemed to think it through for a moment. In doing so, he reveals that he understands several important social facts. First, he knows that Chinese people come from China, where people can read Chinese characters. There is thus something about being in China that facilitates reading those characters, and he recommends to Debi that she go there, because she would also be able to read Chinese. His logic is a bit faulty, but his attempt to sort through the complications of language and ability are striking. He is not confused by Debi's failure and does not persist in his request that she read to him. Rather, he puzzles through her inability to help him and then offers a suggestion on how she might rectify her deficiency. An egocentric child might have insisted on Debi's help, not realizing that other adults might not have skills that familiar family members possessed. Michael quickly recognized that Debi was not Chinese, and he seemed embarrassed. Debi's gentle reminder that she did not speak his language prompted him to offer help to her, a response far from egocentric or confused.

People who were not close to the children routinely dismissed our research and denied that youngsters could use racial or ethnic concepts in any but a rudimentary and disordered manner. The following episode illustrates the strength of this denial. Here Debi is being questioned about her research by a volunteer, David. He had learned from a teacher what the research project entails and seemed upset at the research plan. One afternoon, while the children were engaged in play outside, David sought Debi out and asked her if she would explain to him what she was doing. "Jeanne tells me that you are looking at whether or not children think about race. That's awful! How can you even think these little kids would be racist?" he says firmly. Recalling her interaction with some parents, Debi responds cautiously, "What do you mean by 'racist'?" By this point in the research work Debi had become accustomed to responding to adults who were upset by the idea of researching children's use of racial–ethnic concepts and had prepared herself to answer these concerns in as nonconfrontational a way as possible. Ordinarily, some discussion of conceptual terminology and about how the questioner felt about ethnicity or racism was sufficient.

"I mean," David began, a frown on his face, "I mean . . . I don't know what I mean." He stopped, regarding Debi with an even deeper, more puzzled frown. "What do *you* mean by 'racist'?" he continued, apparently taken off guard by Debi's question. "I don't use 'racist' in my research. I am only focusing on 'race' and then only on the kids' own ideas and behaviors," she answered him, ready to continue explaining the purpose of the project. But David was not satisfied with this. "Well, that's just as bad," David replied, "because they don't know anything about race, and it's wrong to bring it to their attention. They're not ready." He finished his comment emphatically. "I am majoring in psychology, and I know that children of this age simply do not have the tools to understand race. You are introducing it to them too early." He waited for Debi to concede to his academic knowledge.

"I'm not introducing it to them. I don't tell them anything. I just listen to what they say and watch how and who they play with," Debi replied, trying to ease David's concerns. "I'm interested in learning about and describing what they already know." He seemed unconvinced, so she added, "I'm not a teacher, remember. I don't introduce concepts, or try to lead them or discipline them. I'm only here to listen to what they do with whatever they get from the world." David leaned toward her, still frowning. He begins sarcastically, "So what do they do? Are they burning little crosses? Do they call each other 'nigger' or 'spic' or any of that? Of course not." He finished, folding his arms and seeming quite satisfied. "They're too little, and even if they did they don't understand it, not like we do. It doesn't mean anything to them. They're too little." David appeared to be convinced that the children's youth precluded any possibility that they could be involved in any racialized activity, at least as he was conceiving of it. He focused on the lack of meaning that race must have for children, demonstrating his belief in the notion of childhood innocence. He reiterated, shaking his head, "They're just too little."

Debi could now see that her prepared explanation was not going to be sufficient for David. His knowledge was likely grounded in the traditional, cognitively oriented readings he was undoubtedly encountering in his course work, as well as in the commonsense views that most adults hold about preschoolers' social abilities. Further, he was obviously encountering strong emotions about the research, which made Debi's explanatory task more urgent. "Well," she began again, "actually, they do call each other those names, and more, but that's not really what I am most interested in." David's jaw dropped, and he regarded her with widened eyes. "You are kidding, right?" he asked. "They don't really do that, do they?" David had moved from convinced to distressed. "I wasn't serious!" he said. "This is terrible!" David's distress at the news is intense. "Oh yes, they do that, but not often," Debi replied. "But you see, what I am most concerned with is not name-calling. It's the context of how they use those words, and lots of other racial ideas." Debi continued, telling David about some of the episodes of hand painting, Corinne's many dilemmas with her biracial/biethnic history and how the child handled them, and Carla and her cot. She tried to help him understand the broader social contexts of race and ethnicity. He listened carefully, no longer interrupting her. "Well," he said, after she had finished and was waiting for further comments, "I know that you won't find much else. I'm going to listen more carefully to them and teach them that they shouldn't do such things." What is perhaps most significant in this interesting exchange is not that David was very concerned about young children's understandings of racial and ethnic matters, but that he continued to discount Debi's summary of the research and insisted that she would not find "much else" in her research. Like many other adults, David had indicated a strong desire to teach the preschoolers right from wrong in regard to racial matters, a conviction shared by the classroom teachers.

Several weeks into the research project, Debi was asked by the center director to share some of the initial findings from the research with the school staff. She deliberated on how to best present her sometimes surprising discoveries to them. All the teachers in this classroom were certified by the state in which they taught, and all were current with the curricular requirements for teaching. Collectively, they had decades of teaching experience with young children. These were dedicated and serious professionals, all involved in keeping themselves current in teaching methods, and all committed to the goals of the multicultural curriculum. For that reason, Debi decided that a useful approach would be to describe the least-adult research methodology she was using and then to recount a few of the observed accounts of children's actions. She chose to recount the stories about the wagon and "white Americans," Carla's episode with moving her cot, and the hand painting activities. A prepared report was distributed to the staff. Debi expected that the teachers would react with curiosity and professional discussion. Their responses, however, were unexpected.

"My God!" one teacher gasps, as she reads the report. "When did this happen? Did this happen here, at this school?" Another teacher shook her head, with an expression indicating dismay: "Who did these things? Have the names been changed? Are these kids in *our* classroom?" The teachers reacted to the stories with shock. Yet another teacher smiled, then leaned forward and said, "You've got to be making this up. You've got to be. You're making it up." Their responses surprised Debi, who had anticipated that they would have at least been aware of some of the children's activities, even if they regarded them as rare or inconsequential. The friendly accusation that the data were "made up" put Debi at a loss for an adequate response, but the teachers quickly filled in the gap in conversation.

One teacher, Jeanne, asserted, "We have to do something about this and do something fast." "Oh, don't worry, we believe you," she nodded in Debi's direction, "but I never thought the kids were doing anything like this. All I knew about was Carla, and we figured that was because of her parents. Remember that meeting?" she asked Debi, who nodded in reply. "That was awful, wasn't it? And now you're telling us that all the kids do that stuff? When we aren't paying attention?" Jeanne was obviously distressed. "Where did they get this from?" wondered Patricia, another teacher in the classroom. "They aren't getting it from us, from me. I do lots of diversity exercises with them; I always accent diversity." Her expression was one of dismay and concern.

Jeanne continued, "Have you shared this with the director?" When Debi assured her that she had, Jeanne was dismayed. "Why didn't he tell us?" she wondered aloud. "I mean, we're supposed to be a good school. We're accredited, for goodness sakes." Debi tried to reassure Jeanne that there was nothing about the school, teachers, or curriculum that was wrong. "The kids get these ideas from the whole world," Debi explained, "not just from you all, or from school. I think that's the strongest point I want to make. If you need to blame something, blame society. This is society's fault. These ideas are everywhere." Debi tried to continue, but the teachers had apparently tuned her out, for they were already focusing on ameliorating what they perceived as a failing in their instruction and curriculum. The discussion rapidly became a curriculum review, with all the teachers brainstorming ideas for how to overcome this evidence of society's imperfection.

Each teacher immediately centered on what she had been doing with the children. Their ideas focused on their individual abilities to offer accurate instruction to the children. Patricia was particularly distressed, as she devoted much time and attention to bringing diversity and acceptance of differences to the children's attention. She was ever alert for teachable opportunities and active in accentuating positive difference in her interactions with them. All the teachers resolved to devote more classroom time and activities to issues of difference, and one resolved to visit the university library.

There was a striking omission in their discussion, however. None of the teachers acknowledged the more positive racial and ethnic interactions revealed in the report. For example, almost all of the hand painting activities showed that those children had acquired positive and strong self-identities, but the teachers ignored these preliminary findings and concentrated instead on ameliorating the children's negative behavior. All discussion centered on name-calling and children's incivility to one another. The teachers' response was strenuous and resolute. Part of their curriculum, after all, was devoted to ensuring that the children in their care received positive, caring, and accurate racial or ethnic information. They were viewing this report as damning evidence that they weren't doing their job, and they did not like the implication. They were committed to the ideas incorporated in the antibias curriculum and concentrated their energies toward reinforcing the goals of that curriculum.

What Debi had discovered was deeply disturbing to them, to the point that they totally disregarded the subtler, positive use of race.

Another instance of teacher misperceptions was revealed when Marion, a graduate student in another college, contacted Debi about the research at the preschool. When Debi's observations were nearly completed, a brief account of her findings appeared in a local periodical. We had read the piece before it was published and determined that the account was accurate. Marion read the article, and she contacted Debi and told her she had seen the piece. Marion had extensive experience with schools, and she questioned our research. "You are absolutely wrong, you know," she informed Debi. "Your interpretation of what the children say is deeply flawed." Debi was surprised at Marion's statement but responded, "In the traditional view of children's behavior that might be a reasonable conclusion." Marion shook her head and continued, "You obviously have no idea how children's minds work." After Debi replied by suggesting a later meeting, Marion then added, "I've written a letter to the newspaper. You should have spoken with the teachers, or someone who understands children, before you published that." Marion's response to the published account of our research is another verification of the strength of adult denial. Critical of our research, her letter proclaimed, "If Ms. Van Ausdale would have asked the teachers, she would have gotten a much better picture of what children know about race." Although Marion's own research did not involve observations of young children, she had spent much time with them. However, she did not see what we saw, apparently because she was not looking for such evidence and because of the common belief that young children could not engage actively with sophisticated and complex racial–ethnic ideas.

As we pointed out at the beginning of this chapter, there is a strong tendency on the part of adults to consider themselves as experts on matters of childhood. In Marion's case, this expertise appears to be amplified by her experience within schools and her work with children. However, her familiarity with children has caused her to fail to consider explanations other than cognitive ones. For Marion, the best possible explanation of children's behavior arises through teachers' and parents' interpretations. This knowledge seems grounded in her thorough understanding of mainstream child development theory and research. However, her reliance on cognitive/developmental theory had apparently blinded her to what was obvious to us working in the field: children were doing race and doing it on their own. Believing otherwise is a common misconception, and one that we hope our research will help to overcome.

The children we observed were adept at manipulating racial and ethnic concepts and distinctions outside the purview of adults. They exhibited quite a bit of talent in concealing their knowledge and behaviors from adult notice. Some of our findings related directly to the children's capacity to avoid adult intervention in their activities and adults' reluctance to recognize their abilities to conceal. These three-, four-, and five-year-olds were proficient at maintaining private spaces more or less free from adult intervention, and this facilitated their experimentation with racial and ethnic concepts and issues. Despite the teachers' best efforts, children managed to create places for their activities removed from the prying eyes of adults. This is undoubtedly common in all schools, and teachers everywhere are to some degree aware that children hide certain things from them. The children in our classroom seemed to realize early on that adults were sensitive to racial and ethnic issues and that they should take care in discussing these issues with sanctioning adults. When the children were alone, however, racial and ethnic concepts and distinctions figured into their interactions, as the data in previous chapters show clearly. This latter point is an important one, for some recent researchers have argued that young children do not talk about race (Hirschfeld 1997). To some degree, this conclusion may represent the inability of many researchers to hear what children are doing apart from the worlds of sanctioning adults.

Moreover, we are not suggesting that the teachers in this center were ever careless in their efforts to supervise the children or deficient in that supervision. They were invariably *vigilant* and very *concerned* with making sure that children were safe and happy. Their distress at learning of the children's activities was genuine. That children can create private space is an unintended effect of both how many of them there are and how determined they are to avoid contact with adults. No teacher or other supervising adult can possibly keep a close eye on each individual child in any classroom. This preschool held a ratio of about ten children to one teacher, a desirable number. Counting volunteers and other adults who were usually present in the room makes this ratio lower. Still, the children were in an area with several thousand square feet of teaching and play spaces, and, even with several adults present, it was easy for the children to secure some privacy, especially when they were outdoors. As we observed them, they frequently used this private child's space to practice and discuss things that they knew adults would interfere with if they observed or overheard.

We should note here that racial and ethnic concepts and actions were only *one* component of these hidden discussions and practices by children. Talk about bathroom activity was also a domain for such camouflage, as was the use of obscene language, talk of intimate relations, and discussion of other forbidden topics. While we did not conduct systematic observation of these or other concepts, we can offer a dramatic example of what we mean. One afternoon, Debi was seated on the deck, observing three four-year-old white girls at play with dolls. At first Debi notices nothing unusual in this activity, but after a moment or two she realizes that more is going on here than meets the eye. Renee, Jennifer, and Brittany each have dolls and are seated on blankets spread out on the floor of the deck, surrounded by blocks and other toys. Since the blocks obscure vision, they are partially hidden from view unless an adult observer is within a few feet of them. Debi sits only a few feet away from the girls and shows interest in their activity, but does not speak to them. They ignore her.

Renee announces to the other two girls, "She's about to have a baby!" Jennifer and Brittany giggle, glance around, and then return their attention to Renee, who is holding her now unclothed doll in her lap. Renee places the doll on the blanket and encourages it to "push, push, push." The other two girls appear to be hardly breathing, and Renee picks up a second doll, places it between the first doll's legs and announces, "The baby is here!" Jennifer and Brittany clap hands briefly, then glance around again and spot Debi watching them. They turn back to Renee, who appears to be functioning as midwife in this play.

Renee again takes the unclothed doll and stands it up. "Uh oh, here we go again," Renee says solemnly. She pushes the doll over backward, and it lands on the deck with a thud. "She's having trouble," Renee tells the other two. "I have to help her." Renee gets up and places her hands on the doll's stomach, squashing it. "That's it!" she announces triumphantly. All three girls giggle and pick up their dolls. "Mine next," Jennifer demands, placing the doll in Renee's lap. Renee leaps up, saying, "Just a minute." She goes inside the center.

When she returns moments later, she is clutching a collection of wooden play knives and forks in her hands. "She needs an operation," Renee announces to Jennifer. Jennifer nods gravely, and Renee busies herself with her tools. Now there are three naked dolls lying on the blankets in front of the children. Jennifer and Brittany sit expectantly, but just then Crystal, a teacher, approaches the group. The girls immediately pick up their dolls and cradle them in their arms. "Having fun?" Crystal asks the group, nodding at Debi. "Oh yes," Debi responds, "loads." She smiles at Crystal, who promptly turns and enters the playground.

Once the teacher is gone, Renee places Jennifer's doll on the blanket, face up, and picks up a wooden knife from the floor. "Here goes," she tells the other two girls. Renee draws the knife across the doll's abdomen—clearly doing a cesarean section—and shrieks, "The baby's here!" All three girls erupt into laughter, and Brittany insists, "Mine next, mine too, don't forget mine." Renee repeats her performance.

Noteworthy here is the quickness and skill the three children demonstrate as they hide their activity from the approaching teacher. Also important is the fact that they made no attempt to disguise their activity from Debi, who sat within five feet of them the entire time. This shows two levels of awareness in the children. First, they were aware that Crystal would not approve of their activity and might stop it. The intrusion of a *sanctioning adult* dramatically changed the girls' behavior, and this change was due to Crystal's entry to the play area. Second, the children were also aware that Debi posed no threat to their activity, since she was a type of powerless adult, unconcerned with the content of the children's play. The girls showed solid and accurate awareness of adults' state of mind and made accurate predictions of their behavior. In addition, when we recounted this story later on to some parents, they denied that their four-year-old girls could know this information or engage in such behavior—even the parent of one of the four-year-olds in the account!

Occasionally, some adults at the center acknowledged the possibility that children might notice racial and ethnic distinctions. They sometimes looked for signs that this was happening. Thus, one teacher shared the following story with Debi shortly after our research findings were presented at the teacher's meeting. Chris was a teacher in another of the classrooms at the preschool. She approached Debi one day and remarked, "I have something I'd like to share with you. I need your opinion on what to do. Is that OK?" Debi assented, and Chris told the following story to her. The mother of one of Chris's students, a four-year-old Asian boy, approached Chris with a request for permission to provide her son with food from home. "She told me that American food was very strange for him, and she was worried that he wasn't getting enough to eat. She told me that he wasn't adjusting to the changes of being in America and that he wasn't eating properly," Chris continued, "so I said sure, for her to bring a lunch for him was just fine. I told her that lots of the parents brought food for their kids." Chris frowned as she recalled the incident. "But then she told me that she was worried about bringing food because there are Black kids in the classroom." Chris's voice dropped as she moved closer to Debi. "His mom more or less informed me that Black children were thieves and that she was concerned that they would steal Lee's food. She said she heard a lot of stories about Blacks in her home and had been warned to stay clear of them by her relatives." Debi asked, "Are you sure that she thinks Black kids are thieves? Maybe she thinks they're hungry. Sometimes folks from other countries think that all American Blacks are poor." Chris shook her head vigorously and added, "Oh no, she didn't hint at it, she told me that Blacks are thieves. She's not confused."

Debi then asked, "What did you tell her?" and Chris responded, "Well, first I told her that we would not allow any child to take anything from another child's cubby and that we talked about private property and respect and those sorts of things. Then I told her that little children, Black or white or whatever, can't be 'thieves'; they're too little to have such motivations. And I let her know that we were alert for the kids, that we don't just let them rummage around in other people's belongings." As Chris spoke she became more concerned. "I mean really, what a terrible thing to say. It's really hard for me to be nice to her now." Debi replied, "I'm sure she was just making bad assumptions and that she's not still thinking that way." Chris looked doubtful. "I don't know, she didn't seem too convinced, and she hasn't brought any food for Lee. And how am I supposed to teach kids whose parents are at home telling them . . . that?" The conversation ended with Debi suggesting that Chris discuss the matter with the center director and perhaps arrange a meeting with the parents.

This preschool teacher is committed to a multicultural curriculum that embraces respect for all cultures. She teaches it to the children in her charge and practices it in her everyday life. However, when confronted with overt racism, she is not sure how to respond. Her primary objective is to ensure that the children are exposed to other cultures and learn to appreciate and value the differences between people. She proceeds on the assumption that the children are open to her teaching and is angered that a parent would make a blatantly racist statement to her. Yet when Debi inquired about how Chris had resolved the problem, Chris reported that she had decided to do nothing. "I'm just ignoring her," Chris told Debi, "and concentrating on Lee. There's hope for him, anyhow, and it's not my place to try to change the parents. The kids are another matter. We can still reach them." In the end, Chris's decision is to focus positive attention on Lee. Her resolve illustrates the ongoing belief that young children can be salvaged from racist beliefs, if they are taught early enough.

All the center's teachers followed the official curricular goal of instilling respect and consideration for cultural and ethnic differences. In their official capacity as teachers, all adhered to lessons that presented differences in positive ways. Diversity was a valued part of the curriculum, and if the teachers had been questioned about it, all would have professed enthusiastic and genuine support for it. They could not, however, single-handedly counter the impact of race and racism that the surrounding social world routinely exerted on the preschool children.

Most adult Americans, especially whites, have had little formal education in the deep realities of U.S. racism, and this can handicap those who are willing to do something about the racist attitudes and practices they see around them. One basic lesson about this systemic racism is that it has a global reach, thanks to the dominance of the U.S. media around the globe. As we have seen in some of our accounts, even Asian and Latin American peoples, including those who immigrate to the United States, often harbor negative images of and attitudes toward African Americans, views they have picked up from watching U.S. television shows and movies in their home countries (see Feagin 2000). Immigrants from many countries overseas may thus arrive on U.S. shores with anti-Black views already embedded in their minds. This further reinforces systemic racism in the United States.

Moreover, at times teachers and others working in the day care center's community engaged in behavior that was less respectful of diversity. For example, one worker at the center shared the following episode with Debi. "I was listening to two of the teachers talk to Gregory (4, Middle Eastern), and they were teasing him, trying to get him to say his name and to say particular words." Debi asked her, "Why were they doing that?" The volunteer replied, "I think they wanted to hear his accent." The volunteer regarded Debi with a rueful look on her face. "I mean, don't you think that's mean? I think Greggie was upset by it. I was watching, and after a minute he wouldn't say anything for them. They seemed to think it was funny, but I think that's mean, teasing a little kid about the way he sounds." Debi agreed that teasing a child about his speech was not appropriate and remarked, "You should discuss your feelings with the teachers. Perhaps they don't realize that Gregory was upset." The volunteer looked doubtful but replied, "I guess. I suppose they don't mean it, you know, I'm probably overinterpreting it. But I like Greggie, he's so cute." Unsure of how to proceed, Debi reiterated that discussing the matter with the teachers or with the center director might be helpful.

Gregory's accent was charming, and listening to him speak or tell a story was a pleasurable experience. There were several children, as we have related above, who were from other countries and spoke English with noticeable accents. The adults at the center seemed to enjoy listening to them and encouraged them to speak and share with the other children. Yet perhaps this encouragement was misconstrued as teasing, by the volunteer or the child himself. Then the encouragement could be experienced negatively, interpreted as a devaluation of difference. Since Gregory was reported to have stopped talking to the teachers, and to have seemed distressed, it is reasonable to conclude that this lesson in diversity had gone awry. What was intended to be an exercise in valuing difference may have been experienced as teasing from adults, and a young child was potentially silenced.

A few days later the volunteer again approached Debi. "I've been noticing," she began, "that some of the teachers can't pronounce the Asian kids' names." Debi agreed that some of the children's names were a struggle for some of the teachers. "I mean, don't you think that they should at least learn the kids' names?" the volunteer continued. Debi again agreed, but added, "At times I have trouble, too, especially with the longer names. I usually try to make it into a game with the kid, you know, get them to say it several times, to teach me. They seem to like that." The volunteer nodded thoughtfully. "I didn't think of that," she remarked. Debi assured her that she would be alert for such behavior in the future. Later in the afternoon, Debi listened to two volunteers discussing Ling-Ling (5, Chinese). This child speaks no English, except for a few essential words such as "toilet," "teacher," and "you know what." Debi had often heard Ling-Ling approach a teacher or volunteer, announce, "You know what?" and proceed, in Chinese, to inform the listener about his concerns in long and torturous sentences. One volunteer remarks, "I just can't understand a word he says!" The second nods in agreement, but points out that Ling-Ling seems to get along fine with the other children: "He has no trouble at all; he just plays and has a good time." The first volunteer adds, "Yeah, they don't care about English. They just know play."

Yet Ling-Ling does have some trouble. Over time, Debi's observations revealed that his lack of experience with English worked to his detriment. This little boy is an active child and enjoys rough-and-tumble play. Occasionally, his playmates suffer unintended injury. Someone gets hurt, but it is not always Ling-Ling's fault. However, he cannot explain what happened to the intervening authority, and he is rarely crying. He invariably ends up punished, usually put into time-out, and the other child goes free. We can speculate that his experiences will shape his evaluation of life in America. Yet the adults involved in his education seem to view him as doing well at the center.

Teachers, volunteers, and other adults at the center often remarked on how well the children got along together despite their differences in gender, racial, ethnic, and linguistic backgrounds. On several occasions, adults would comment to Debi about how wonderful it was that the children played so well with each other. From the inception of the research project, however, Debi's field notes are filled with observations that the children routinely segregate themselves by gender, racial group, and language. The notes reveal many situations where boys played almost exclusively with boys, girls with girls, Blacks with Blacks, Asians with Asians, and whites with whites. For the first few months these findings were daily observations, until finally Debi decided to note that such voluntary segregation continues unabated. She decided it would be more productive to note when the children failed to segregate themselves, for group segregation was common. The exceptions to this general rule were notable.

Other adults noticed this pattern also and remarked on it on several occasions. One Asian father commented that it was rather strange that the Asian boys often played together at school. "They don't play together at home," he told Debi, after watching the children on the preschool playground. Some of the Asian children lived in the same housing complex and thus knew each other well. "Well, I suppose it is because they all look alike," he concluded, smiling at Debi. "They don't know any better yet." He concluded that the children's criteria for selection of a playmate was their physical similarity. But if this is the case, why is it only practiced at school? That is, if one child's physical similarity to another functions as a guiding criterion for playmate selection, then we would expect that these young children would adhere to this standard regardless of location. What is happening at school that encourages children to form play groups based on racial and gender elements? We can only speculate, but perhaps some of the children of color opt to play together for defensive reasons.

CONCLUSION

Adult explanations often maintain that young children either have no consciousness of racial distinctions or hold naive and shallow conceptions easily amenable to change. As we have seen in this and previous chapters, the parents, teachers, and volunteers routinely dismissed or denied the extent of children's racial–ethnic knowledge. Some adult observers were distressed when learning of children's racialized behavior. For their part, most of the children seemed aware that adults did not expect them to understand racial and ethnic matters. The children would regularly disguise or conceal their activities from adults when there was a racial or ethnic component, especially if they were acting in negative ways. In effect, there are three social worlds here. In one social world, adults interact with other adults apart from children, with racial–ethnic distinctions and concepts central and essential for social life. In a second social world, children interact with adults and pick up many of the racial–ethnic images and understandings of the adult world, often without letting adults know they are doing so. In the third social world, children interact with other children, apart from adults. It is especially in this interactive world where children experiment with the racial–ethnic images, insights, and tools picked up from the larger society. In this third social world, children do much of their probing, experimenting, and learning that cultivates them into adults. We are suggesting that this third world of social activity is the most unknown to adults, and indeed to many researchers of children's lives.

Children are far more capable of keeping their activities hidden from adults than we are of disguising ours from them. The first world, of adult–adult interaction, is probably far more accessible to children than we acknowledge. Recall the episode above, where a teacher's aide discussed one little boy's ethnic heritage with Debi, in front of the child. She behaved as though the boy was unaware of her dialogue, despite the fact that she was discussing his looks and parentage. But certainly he heard her: he was sitting in her lap, and she directed her conversation with Debi right over his head. Yet she behaved as though he could not possibly understand the implications of her remarks. Should we then be more careful of our discussions about race and ethnicity? Do we unwittingly encourage children to focus on racial and ethnic ideas? Perhaps. But children still have tremendous abilities to deal with information and will often seize on and use compelling, powerful notions like these. Regardless of whether or not we are unconsciously indoctrinating children with racial ideas and propensities, it remains that the pervasiveness of race in our society does not allow us to ignore our children's capabilities.

6

WHAT AND HOW
CHILDREN LEARN ABOUT
RACIAL AND ETHNIC MATTERS

During the first week in this research study, Debi watched this next event. Since it is raining, the children are playing on the covered deck of the playground. Play is rambunctious and loud and seems even louder in the rather confined space. Francisco, a very small Latino boy, three years of age, is playing with a small group of children. He suddenly starts a fight. Francisco pushes Cheng-Li (5, Asian) over and topples the Asian boy's Lego tower. Cheng-Li begins to cry. Francisco parks himself down with a white girl a few feet away from the Asian boy. He declares to her, "I don't like him. He looks funny. But I like you." Francisco pats the girl on the face reassuringly. A teacher intervenes as soon as Cheng-Li's cries are heard, and she removes both boys from the play area, taking them aside. She stoops down and says, " Francisco, you need to be good friends with Cheng-Li. Use your words. You need to work it out." She remains with the boys, but they make no move to reconcile. Instead they just glare at each other. By now the Asian child has stopped crying and stands waiting for Francisco to apologize, but he never offers any expression of regret. He backs away slowly, waiting for the teacher's patience to wear out. He is soon rewarded, and the teacher moves away, to come speak with Debi. She tells Debi that Francisco is in a bad temper today but is usually not like that.

In our initial evaluation of this incident we accepted the teacher's evaluation, not considering that Francisco's attack on the Asian boy could have been racially motivated. Debi's field notes contained this entry: "It seems likely that this little boy was tired or temperamental. Three-year-olds are like that sometimes." Our own personal experience in raising children also seemed to fit with the teacher's explanation of Francisco's behavior. Common sense and personal knowledge of children's natures told us that the

175

teacher's evaluation was reasonable. Over time, however, Debi discovered that Francisco picked fights with or teased Asian children far more often than he did any other children. It is probable that Francisco wasn't just tired or cranky that first day—his actions were directed specifically at Asian children. Moreover, Francisco probably had shared his physical evaluation of Asians with at least one other child, Roger, whose antagonism toward an Asian child ("You look ugly") was recounted in chapter 4.

Once again, learning about racial identities had passed from one child to another, embedded in similar language. Both Francisco and Roger demonstrated similar animosity toward a child of a different racial–ethnic group. In this book we have shown that children's lives are much more complicated and involved than many analysts, including researchers, teachers, and parents, are willing to acknowledge. Racial group and ethnicity, in their complex variations, are integral components of children's daily living. At the beginning of our research process we, too, were inclined to believe that small children could not behave in overtly racist ways. Our experience with our own children confirmed this belief, and we were supported by most of the existing literature on young children. However, our field research data solidly refute this widespread presumption. Once we began to gather in-depth information about these children—which included their personal histories and careful long-term observations of their relations with others—we realized that many years of previous research findings and our initial reactions were inadequate or mistaken. Concrete reality has a way of contradicting our commonsense notions.

More than a half century ago, in a landmark study of anti-Black racism in U.S. society, Swedish social scientist Gunnar Myrdal (1964 [1944], 612) argued that a system of racist etiquette prevents American whites from truly knowing Black Americans like they know whites. Because interracial contact was so circumscribed and ritualized by an elaborate etiquette system, attempts by individual whites or Blacks to gain genuine knowledge about each other were usually doomed. Myrdal argued that the structure of this etiquette was un-American on its face. Still, racist thought and practice so pervaded everyday life that it assumed a sort of normalcy for both groups. Racial categories mattered and shaped conventional behavior by whites, very few of which questioned or even acknowledged the extent to which their lives were bound up in and controlled by this racist structure. According to Myrdal (1964 [1944], 615) this caste etiquette "indicates the split in the American's moral personality." (We should note that, in spite of his language, Myrdal was not actually speaking of all Americans here, but only of white Americans' moral schizophrenia. Of course, Black Americans did not have such a reaction, for they were acutely aware that the daily system of oppression was both painful and immoral.) The pressures of the system of informal discrimination and segregation were at least as powerful as those brought to bear by legal measures. And this was as true in the North as in the South. Myrdal argued that everyday pressures exerted great influence on social behavior, although at times this influence could be modified by the context of an interaction between Blacks and whites. The context of everyday life in a racist society was critical for understandings of racial relations.

For contemporary society, social context remains very important for understanding what might better be called racist oppression and resistance. While most types of overt legal discrimination against African Americans and other Americans of color have been eliminated as we move into the twenty-first century, a vast informal system of racism remains substantially intact. Recall from chapter 1 that the system of racism in the United States has several important dimensions, including the racist attitudes and discriminatory practices that still involve the majority of white adults. Surveys show that many white Americans admit to being racist in their thinking about African Americans, and in-depth interviewing indicates that many hold such views in a deep and emotional way. Many whites also hold negative views of other Americans of color. In addition, research on housing discrimination suggests that, when given an appropriate opportunity such as renting an apartment or selling a house, a majority of white adults in those situations will place overt or covert barriers in front of African Americans, and large numbers will do the same for Latinos and Asian Americans. Many whites try to impose a subordinate position on African Americans and other Americans of color. Preferably, Americans of color are supposed to stay mostly in their own housing areas and schools, where many whites assume they are happy to be with "their own kind." The white majority is today less overtly racist than it was a few decades back, but many whites still accept African Americans and other non-European Americans only on white terms and in places and circumstances that whites determine. Racialized ideas and pressures are thus foundational aspects of U.S. society and affect Americans of all backgrounds in their interactive behavior and interpretations of racial–ethnic contacts.

Not only white Americans but also Americans of color are influenced in thought and action by the larger racialized context in which they live. White Americans have built, now over nearly four centuries, an institutionalized framework of racial subordination and typification for all non-European groups that entered after whites conquered Native Americans. Constructed from the beginning of the new European American society, this racialized framework has been most thoroughly developed in regard to African Americans—who were first enslaved, then were legally segregated, and now are discriminated against without legal sanction. Later on in the nineteenth and early twentieth centuries, when large numbers of Asian and Latino Americans (as well as other non-Europeans) began to immigrate into U.S. society, they entered a system where anti-Black racism was well institutionalized across sectors of society. Thus, most whites have viewed, and discriminated against, the newer non-European groups from within this long-standing system of anti-Black racism. Not surprisingly, then, negative views of newer non-Europeans, such as Asian and Latino Americans, have often been similar to older views of Black Americans. Over time, moreover, the newer groups not only suffered racist prejudice from whites but also picked up—and at times implemented—anti-Black ideas from the white racist context. We have seen in our research work how sometimes other adults or children of color can take an anti-Black stance in regard to an African American child. Such prejudice or discriminatory action is yet another manifestation of white racism, yet this time indirectly manifested. Moreover, when one child of color takes a negative, racialized action against a child from another non-European group— be they Black, Latino, or Asian—such action is usually yet another example of white racism expressed by proxy. Since whites have held the major positions of power and control for centuries, it is they who are most responsible for the creation and maintenance of this racialized system in the United States. Both children and adults, in all U.S. racial and ethnic groups, reflect the deeper racial realities in their everyday thoughts, propensities, and actions.

From an early age, children are immersed in this pervasive and informal system of racism, and during the course of their daily interactions with others they acquire the techniques of dealing with members of other racial and ethnic groups. Our research has shown how widespread racial and ethnic concepts are in children's lives and how children handle the complexity and implementation of these concepts. Particularly important for understanding the meaning of racial group membership and ethnicity in children's lives is a careful consideration of how they put these critical social concepts to practical use.

CHILDREN AS PRODUCERS
OF RACIAL–ETHNIC MEANINGS

Learning the Rules

In this study we have captured the richness of children's racial–ethnic experiences by means of extensive observations of their activities. The racialized nature of children's language, concepts, and interactions only becomes fully apparent when their activities are viewed over time and are contextually understood. Close scrutiny of their lives reveals that they are as intricate as adults' lives, even though children have a more limited experience with the social world. The limitations to children's experience derive from their relatively brief time in social contact with others, not from deficits in ability, engagement, or facility with interaction. They are simply not as practiced or familiar with social life. Despite their status as relatively new members of the social world, most young children quickly develop complex social capabilities, refining and honing their interactive abilities over time as they gather much new information. The accounts presented in this book are drawn from real, everyday experience and are generated in intimate and recurring social relationships. From these research data we have gained considerable insight into the significance of racial and ethnic concepts in young children's everyday lives.

Young children's ability to manage and understand the social world is not nearly as restricted as mainstream theories of development would have us believe. Most children are accomplished at deciphering and manipulating the social world and its complexities. They begin to do so soon after birth, establishing social relationships with their immediate caregivers and building up social understanding from this base (Vygotsky 1978). Most children are involved in an intricate web of social relationships. While children's contact with other people might be fairly limited, usually only to parents or other caregivers, these adults bring a vast array of their own experiences to bear in creating social life for their young children. Their experiences are presented to their children, again perhaps not directly and intentionally, but certainly vicariously. We do not hide our lives from our families. In fact, home is the one place where we can feel somewhat free of the societal constraints imposed on us in our more public lives. Interpersonal experiences are transformed into individual ones, not the other way around. Children have social experience first, then incorporate these experiences into a personal framework of action. This transformation is a result of many interpersonal events taking place over a long period of time.

Our method of relatively long-term, in-depth observation of children's everyday lives led us to discover how important the interactive process is for understanding racial and ethnic concepts. The idea that young, allegedly ego-centered children are somehow disconnected from the larger social world and its deeper understandings does not hold up in the light of field observations. This perspective seems to be based on adult unfamiliarity with how children relate to each other when away from the controlling influence and surveillance of adults. Most previous investigation of young children's activities has not been conducted within the children's own social worlds. Such detachment introduces an element of artificiality to the extant research findings on children. Mainstream perspectives accent individually focused, cognitively based theories of children's abilities and neglect the social complexity of their worlds.

Because racial–ethnic understandings and behaviors are embedded throughout the larger society, they quickly become important in children's lives and assume a complicated and evolving character. Blumer (1969, 138) suggested that any sociological variable is, on examination, "an intricate and inner-moving complex." Dunn (1993) notes that complexity and multidimensionality characterize children's relationships, even within their own families. This evaluation is accurate outside families as well. In the case of the boys Jason and Dao (who developed their own language), for example, their interactions were not only creative and complex but initially beyond the ability of the surrounding adults to comprehend. Their interaction evolved over time as they came to develop a hybrid language that enabled them to play together. By exploring the use of racial and ethnic concepts within a child's own world, instead of trying to remove either the child or the concepts from that world, we glean a more nuanced and complete picture of how children speak, mold, and manipulate these concepts.

Racial and ethnic issues arise forcefully within the context of everyday interaction with other children. Most of the young children that we observed apparently had little interactive experience with people of other racial and ethnic groups outside the center. For these children, many of whom were having their first extensive social experiences outside the family, racial and ethnic differences became important in youthful explorations and experimentation. Children became more active in their social agency within a larger system focused on race and ethnic realities. The racial–ethnic distinctions thus became powerful identifiers of the self and of the other. Whether this is also the case for children who do not experience substantial exposure to racial–ethnic differences in a diverse social environment, we can only speculate. However, over eleven months of observation, we watched slowly evolving transformations in these children in their explorations and understandings of racial–ethnic roles and identities. For many there seemed to be some increase in racial–ethnic awareness over time. Some regularly explored racial identities by comparing their skin color with that of others. Others faced recurring dilemmas about self-image. Indeed, one child, Renee, used racial group as a method of self-identification in one scene, as a way to define a partner in another, and as an exclusionary tool in yet another. For still others, racial or ethnic issues arose intermittently during our observations, and these issues did not seem to be as central to their everyday social relations, at least at the day care center. There was variation in how often children openly expressed or indicated racial and ethnic understandings.

For children of color, particularly for African and African American children, notions of color, race, power, and white superiority were constant pressures. Learning race and coping strategies were more a matter of survival than experimentation. Taleshia and Corinne faced challenges almost daily, Taleshia because of her dark skin and Corinne because of her complex ethnic and racial identity. Mike, the four-year-old who declared that he was "Black and strong" to other children, also produced challenges regularly, since he eventually was shunned by most of the other children. He was indeed stronger and larger than the rest of the population, and he experienced increasing difficulty in maintaining friendships. By the end of our observation period, Mike was headed to a private kindergarten, where hopefully he would encounter other children who could keep pace with him. However, he brings his experiences at the day care center with him, and these experiences are sure to shape and inform his continued growth in the world.

As we see it, in order to understand fully the importance of racial and ethnic understandings for children, researchers must come to recognize the nuanced complexity and interconnected nature of their thinking and behavior. Studies of concept awareness need to incorporate not only the cognitive level of the child but also relationships the child has developed in social situations. Corsaro (1981) has proposed that conventional cognitive-development models do not offer much analysis of children's communicative skills in regard to social status issues. Other researchers (Graue and Walsh 1998, 44) suggest that viewing children through the lens of traditional theory produces "remarkably myopic" perspectives and note that even Piaget himself stopped using the concept of egocentrism nearly three decades ago. Yet, until fairly recently, individualistically focused developmental perspectives held sway in the research community without much opposition (for a new critical approach, see Rogoff 1998), and these notions continue to inform commonsense interpretations of children. Yet interaction with other children is important for exploring social status. Children can investigate what social authority or status means when they are apart from the adults and older siblings they are in contact with at home (Troyna and Hatcher 1992; Connolly 1998).

Social status and its accompanying power and prestige are important for young children at a preschool. In our observations we have seen young children experiment with and develop a consciousness of racial–ethnic statuses over some period of time. Certainly, in the classroom hierarchy teachers hold the highest status, and children acknowledge this by generally acquiescing to them. As we have indicated in previous chapters, Debi's usual position as playmate–observer was affirmed periodically; she was not seen as a sanctioning adult in the children's eyes. When she approached children playing, they usually did not alter their activity even if the activity was one likely to be sanctioned by a teacher or parent. This gave her unique and substantial access to children's social worlds.

CHILDREN LEARNING SOCIAL
RULES AND IDENTITY–ROLES

A key finding in our research is that young children quickly learn the racial–ethnic identities and role performances of the larger society. They take the language and concepts of the larger society and experiment with them in their own interactions with other children and adult caregivers. There are, of course, variations between children and over time for a given child. Children may accept these status roles in whole or in part. Their cultural understandings and social performances evolve over time. Many of them play and experiment as they learn and remold the identity–roles of racial superior or inferior. Thus, as white children grow up, they learn, develop, and perform the meanings associated with the white identity–role. Black children and other children of color often must cope with the subordinating expectations imposed on them, expectations that they may accept or resist. In the process most children, like most adults, come to see racial and ethnic categories as more or less permanent parts of their environments.

We see this permanence clearly in numerous accounts in this book, such as the case of one child's expressed understanding that only white Americans are eligible to pull a wagon. White children frequently use social tools from the toolbox provided by the larger society. Gradually, they take on the language and behaviors of whiteness and construct them actively in their own lives. In contrast, those children who have the inferior identity–role imposed on them may resist in varying ways. They resist and counter white impositions and understandings. Recall, for example, the case of Taleshia and the hand painting exercise. Told to pick a color that looks just like her skin, Taleshia has her hand painted pink. Robin, a white child, protests, exclaiming, "She's not that color. She's brown. Look, Taleshia." She holds her arm next to Taleshia's and again insists, "She's just not pink, can't you see that, she's Black." Soon another white child joins the chorus, telling Taleshia that she is not pink and thus should not choose the inappropriate color. Still, Taleshia insists and finally has her way. These white children have an idea of the choices and identity to which Taleshia should be adhering. As they see it, Taleshia should pick a color that goes with her socially constructed racial makeup. They insist with vigor, to the point of grabbing Taleshia's arm. In this case, however, Taleshia does not capitulate, but holds her ground. Clearly, how social identity–roles are seen varies between those imposing the understandings and expectations and those who are pressed to endure these expectations. In the case of identity–roles that are part of an oppressive social hierarchy, there will likely be some, or great, resistance to the imposed social expectations.

Using the language of skin color, the white girls actively perpetuate boundaries between Taleshia and themselves. These young white girls are already experts at the social construction of physical reality. This and similar accounts in our book are not about the biology of the children involved, but rather are about the active construction of physical reality in ways to sustain social group boundaries. As we have suggested throughout this book, *doing* racialized power is central to many events at the day care center. In our data we see the categories in which children and other people are defined, but we also observe the moving reality of everyday practice that reshapes or perpetuates these categories and associated behaviors. Doing race is a complex of socially shaped and constructed behaviors that are constantly interactive with others and that have significant social consequences (on similar issues for gender, see West and Zimmerman 1987, 126). It is in the doing that the oppressive social relations we call modern racism are often constructed and reconstructed.

Modern racism is fundamentally about a severe imbalance of power— the power of whites to control society's social resources. Being white means having power over Blacks and other people of color. Significantly, in our observations *no* child of color used racist epithets to control white children.

They did fight back when challenged and sometimes used constructed racial distinctions to create their own exclusive play groups—perhaps as a defensive reaction to the white exclusion they had felt inside and outside the preschool setting. While we do not have enough data to draw firm conclusions, it seems important to distinguish the use of racial markers by white children against children of color from what might appear to be a similar use of racial markers by children of color against white children. In both types of settings the excluded children may feel some pain, and we suspect that the two situations are not equivalent in their impact on the children, either for those who are the perpetrators or for those who are the targets. The reason for this is that the exclusionary actions carried out by the white children replicate and reproduce similar exclusionary actions that children of color and their parents face regularly in the larger society. There is a close social fit between what happens in the school and what happens outside. In contrast, when a white child in the preschool suffered some attempted exclusion, he or she was not likely to view that exclusion as part of a lifelong struggle against exclusion by people of color in the larger society. Much research suggests that whites learn to view their lives as neutral, average, and ideal (McIntosh 1988), and never recognize themselves as highly privileged oppressors. This learning also begins early and is constantly reinforced in daily experience. Lillian Smith's (1949) riveting *Killers of the Dream* recounts the depth and extent of growing up with white privilege; her experiences began in early childhood.

As we have suggested previously, the social roles of student, parent, and teacher are not performed all the time. Imposed racial identity–roles, in contrast, pervade daily living and persist for lifetimes. In our data we see many a child who is regularly constructed in social terms as Black by others in his or her environments. Categorizations such as "Black" and "white" are socially recurring and shape the social interactions in which each child or adult participates. They become accepted as permanent parts of the social milieu. Still, an element of resistance is characteristic of much everyday interaction, particularly interaction of members of subordinate groups with members of the dominant group. Change often results from this resistance.

Layers of Social Rules and Requirements

A fundamental task of childhood is to develop comprehension of critical social language, rules, and norms. This evolving understanding enables young children to recognize appropriate social behavior, forming the foundation for organizing their own interactive behavior in the future. Smetana's (1993) explanation of the nature of social rules and her conceptual model for understanding the differences between levels of social rules are useful for probing the nature of racial and ethnic distinctions in children's relationships. Smetana differentiates between two domains of social rules: higher-order moral rules and lower-order conventional rules. The lower-order conventional rules are those drawn from the everyday customs of a particular society in a certain period of time. "No shoes, no shirt, no service" is one example of a lower-order convention of behavior. It dictates the socially accepted mode of dress in certain places, primarily public places of business, but no immorality is associated with it, whether individuals adhere to or breach the rule. In contrast, the higher-order moral rules deal with issues that are common across most societies and that shape the deeper values and orientations in a society, those that relate to others' welfare, such as their physical survival. "Thou shalt not kill" is an ancient example of such high-order moral rules. This is an interesting distinction, for the focus in children's research to date has been almost entirely on the higher-order moral aspects of children's racial attitudes and actions. However, because children have varied social experiences, their exposure to and understanding of the many rules structuring social life are complex.

According to Smetana, children do not treat all rules the same, as cognitively based theories have suggested (Piaget 1965; Kohlberg 1969). Her model of rule-making and rule-following behavior proposes that children's differing experiences inform them on how to make decisions about what constitutes appropriate social behavior under varying conditions. The perceived differences between moral and conventional behavior are what children rely on to make judgments about social behavior. Additionally, children as young as two and a half years old are able to distinguish between moral and conventional rules (Smetana 1985; Smetana and Braeges 1990), leading us to suggest that most of the children at the day care center had this process of differentiation substantially in hand.

Before we can show how the differentiation between moral and conventional rules figures in children's racial experiences, we should explain how these two domains are understood in the literature. First, the higher-order moral rules are those that deal with issues of seriously hurting other people. For example, children realize early that hitting behavior is heavily condemned (although adults are often exempt from their own professed rule). Hitting or hurting another person is a transgression of a moral rule because the action has direct consequences for the other person. Moral rules are broadly agreed upon and are generally unchangeable, binding on all persons across many social categories, and pertain to all situations, with the wrongness of the act not contingent on either the context of the interaction or the companion with which the act occurs. The admonition to "use your words" to resolve disputes in the day care center is another aspect of moral rules of behavior. Few sanctions by adults were delivered with more gravity than these three simple words, imparting their importance to the children in no uncertain terms.

Conventional rules, on the other hand, are characterized by their contextual dependence. They are constructed from knowledge of experienced social settings and the norms of behavior in those settings. One simple example is a conventional rule of dress in our society: girls wear dresses and boys wear pants. This is changeable across societies and is not dependent on a deep concern for the physical welfare of girls and boys. Breaking this rule usually elicits a distinctly different reaction from observers than does breaking the rule governing a moral behavior, such as violent hitting. In the literature there also is a third distinction, that of prudential rules, but these social rules usually pertain to governing the physical safety of self. An example of a prudential rule would be to carry an umbrella if the skies are cloudy or to wear a helmet when riding a bicycle. Breaking one of these rules harms only the rule-breaker and has little or no impact on social interactions.

Traditional research on how children employ social rules has often focused on the higher-order moral aspects of rule-breaking behavior. In this research children usually are asked brief and pointed questions on the rightness or wrongness of hypothetical social situations. Their answers are analyzed to determine the extent to which they comprehend the moral significance of the rule infraction. According to scholars who work on these issues, children acquire this general sense of morality through the transmission of cultural attitudes from significant adults in their lives (Turiel, Killen, and Helwig 1987). Moral behavior comes to be a part of children's lives as it is filtered to them by parents and other significant adults. The mechanisms for this transmission are the regular practices of family and social life, which provide children with models for evaluating whether a rule is moral or conventional.

As we see it, conventional rules and behavior are also transmitted to children in this way. Much of the literature on children's racial attitudes and behaviors seems to assume that racial concepts are higher-order moral issues, which are best understood through attempts to determine children's level of higher moral functioning. We propose that, because of the embeddedness of racism in the routine operations of U.S. institutions, racial understandings and usage are more often matters of conventional behavior and everyday customs than they are matters of higher moral prescriptions. This is true both for adults and young children.

One question that has been little addressed in previous research is the issue of whether racial and ethnic distinctions, including prejudice and discrimination, are morally or conventionally based matters. Issues involving racial and ethnic matters pose a dilemma for research because of the changeable nature of racist thinking and action over long periods of time. There is variation both within and across societies. Historically, in the United States the rights of individuals have been determined by relying on racial categories and distinctions. For example, in the infamous 1857 *Dred Scott* decision, a majority of the Supreme Court's justices articulated the opinion that Black Americans are "beings of an inferior order, and altogether unfit to associate with the white race, either in social or political relations; and so far inferior, that they had no rights which the white man was bound to respect." African Americans have long had to fight hard to secure even the basic rights and respect taken for granted by white Americans.

For example, today many Black men report that when they approach a lone white female in a public place, she often reacts with an overt display of fear and defensiveness. Car doors are locked, purses are clutched, and streets are crossed by white women (and some men) in order to avoid contact. Their behavior is conventional in the sense that it is automatic, and no regard is given by the white women for the potential adverse impact their behavior provides for Black males. White women's response to Black men often does not derive from actual, personal, negative experiences with them. Instead, this behavior relies on long-lived conventional messages taught to whites of all ages that Black men are dangerous and not to be trusted. Recent research has shown that these messages, often in the form of negative images in the media, are ubiquitous and unavoidable, even for Blacks who have obtained all outward signs of achievement (see Feagin and Sikes 1994).

The ubiquitous nature of this everyday racist practice, coupled as it usually is with negative images of Blacks or other Americans of color, has a significant impact on children. Given the facility most young children have with concealing potentially punishable behavior from adults, it is not surprising that much of their experimentation with race and racism goes unnoticed. As is the case with many other taboo topics (sex, bathroom functioning, and the like), the need to conceal racist behavior results in racial identity becoming a central part of young children's social repertoires. This is particularly true for children in this study, who were immersed in a relatively diverse racial–ethnic environment. At least for white children, racist thought and practice are "normal" and conventional, and they make use of learned distinctions to structure their behavior toward others. Children's strategies of action involve the use of racial and ethnic distinctions as part of an accepted cultural pattern. Their actions have incorporated racial and ethnic concepts and understandings because they are central to the larger society's way of life. We use the term *strategies* here not in the sense of a conscious plan for organizing but rather as "a larger chain of action beginning with at least some pre-fabricated links" (Swidler 1986, 277). Racial and ethnic thinking is, at least in part, prefabricated for children, and it makes as much sense for them to use it in their daily interactions as it does for adults. Unfortunately, for most white children, as for most white adults, there is little in the way of a broad moral dilemma posed by racist thinking and action. What has often been framed as a basic moral issue is really an issue of everyday routine apart from some asserted morality. Racism is today, as in the past, the usual state of affairs, and few whites openly question its reality and privileges.

Many white analysts have taken a different point of view. For example, in his classic 1940s research study, *An American Dilemma*, Gunnar Myrdal (1964 [1944], lxxi) argued that U.S. racism involves a broad moral dilemma pressing on white Americans:

> The American Negro problem is a problem in the heart of the American. It is there that the interracial tension has its focus. It is there that the decisive struggle goes on. This is the central viewpoint of this treatise. Though our study includes economic, social, and political race relations, at bottom our problem is the moral dilemma of the American—the conflict between his moral valuations on various levels of consciousness and generality. The "American Dilemma," referred to in the title of this book, is the ever-raging conflict between, on the one hand, the valuations preserved on the general plane which we shall call the "American Creed," where the American thinks, talks, and acts under the influence of high national and Christian precepts, and on the other hand, the valuations on specific planes of individual and group living, where personal and local interests; economic, social, and sexual jealousies; considerations of community prestige and conformity; group prejudice against particular persons or types of people; and all sorts of miscellaneous wants, impulses, and habits dominate his outlook.

We should first note again that, like most white analysts before and since, Myrdal here uses the term *Americans* here for *white* Americans.

Second, we should note the strong argument that for (white) Americans there is a broad moral dilemma, a tension between the democratic creed alleged to be dominant and the discriminatory practices. Later on, in a 1960s preface to a later edition of *An American Dilemma*, Myrdal (1964 [1944], xxiii) continues to take an optimistic view that the ongoing civil right changes and laws are a working out of some higher-order moral pressure, the American creed of equality and justice, on white Americans. Here Myrdal agrees with his 1940s view that there are great changes going on in U.S. racial relations in the direction of the elimination of racism from the society. Yet from the perspective of the present, the early twenty-first century, Myrdal's interpretation is too hopeful. As we have documented previously, racist attitudes and practices are commonplace today among whites in the United States—toward not only Black Americans but also other Americans of color. The continuing reality of this prejudice and discrimination calls into question whether there is any such moral dilemma as the one described by Myrdal. Today, a majority of whites seem to have a limited, and often verbal, commitment to the ideals of racial equality and justice. Most whites do not yet wish to see them actually incorporated as the foundation of the society. At best, the supposed "American creed" is hypocritical, for it represents what whites say, not what most whites do in practice. Conventional racist behavior, one might say, has established its own morality—or immorality—involving patterns of everyday injustice. This is nowhere more revealed than in the actions of three-, four-, and five-year-old children.

ADULT MISCONCEPTIONS

In our experience, children's active construction of racial and ethnic meanings and attitudes occurs early and is in important ways very similar to the meanings and attitudes held by adult Americans. Despite the sometimes contradictory nature of research findings, most researchers agree that the majority of children have a solid conception of racial and ethnic distinctions by the time they are about six. In fact, even children of this age who have had little or no direct contact with people from other racial and ethnic groups have been found to understand the social meaning of racial–ethnic distinctions (George and Hoppe 1979; Radke and Sutherland 1949; Ramsey 1991). Our data extend this finding to include much younger children. Well before they can speak clearly, children are exposed to racial and ethnic ideas through their immersion in and observation of the large social world. Since racism exists at all levels of society and is interwoven in all aspects of American social life, it is virtually impossible for alert young children either to miss or ignore it. Far from being oblivious to racial group and racism, children are inundated with it from the moment they enter society.

Despite this evidence, certain "commonsense" conceptualizations of children continue to drive much research. Adults often experience deep denial when it comes to acknowledging racism, especially in young children. This denial can be seen in the 1967 report by the Plowden Committee in Great Britain. It concluded that

> Most experienced primary school teachers do not think that colour prejudice causes much difficulty. Children readily accept each other and set store by other qualities in their classmates than the colour of their skin. Some echoes of adult values and prejudices inevitably invade the classroom but they seldom survive for long among children. It is among the neighbours at home and when he begins to enquire about jobs that the Coloured child faces the realities of the society into which his parents have brought him. (Plowden Report, paragraph 179)

This conclusion is similar to the reaction that the director of the center had when he learned that Carla, a three-year-old child, had used explicit racial slurs (see chapter 1). He tried to discover the source of the child's behavior, apparently assuming that she had learned it at home. However, when the parents were called in, they denied ever using such language around their daughter. They blamed a neighbor and his child. Another parent, curious about our research, informed Debi that her daughter would never do such things, just like all little children. "If you didn't teach them about it they wouldn't notice." Here "it," of course, is racial concepts and thinking. Indeed, with the exception of a Black teacher at the day care center, all the adults employed there were surprised or shocked at the results of our observational research.

Many adults are concerned about the impact of racial–ethnic relations on children's social development, but they—mainly white adults— often fail to understand the importance of racial and ethnic matters for children. This failure to acknowledge the importance of racial groups in children's lives arises from the twin adult convictions that children are naive and that color blindness is not only desirable but achievable. To reach this goal, many adults verbally discourage children from recognizing that skin color is a critical social marker. This professed color blindness denies the racially and ethnically divided world that kids observe and function in on a daily basis. Frankly put, many white adults insist that racial distinctions do not matter, while all around them children see ample and compelling evidence that they do matter, and matter very much indeed. One practical response to this ideological contradiction by white children is to conceal the creation of their own racial understandings and relationships, at least while the prying eyes of adults are on them. This enables them to reproduce the racial–ethnic hierarchy in their own relationships without interference from adults.

Perhaps the strongest evidence of white adults' conceptual bias is seen in the assumption that children experience life events in some naive or guileless way. This perception of children leaves unaddressed the wide variation in children's life experiences and coping skills and perpetuates the theory that children are all the same. Yet there is ample evidence that this just is not so. For example, a large literature has demonstrated that Black children tend to be precocious and knowledgeable about matters of racism. Thus, in his development of a model of Black child socialization, William Cross relies on W. E. B. Du Bois's concept of dual Black identities. Cross discusses the *bicultural* competence that American Blacks develop out of the necessity of living in close proximity to whites (Cross 1991). They must know what the imposed image of Blackness is, and they must develop a potentially divergent sense of themselves. They must know the white world and be able to operate in the Black world (for example, at home) as well. In general, as we have seen in our data, Black children are adept at negotiating racial groups and racist structures.

This is not surprising once the deeply racist nature of U.S. society is acknowledged. Black children are fully functioning members of a society that automatically reduces them and their life potential because of the racist hierarchy privileging whites of all ages. They are immersed in a society that continually presents them with negative images of Blacks. They are the targets of the conventional rules and behavior that literally become second nature for most white Americans. To survive, Black children must develop skills that can guide them through life with a minimum of damage. It was neither coincidence nor accident that the children who developed the most racial acumen in this study were Black females. The accumulation of experience with racial group and racism influences young Black children, as it does adults, helping them to develop an array of techniques for dealing with racist situations (Feagin and Sikes 1994). For example, even at three and a half years of age Taleshia had already developed a wide variety of coping techniques for dealing with the racial categorizing and discrimination imposed on her by her non-Black peers. She selected her countering strategies, from active resistance to passive withdrawal, based in part on the context of her interactions. How she managed her life was inextricably bound to how racism shapes the social character of her world, and she managed with extraordinary intelligence and sophistication. Moreover, as we see in our data, many of the same sophisticated coping strategies can be seen in the actions of other children of color.

The conception of children as racially naive is a construction of white adults—a type of wishful thinking that is not borne out by observation. Adult bias in general leans in favor of viewing children as sweet, ingenuous, and in need of protection. This tendency leads us to false assumptions about children's abilities in the social world. Yet it is hopeful bias, grounded in our American Dream of equality and fairness. We want very much to hope that children, in their innocence and purity, will overcome the massive structure of racism that undergirds our society.

RACIAL GROUP AND ETHNICITY IN CHILDREN'S SOCIAL HIERARCHY

Young children, whatever their own backgrounds, often understand that in U.S. society greater privileges and higher social status are generally awarded to white people. Many understand that by virtue of certain physical characteristics such as skin color, whites are accorded more power, control, and prestige. Young children have the racial knowledge necessary to carry out interactions in which one's racial group is salient. The possession of this knowledge is situational, and children are capable of making the basis of interaction race-based or not-race-based, according to their own evaluations of appropriateness.

The social conventions of racial hierarchy are as observable as are those of the age hierarchy. Almost any child with a little experience at observing the world can explain to any adult that children have a different status in society. Most children can provide descriptions of this status in great detail. Since this idea of hierarchy, or ranking, of society is familiar to them through their recognition of their subordinate status as children, even a child who has had limited exposure to society at large has observed and recognized the racial hierarchy in action. They are attuned to matters of status through their own subordinated position. The mass media, parental behavior, peer attitudes, and experience with other adults also provide young children with a wealth of information about how U.S. society is structured. Hence, young children's social judgments include at least an inchoate recognition of racial relations and whites' superior position within the racial structure.

What the children did in this preschool setting is doubtless not unique but is likely to be repeated in other settings. Even the traditional research literature accepts the fact that children display racial and ethnic prejudices by the time they arrive at elementary school, but it usually offers no explanation about the acquisition of prejudice beyond imitation of parental behavior. We would expect continuity of the children's racial–ethnic categories across a variety of social settings, for children reveal a readiness to employ their knowledge of racial group and ethnicity wherever it seems relevant to do so.

Our observed accounts of children's interaction underscore numerous problems in traditional theories of child development. Researchers too often conclude that children do not have the cognitive capabilities to understand racial groups because they often fail conventional cognitively based tests designed by researchers. However, a few other surveys and observations of children in natural settings support our argument that children as young as three often have constant, well-defined, and negative biases toward racial or ethnic others (see Ramsey 1987). Rather than insisting that young children do not understand racial–ethnic ideas and meanings because they fail to reproduce these concepts in certain researcher-mandated ways, researchers should determine the extent to which the racial–ethnic concepts used in daily interaction are salient definers of children's social reality. Some previous research (Thorne 1993) on children's use of gender concepts suggests that the more a research design allows entry into the real life of children, the more that research can answer questions about the nature of gender in action in children's everyday lives. We have found the same to be true for racial meanings and identities in young children's lives.

Anne Wilson (1987) has suggested that the wider social skills acquired after entry into school complicate investigation on how children come to know the meaning of racial groups and ethnicity. However, as we see it, it is this wider exposure that facilitates investigation, because it is through social interaction that children begin to actively construct racial groups, complex racial identities, and racial relations with each other— and reveal this developing knowledge to those adults willing to pay attention. Wilson (1987, 105) suggests that

> It is not difficult to offer hypotheses about why even young children develop clear and complex category sets in the context of poverty, racial tension and racial diversity. Where there is a wide range of skin colours and cultures and where the child's everyday linguistic experience is not sheltered by euphemism, racial categorization is likely to be open and to the point.

However, in her research on the racial messages that mixed-race children receive from home environments, Wilson gives little attention to the barrage of such messages sent out by the larger society. Instead, she seems to assume that children do not understand the standard euphemisms about racial matters until they are older. She proposes that in the more middle-class, white setting a mixed-race child will receive a more limited exposure to racial slurs, implying that this is the primary way children learn about racial distinctions and employ those distinctions in their everyday lives. The white middle classes, Wilson seems to assume, are more subtle about racism, making it more difficult for children to acquire the proper tools for both creating racism and dealing with it. This conception of white middle-class society as being only subtly racist is in error (see Feagin and Sikes 1994; Feagin and Vera 1995; Feagin 2000), for middle-class whites account for much of the overt and covert discrimination in housing, employment, and public accommodations that is faced by African Americans. Moreover, our field research shows that racial concepts are quite accessible and easily worked into daily interaction among preschoolers of all backgrounds, including those from middle-class families. We further speculate that this implied subtlety of racism among the middle class might serve to make it more seductive for children in these families. It seems more mysterious and elusive. Their parents' use of racist behavior or thought might create contradictions for children of the middle classes, who are actively comparing what goes on at home to what they are encountering in the rest of the world. The hushed and careful attention that middle-class parents often give to racial matters might serve to enhance their children's attention to it, just as our attempts to disguise sexual matters from children often serve to foster even more curiosity about it.

UNDERSTANDING RACIAL ISSUES IN CHILDREN'S LIVES

Most traditional Piagetian approaches allow little room for differences among children by class, racial group, or gender. That is one reason they cannot account for the large variability in children's everyday experiences. Accompanying the assumption that all children behave more or less the same way is the pervasive belief that children actually behave and think in the ways adults believe or describe. As we have pointed out before, the most common theory of children's minds is formulated substantially from measurement of their failures to achieve adult levels and forms of thought. Doll tests, often modeled on the Clarks' pioneering work in the 1930s and 1940s, are still in use and continue to provide contradictory information on the nature and extent of children's racial knowledge. Like many other measurements, they involve contrived research arrangements that may or may not tap the knowledge that children gain in their own everyday worlds.

A deterministic and romanticized model of early childhood as a more or less idyllic time ordinarily devoid of stress and responsibility is probably responsible for the misinterpretations of some scholars who have come to be known as the "hurried child" theorists (Elkind 1981). However, the modern "hurried child," one who is forced by the increasing social pressures of contemporary times to grow up too quickly and to thus forego the leisure and purity of past-times childhood, is a pervasive myth. There is ample evidence to suggest that childhood in the past was as tough or tougher on kids than it is today (Aries 1962). Even more important is the fact that childhood was, and still is, experienced differently by children in varied social groups and classes (Dunn 1993; Lynott and Logue 1993). As a group, children are not socially naive and inexperienced, but develop complex social skills for dealing with a variety of people and situations that they are likely to encounter throughout their lives. These skills are located in the way that they negotiate their daily activities, whether with adults or with other children. They move within and between a variety of realms and relationships, changing their approaches to life to meet varying situations. The way that we observe and interpret children's lives needs to incorporate the complexity of the world that they encounter and help to build for themselves.

In their examination of children's development of role categories and social organization, Emler and Dickinson (1993) suggest that all people are amateur sociologists by necessity. The fact that each day virtually all people negotiate the social world, making decisions about a large variety of social interactions, creates a need in each individual for social analysis skills. They suggest that the larger social structures of status roles and inequality facilitate these everyday interactions, because these structures provide us with knowledge of how people come to occupy their social positions and what is expected of us in our relations with others. In addition to gender, wealth, and prestige as social organizers, racial distinctions are central to the organization of U.S. social relations. Thus, any theory that seeks to explain children's understanding of social structure must include racial relations.

Young children can explain income and status inequality by drawing on their observations that some people are treated differently than others and that this differential treatment revolves around the power and value of various occupations (Tajfel 1984). To some degree, social structure is given attention in this explanation. However, our society's racist structure is rarely offered in explanation for the differences among racial groups, even by white adults. Individualistic explanations for why some people are more powerful or important than others are usually relied upon, even into adulthood (Dickinson 1986). People become powerful, successful, or even happy because of the effort, hard work, and determination they bring to action. Those who fail to succeed in life come to this end because of their own, individual choices. The importance of social structure is rarely acknowledged beyond references to vague forces such as "political power" or "market forces."

If three- to five-year-old children can to some degree cite and understand class and occupational differences, as some earlier research concludes, then it should not be surprising that our research shows that they can also interpret racial and ethnic differences with some degree of sophistication. The level of abstraction required is similar between the concepts, and the children have access to all social structures, through their exposure to the social toolbox. Emler and Dickinson (1993) also suggest that these explanations are the result of a process of social consensus. Consensus building occurs as children use racial and ethnic understandings to organize play spaces, like Rita did when she invented her rule that Spanish language use was necessary for entry into a play area. Consensus is not clear-cut, however, but changes as the social knowledge of racial groups and ethnicity changes, over time and with much practice. Everyday discourse provides children with reasons for why racial and ethnic distinctions are important and when they can reasonably be included as justifications for social action. The social toolbox is wide open and ready for children to use as their skills develop. When the nature of everyday discourse and practice is laden with racial–ethnic meanings, children, too, will make much practical use of that discourse in everyday life.

Clearly, the building of the edifice of racialized power in the United States begins at an early age and requires many new hands from each generation to keep it in place. Some of these hands, sadly enough, are very small.

7

POSTSCRIPT: WHAT CAN BE DONE?

No social study that does not come back to the problems of
biography, history, and their intersections within a society has
completed its intellectual journey.

—C. Wright Mills (1959)

Wdon't know about that stuff. They don't understand." We received polite
smiles, shaking heads, and gentle suggestions to look elsewhere. This reaction compelled us to look further.

There are two pieces of conventional wisdom that crumble under the
research scrutiny we have given to young children's lives. The first is the
insistence that racism is impossible for young children—they simply do
not understand and cannot engage in such ugliness. The second is that
racism is a fading societal reality destroyed by decades of legislation and
reversals of negative attitudes in the white population. From this perspective, racism cannot be an important part of children's lives; their pre-
sumed incapacity to comprehend it is coupled with its allegedly rapid dis-
appearance from public life. These two notions together present a
formidable barrier to understanding children's lives. Those who accept
them cannot understand the meaning and implications of continuing
racial and ethnic inequalities for themselves or their children.

The more central question, as we see it, is not how children become
racist but rather how racism is sustained and perpetuated in a society that
insists it is either dead or mortally wounded. As we have demonstrated in

197

the survey in chapter 1 and in our data, racist thought and practice remain strong in the United States, and young children cannot avoid participating in and perpetuating them. Racism surrounds us, permeates our ideas and conversations, focuses our relationships with one another, shapes our practices, and drives much in our personal, social, and political lives. There are few social forces so strong. Children are neither immune to it nor unaware of its power. A social reality this mighty is bound to become an integral part of their lives, and thus it endures from generation to generation, perhaps changing somewhat in form but still strong in its impact.

We should not look at the lives of children in isolation and without accounting for their context. We cannot understand children's lives without incorporating a thorough understanding of both the past history and the contemporary manifestations of racial relations in North America. Children are engaged with the world in its rich beauty and profound ugliness, and within their contained, immediate milieus they construct ideas, meanings, and actions while learning to make sense of society. Each child in our study possessed connections with family, friends, teachers, and playmates at the center. They were part of ever larger social circles and networks—and were thus part of the larger racialized society of which we are all members. How they have managed to create, re-create, and reinvent that racially stratified society in their own discourse and practices is at the center of our analysis. Racism intersects with their lives in a flood of elaborate, blatant, and subtle ways—from the definition of identity and self, to the performance of hurtful practices, to various articulations of dominant group power. It is this complex array of social realities that has defied much previous analysis trying to make sense of children and their racial–ethnic attitudes.

In much social science research there is an intellectual bias that inclines us to see the social world as something for us only to interpret, rather than as a set of concrete problems that also need to be solved. Much of the research on race, ethnicity, and children has attempted to interpret children's behaviors and attitudes outside the context of a larger society with continuing racial problems that need to be aggressively attacked and solved. Traditional theories viewing children as egocentric and limited social beings have often combined with commonsense inclinations in the viewing of children as cute naive beings who possess few or none of the repugnant behaviors adults direct toward each other—unless they were taught such behaviors by adults, of course. Some research has perpetuated this commonsense view. Few analyses, whether scholarly or popular, have proposed that children themselves are teaching each other in detail about the many faces of racism—and are unfortunately doing a good job of it. While a few studies (see Connolly 1998) on race issues and children have called attention to the importance of peer group learning, none that we have seen examine the ways in which white children and children of color—both within their own groups and across the color lines—work interactively to develop and implement racial ideas, discourse, and actions. Most scholarly assessments have suggested that racial ideas and behavior among young children are naive or transitory and can be easily eradicated with a little instruction in tolerance and respect for others. From this framework, persistent negative attitudes toward other groups is an indication of perverse adult indoctrination. As the words of a song in the musical *South Pacific* suggest, "they have to be carefully taught" about hatred, bigotry, and prejudice.

Suggesting that children remain largely unaware of racial and ethnic matters until they are taught by adults, however, denies their ability to absorb and manipulate the social world. This is akin to insisting that children cannot speak unless they are formally taught language by adults. Of course, we are not systematically taught the early language we use. Infants mostly learn to speak by being spoken to, from the time they are born. Children are immersed in their language and, with few exceptions, become accomplished speakers within a few years in this informal and unstructured format. Drawing from our data, we view children's learning about racial and ethnic matters in a similar way.

The problems for parents, educators, and others concerned with the mental health and welfare of children are certainly abundant and complicated. Addressing racial and ethnic hostility and negative actions in the schools and in the lives of our children requires that we rethink our ideas about several dimensions of everyday life, including the nature of racial and ethnic oppression, the intellectual capacity of children, our willingness to effect changes in oppressive social conditions, and the extent of children's social skills. Some curricula and programs attempting to reduce prejudice and discrimination and increase diversity in schools have been in place for several decades. And some recent studies of older children, such as high school students, indicate that they publicly express greater acceptance of racial–ethnic diversity, at least verbally (see, for example, Bachman, Johnston, and O'Malley 1997).

Yet the actual racial and ethnic relations in many of our schools are often tense, if not openly hostile and conflict-ridden—in some areas as much as at any time since the civil rights movements of the 1960s. This suggests that in many school systems applying the usual multicultural thinking about children and racial matters has had, at best, modest effects in the direction of eradicating racial prejudice and discrimination. Now at least a full generation of children has been subjected, in varying degrees, to some instruction that declares "tolerance" to be appropriate and "intolerance" to be immoral; the positive valuing of all children or people is often said to be a virtue.

Why have many such well-meaning programs had apparently modest effects? We suggest that one reason is that these approaches rely on a limited and incomplete understanding of children that effectively reduces their impact. In our educational systems, as a rule, we start countering the pernicious effects of racial and ethnic prejudices and discrimination far too late and with too little energy and sophistication. Thus, in most settings we have no, or limited, antiprejudice and antidiscrimination programs for young children. As we see it, the most effective antidiscrimination programs will be those that vigorously attack both individual and institutional patterns of racial and ethnic oppression at all points in society, from the highest levels of government to the ordinary world of the playground. Successful antidiscrimination action cannot be limited to a few places, at certain times, and with only some groups in the population.

What are some solutions for the problems that we have discovered with the ways young children are taught in school classrooms? One of our goals is to get educational and other researchers and public commentators themselves to understand the realities of the social worlds of children. Racism is real in its effects on children's lives and in its impact on our continuing relationships with each other. There is perhaps no stronger evidence of this reality than our data on its imprint on the lives of more than fifty small children. Children make use of its power and importance in social life from at least the time they enter the public sphere, and probably well before. It is likely here that no adult has actively taught most of these three-, four-, and five-year-olds about white power, racial self-identification, racial–ethnic exclusion, and racial–ethnic discrimination. Certainly, the day care center's staff uniformly and overtly taught tolerance, value, appreciation, and consideration for all children of all backgrounds and colors.

So how did little children become so adept at race-centered behavior? One major answer lies in the fact that they are surrounded with racial imagery, thinking, discourse, and behavior. They observe it, experience it, and absorb it in different places and from the people they encounter. It is ubiquitous. Children use the social tools they find most convenient and efficient, as all of us do, to accomplish the social ends they seek. Most human beings of all ages combine and arrange many elements from their social contexts in order to construct a personally adaptive and meaningful life, generally adapting to their immediate situations but utilizing the social tools picked up in many settings. Part of the task facing educators and others seeking change is to recognize first how central the tools of race and racism are in the social toolbox. Once that is fully realized, we can begin working toward rendering the tools of race and racism obsolete. A first step must be to address, reduce, and eventually vanquish engrained racist ideas and discriminatory practices in all social settings and institutions. For all our efforts in the past, we have made modest progress, primarily, we suspect, because most whites deny the deeply racialized organization of our social worlds. We will now look briefly at three relevant areas of U.S. society where the reality of race and racism still remains all too clear for both young and old Americans.

THE CONTEXTS OF RACISM IN U.S. SOCIETY

Education and Neighborhoods

In recent years numerous U.S. educational institutions have moved to reverse the progressive trends stemming from civil rights activism in the 1950s and 1960s. Legislation in several states, such as California, has effectively eliminated programs of affirmative action in education at many levels. Mandatory busing programs for school desegregation are being eliminated despite evidence that many schools are becoming ever more segregated. According to the Harvard Project on School Desegregation (Orfield et al. 1997), U.S. public schools became *more racially segregated* in the years between the early and mid-1990s than at any other time since the historic *Brown v. Board of Education* Supreme Court decision in 1954. De facto segregation remains in place at all levels of the public school system, where most children accomplish their educational careers—from preschool to high school.

The design and operation of public school systems almost guarantee that they will remain segregated. One issue is funding for public schools. It is a matter of widespread policy that public school funding is a local function, and most money for schools is usually derived from local tax coffers, primarily property taxes. This results in affluent neighborhoods typically being endowed with good schools, where teachers are better paid and supported with good resources and parental involvement. Such schools are usually located in suburban, predominantly white areas.

Schools located in neighborhoods with fewer tax-generated resources generally offer much less to their students. While some studies have shown that the amount of money invested in children's schooling has a negligible effect on learning, when scant resources and poorly compensated teachers are combined with rundown neighborhoods and high rates of joblessness and underemployment, the negative effects on children's learning are amplified. Such conditions are the result of social policy choices in regard to school funding and employment practices that advantage white, middle-class, and suburban populations. The dynamics and impact of funding choices have been amply discussed in a variety of research studies now over several decades (for example, Kozol 1988), but most states in the nation have as yet seen little significant change in funding policy or public attitudes on behalf of changing such policies. Many affluent Americans still seem reluctant to fund schooling for "other people's children."

Many children of color realize that they are not a funding priority when they attend their problem-ridden or deteriorating public schools. Most children now attend schools in or near their home neighborhoods, especially since many busing mandates for desegregation have been struck down across the nation. This tendency exacerbates school segregation, since neighborhoods themselves are often racially segregated. There are relatively few racially mixed communities that endure over the long term. The practice of living primarily within racial-group boundaries means that most children begin to see these racial groups as distinct. While adults may present images of alternative living arrangements and neighborhoods to preschool and older children, such as in optimistic storybooks and similar media, the unyielding reality of racial segregation at home remains an important and conspicuous part of most children's everyday lives. As the old adage warns, "Children learn what they live." If the majority live in more or less racially homogeneous and segregated environments, they learn that people group together by skin color and language—and usually that where light-skinned people live is the preferred territory. Living in such separated places undoubtedly affects, often in negative ways, how children interact in schools, even if they are placed in school settings where there is greater diversity than in their home neighborhoods.

Employment Policy and Practices

Gaps in unemployment between Blacks and Latinos, on the one hand, and whites, on the other, remain more or less large, and many occupations remain racially segregated. On the average, Black workers and other dark-skinned workers continue to earn less than white workers, and Black and Latino families continue to have less income and much less wealth (net worth) than white families. While in recent decades more Black Americans have entered the middle class, their proportions are still significantly lower than that for white Americans. Whites continue to occupy very disproportionately the vast majority of job categories commanding respect and higher wages.

While one might expect that young children do not realize the varying nature of work and occupational prestige, a quick trip into the world of children will dissuade the reader from that opinion. Go to the places where many children go. In most of the public places that children frequent, such as grocery markets, fast-food restaurants, and retail stores, many of the people doing the low-paid work are not white. Whom do children see performing many of the cleaning and serving functions in the social world? Who mops the floors at school? Who bags the groceries? Who digs the ditches and mows the lawns? This daily exposure to the world of work might prompt many children to automatically assume that Blacks and other people of color are mostly relegated to the worst jobs. Certainly, few teachers actively instruct children that people of color should be limited in their occupational placement because of skin color. Indeed, most teachers may propound an equality of opportunity vision of U.S. society to their pupils. However, given the children's other daily experiences, such a teacher's vision probably does not dissuade them from the idea that certain types of people have certain jobs and that these jobs are often allocated by skin color. Once again, children learn what and where they live.

Issues of Crime and Violence

Americans of color, and particularly African and Latino Americans, are disproportionately involved with crime and the criminal justice system in the United States. First, they are more likely to be the *victims of crime* than white Americans. Second, the blue-collar crimes some of them commit are much more likely to be targeted for punishment by the criminal justice system than the white-collar crimes that are more common among whites. Proportionally, a larger number of people of color, especially Black Americans, is either incarcerated or has been jailed. Incessantly replayed and highlighted by the mass media, this reality is not missed by children, who likely notice that men and women in communities of color typically have a different experience with the criminal justice system than do white men and women. The constant media reiteration of the differential representation of Black and Latino Americans in the criminal justice system, including prisons, undoubtedly feeds the conviction among many whites, young and old, that average Black and Latino Americans are somehow much more criminal, violent, and dangerous than whites. In addition, the media blitz likely leads many whites to support aggressive get-tough, three-strikes, and racial profiling policies on the part of police agencies, which unevenly impact communities of color. Few whites bother to examine the realities of racial discrimination in policing and other parts of the criminal justice system. And many white parents likely communicate their stereotypes and misunderstandings about race and crime to their children (on the actual realities of crime, see Feagin and Feagin 1997, 269–309). This means that children, especially white children, are likely to associate criminality, and violent criminality, with the people of color with whom they come in contact. Many white Americans, both adults and children, seem to live out their lives convinced that the numerous misrepresentations of Americans of color as particularly violent or criminal are accurate in regard to a great many Americans of color. Such misrepresentations and gross exaggerations provide yet more fuel for white children's racial fires.

To illustrate the power of race for informing young minds about the nature of people considered socially deviant, we can turn to an incident that a young mother recently shared with us. While in New York City, the first author spoke on our field research at Columbia University. She recounted several episodes outlined in this book. When she finished the presentation, a mother in the audience offered this story of her own experience with children and race.

This woman, whom we will call Maria, had two children, a toddler aged two and a half and a seven-year-old. Since she and her family lived in the heart of New York City, one of the preferred methods for getting around town was to bundle the toddler into his stroller and maneuver the city sidewalks that way. It was quick and offered less potential for the little boy to become detached from his family. In the family's neighborhood there were usually several panhandlers on the street, almost all of them Black men who solicited change from passersby. Maria made it a habit to sidestep the area that these men frequented, giving them a wide berth. She was not fearful of the men, she said, for they were invariably polite and never demanded money. However, she usually was not able to offer them change and did not wish her children to think that she was not kind. Over time her practice of avoiding the men became routine. She and her children wheeled out the front door of their building, made a wide circle around the panhandlers, and headed for school or the train station.

One afternoon, her two-year-old bounced down beside her on the couch and announced, "Black men are bad." Maria was horrified: Where did this come from? She had never told him anything like this. His older sister, sitting alongside them, was equally stunned and asked, "Where'd he get that from?" Maria's husband was queried along with friends and other family members who had access to the little boy; all were shocked.

Like some mothers in our own accounts, Maria and her acquaintances considered themselves to be liberals who would never instruct any child in such blatant racism. The family soon dismissed the child's remark as a repetition of something he must have heard from outsiders. However, when Maria began to describe the incident to Debi, she became aware of how her toddler might have arrived at such a conclusion. Maria had decided that her regular avoidance of the Black panhandlers in her neighborhood must be the behavioral reality that her son had used to make his generalization. He had been wheeled past these men every day, and every day Maria took precautions to keep a distance from them. "We've been actively teaching him to stay away from 'bad' things, like stray dogs, electric outlets, stuff like that," she told Debi, "and I'm guessing that he's extended that to those poor guys." Maria's analysis was tentative but seemed reasonable to her: "I mean, he's really been into this 'good/bad' stuff, since he's learned it. He runs around naming stuff 'good' or 'bad.' I guess we overdid it," she said sorrowfully. Her everyday action, apparently taken out of nonracial motivation, had the potential to deliver racial messages to a young child. In his growing sense of the world "bad" things were avoided and "good" things were brought close. He shared his newfound evaluation of this part of the world with those closest to him.

The world of a toddler is fairly confined and constrained, and Maria kept a close eye on her son's association with others. Still, her analysis might not be accurate: her son may have learned to name Black men as bad from some casual acquaintance or from viewing television. Perhaps he learned it from his sister, who only pretended to be shocked to avoid reproof. Yet an examination of the events leading up to the boy's pronouncement does suggest that he may well have learned this on his own, from observing and dissecting his social world. And it is also possible that he joined his own observations on the street to what he had learned in other settings. In any event, like the older children in our study, this two-year-old toddler's growing contact with the world—and accurate observations of it—is already furnishing lessons on racial stereotyping and avoidance.

Recognizing Racial and Ethnic Oppression

We have outlined only a few of the many types of social settings and institutions that surround and have great bearing on the lives of children. These settings, moreover, are intimately interconnected. There is a web of social and institutional activities. Schools are linked to neighborhoods, which are in turn linked to employment and patterns of crime and crime perception. One cannot understand the problems of schools in the absence of understanding economic or community problems. The proper unit of analysis, for an understanding of racial or ethnic oppression, is the entire society. In many cases, one component institution enables or constrains yet another institution, and all institutions enable or constrain the individuals operating within them. All U.S. institutions are shaped by racial and ethnic histories and concerns. This is a fact of American life. Children are certainly important actors in this broad expanse of societal activities, and they often experience many of the contradictions and quandaries that adults experience. Children are not ordinarily disconnected from the larger social worlds.

In order to make positive progress, we should not limit change-oriented action to the individual level of each child or adult, nor should we make our solutions only individualistically oriented programs such as antibias curricula in schools and multicultural sensitivity training for teachers or students. These approaches help, but at best they ameliorate the effects of racial and ethnic discrimination rather than eliminate that discrimination. The deeper social changes we see as necessary should begin with a serious recognition of the endemic character of *individual and institutional* discrimination along racial and ethnic lines in the United States. This recognition will require not only more field research on the ways in which racial–ethnic discrimination works in the society, but also a willingness to face the likely disturbing results of that new research—and of the existing research that currently shows just how foundational and persisting racist thought, emotions, and practice are. We sketched out some of this reality in chapter 1. Whites in particular will find this facing of reality difficult, since they have been inculcated with a sense of superiority and privilege throughout U.S. history. For most whites, even acknowledging the racist nature of their own thinking and action, and their white privileges, is a difficult step (see McIntosh 1988). Understanding the institutionally racist character of the larger society is an even more difficult step. Yet, fully understanding and admitting to racism is more than an acknowledgment of personal responsibility; it also involves an awareness of the adverse impact that racism has on all Americans—and particularly on children. Such an admission is not one of guilt but of hope for a better future for all Americans.

Clearly, too, no real progress can be made until those white Americans with influence and decision-making power see institutionalized racial and ethnic discrimination as the societal curse and cancer—for all Americans, including whites—that it really is. Once there is such a recognition—a step we recognize is extraordinarily difficult and currently unlikely—then we as a nation can proceed to devote the major time, effort, and resources that are necessary to undo and eliminate the perverse reality of racial–ethnic oppression and provide compensations and reparations for its centuries of negative effects (see Feagin 2000).

WHAT CAN TEACHERS DO?

In the busy world of preschool and elementary school education, teachers have little extra time. Teaching at this level is demanding and exhausting, and while the intangible rewards can be great, the personal investment in energy and time is large. Teaching small children can be one of the most difficult jobs; indeed, just watching the teachers at their task was often an exhausting experience for the first author throughout her fieldwork. Adding the task of implementing programs to eliminate racial prejudice and discrimination is a lot to ask of teachers who are overburdened and, all too often, poorly respected and inadequately compensated. However, there are things that teachers can do now to promote active antidiscrimination agendas in their classrooms and schools. Here we draw on the findings of our research, as well as on ideas that are incorporated in some of the antibias curricula we have examined and in certain "teaching tolerance" programs such as that administered by the Southern Poverty Law Center.

First, each teacher should make sure that she or he deals with personally racist inclinations and actions, no matter how subtle. Researcher Paul Connolly did an interview study with five- and six-year-old children in an inner-city, multiethnic school in England. He found that "some teachers may be influenced (either directly or indirectly) by a set of racist beliefs which encourages them to think of White children as being more intelligent and well behaved than Black children" (Connolly 1998, 21). So the first admonition is clear: Deal seriously with your own internalized negative constructions of the children with whom you interact.

Second, and very important as well, take instances of racist talk or discriminatory behavior on the part of your children *very* seriously. We have amply demonstrated that young children's ideas of race and ethnicity are often much more sophisticated and organized than most adults assume. Don't dismiss their activities as fleeting, uninformed, or inconsequential. Instead, cultivate an attitude that recognizes and acknowledges their ideas and accepts their insights. Work to ensure that people of diverse racial and ethnic backgrounds are viewed positively. Seize opportunities to talk to the children about differences, prejudices, and discrimination, but be sure to locate the source of these things as mainly *outside* an individual child. That is, don't encourage children to believe that negative racial talk or discriminatory action is the conduct only of "sick" individuals or that it indicates a peculiar character flaw or just "bad" behavior. Talk about the fact that the social world we live in is often unfair to people of color simply because they are people of color and that persisting racial–ethnic inequalities are unjust and morally wrong. Make it clear that racial–ethnic prejudice and discrimination are part of a larger society that needs reform and not just something that individuals do. Generally speaking, we and other researchers have found that children have a strong sense of social justice and do appreciate an adult's honest confirmation of the troubling facts of persisting social injustice. Candor about the social world often makes a child's life less, not more, confusing.

Also, take opportunities whenever possible to introduce yourself and your children to the history of racial and ethnic relations. There are many fine books and publications for teachers and children that address this often oppressive history in honest and candid ways. Ask your school librarian to identify books that treat the history of racial and ethnic relations without whitewashing its seamy side. We are not suggesting that you try to frighten your young charges with stories of great brutality or violence, but rather strive to select books that are as realistic and relevant in regard to social injustice as your children can handle. Try to move beyond the usual selections that feature the struggles of a few famous personalities such as Rosa Parks, Dr. Martin Luther King Jr., or Jackie Robinson, and search for books that focus on common folk, especially children, in everyday settings. Look for stories that the children can easily identify with and that actively promote gaining a greater understanding of the many kinds of peoples—including recent immigrant groups—that make up this multicultural nation. Also, do not limit books to stories that have a happy ending or that present African Americans or other Americans of color as always winning battles against unfairness and discrimination. This last suggestion may be difficult to achieve, because most adults, including parents and teachers, seem concerned with protecting children from the ugliness of human society. But it is not really helpful, in the short or long run, to present children who are experiencing (or generating) racism first-hand in their everyday worlds with the idea that racial oppression is a minor condition or that victory over it is just around the corner. As individuals and as a society, we have a long and arduous battle ahead of us in order to eliminate racial–ethnic discrimination and its many individual manifestations and institutional roots. The more children know about the seriousness of racial–ethnic oppression and its consequences, the more they will be equipped to contest it in their present and future lives.

Be watchful, too, for instances of people combating racism in the larger community, and bring those positive examples of antiracism to children's attention. Invite parents, other teachers, and community figures that have experience in antiracist activities to visit the classroom and talk with the children. If you have the resources for field trips or other excursions, try to identify and visit exhibitions and cultural events that feature the histories and current realities of racial–ethnic discrimination as well as of social activism directed against that discrimination. Exposing children to a wide variety of people and organizations that are invested in documenting or eliminating racism will present them with alternative ways of viewing the racial–ethnic worlds they are coming to know. Most of the time, in most places, children do not see anyone fighting aggressively against social inequities and injustices. In particular, white children are vulnerable in this regard, since they get little personal experience with people of color, other than perhaps in a desegregated school, and often have adults in their social fields who will communicate negative messages about the racial others to them.

WHAT CAN PARENTS DO?

There is much that concerned parents can do to break down the racial and ethnic barriers in this society and create the truly fair and just society that we often proclaim. Educate yourself about the realities of racial discrimination against various groups and about the many aspects of individual and institutional racism. Read more about American history on racial–ethnic matters. There are many good books, some of which are cited in the references at the end of this book. The burden of action here is heavily on white parents, since most parents of color are very knowledgeable about—and are usually proficient in negotiating—the racialized worlds of the society. Indeed, white parents can join with other citizens concerned with learning more about racial–ethnic oppression in the growing number of antiracism groups that have sprung up around the country, such as the numerous Institutes for the Healing of Racism (see Rutstein 1993; Rutstein 1997).

Perhaps the most difficult problem that most white parents and other adults will experience is understanding and accepting that they are very privileged participants in a racially rigged game. It is discouraging to discover that one's hard work, determination, and effort are often no more important to one's long-term achievements and social position than is one's skin color. For many generations now, most whites have been privileged members of society in more ways than they recognize—from privileges in business and employment, in access to good housing and educational opportunities, and even in regard to such mundane matters as not being followed around when shopping in stores. In U.S. society the smaller concerns of everyday life are too often riddled with racism. To help explain this ubiquitous privilege, try this experiment: in a nearby store try to locate a greeting card congratulating the parents of a new baby that does *not* feature a cherubic white child on the cover. The best that one can find is a card featuring a bunny or baby chick, which are hardly flattering to the mothers of African, Asian, Latino, or Native American children. One may be fortunate and stumble upon an "ethnic" card section, but chances are you will have to search. Similarly, try to find "flesh color" bandages in your local store that match the skin color of most African Americans. The smallest and seemingly most inconsequential activities are often shaped by racial differentiation and bias.

Realize that racial prejudice and discrimination are omnipresent, recurring, and systemic in this society. Racism involves much more than personal choice, and it usually is not an indicator of serious mental illness. Moreover, racism is not limited to the activities of a few bigoted and demented extremists that play war games in the woods, nor are racists only hood-wearing, cross-burning fanatics that burn down churches under cover of darkness. Believing that these people are the only serious racists left in this society encourages a white individual to excuse himself or herself from responsibility for the perpetuation of white privilege and power. Racism reveals itself in ordinary whites' employment decisions, housing choices, friendships, voting habits, and patronage of businesses. Doing discrimination does not even require that a person hate the racial others, but only that the person doing the discrimination wants to avoid people of color.

Also, abandon the notion that racial and other major social inequalities result from the personal failures of persons of color, arise out of poor motivation, or reside in a culturally determined aversion to work. While in some individual cases these factors can be important (as they are with whites), looking at them exclusively—without considering the deep and long-term structural constraints that shape and influence social opportunities—produces a myopic perspective that encourages denial or cynicism. Relying on individualistic explanations for systemic problems effectively evades the possibility of solutions to long-standing racial–ethnic prejudice and discrimination.

There are yet other things that you as a parent can do. Actively form friendships with adults who belong to other ethnic and racial groups. However, do not place these friends in the position of being "experts" on racial and ethnic issues. Condescending and patronizing behavior is too easy to fall into, so you must be alert for it and avoid it. Approach your efforts to make new friends with the intention of discovering good company in new places.

Recognize and encourage children's curiosity and their abilities to explore the social world with a sense of fairness. A first step is to accept the fact that most youngsters have much more social insight and understanding than adults would like to admit. By the time they are three or four years old, most are not sheltered, isolated babies, but agile and active social participants, busily constructing the world that we will all live in. Consider, too, that the preschoolers of today are going to be in charge of policy and decision making about adults' lives as they age. Do we want them to be equipped with the best values and information that will help to make this nation and world a better place, one free of discrimination and inequality?

Point out instances of everyday racism and discuss them, even with very young children. As you yourself learn better how to recognize the range of racial–ethnic discrimination and of inequality, bring these conditions to your children's attention and discuss with them the ways of eliminating such injustice. Children are attuned to issues of fairness and are often interested in assuring that everybody gets the same conditions or amount, whether it is of ice cream or turns at bat. And make sure that this interest in fairness prevails throughout their young lives, so that they are as invested in fairness as they are in their own material comforts.

Take your children to multiracial events and multicultural activities in your community. Encourage them, too, to make friends with children of many racial and ethnic groups and then incorporate these friends and their families into your family's activities. Expand racial–ethnic horizons and frequent with your children businesses in neighborhoods other than your own. Introduce other cultures to your child, from an early age and as often as possible.

HOW CAN RESEARCHERS CONTRIBUTE?

Over the last few years new challenges to traditional cognitive theory have been made. While most mainstream theories of child development are still influenced, often heavily, by the ideas of Piaget, moving into this main-stream today we see Vygotskian and other innovative approaches that accent much more than the Piagetian tradition the importance of the social context and argue that there are multiple pathways and varied paces of child development. Still, in much mainstream child development teaching and major textbooks (see, for example, Siegler 1998), Vygotsky's ideas receive only passing attention. More important, the pioneering field studies of children interacting in natural settings, such as those of Corsaro (1997) and Thorne (1993), receive no attention or analysis in key handbook articles and textbooks (see Siegler 1998; Gelman and Williams 1998). Even prominent discussions of the conceptual development of young children seem skewed to extensive research on understandings of physical objects and of concepts such as time, space, and number—with little or no attention to children's learning about such social concepts as gender, race, or class (see Siegler 1998; Gelman and Williams 1998). And the focus is heavily on the individual and on individual learning. Indeed, a few developmental psychologists such as Rogoff (1998, 680) have noted that the idea that cognitive development entails "more than the solo individual is still new to many cognitive developmentalists." Her suggestions are in line with our view that a major paradigm shift is needed and perhaps under way. Moreover, the new empirical fieldwork on children, with its many new understandings of children gained from research in their own natural settings, needs to be much better integrated into mainstream teaching and textbooks on child development.

Continued work in the ethnographic and field study vein needs to be encouraged among all levels of researchers, especially graduate students. Various novel and nontraditional methods of exploration can be implemented, with a striving toward investigating the fullness and complexity of children's lives from multiple vantage points. The notion that we can isolate children from adults and analyze their experiences separately should be abandoned.

Furthermore, the assumption, however implicit, that three- to six-year-old children are naive and guileless beings basically different in mental functioning and social activity from adults should go the way of the horse and buggy. While there are, of course, significant differences between average three-year-olds and twelve-year-olds, as well as between the latter and thirty-year-olds, on such dimensions as knowledge of the world and ability to engage in abstract discussions, these are mostly matters of degree and not of kind. While developmental questions about changes in the organization of human selves, cognitive and abstraction abilities, interactional skills, and emotional propensities need much further research, we think that researchers should concentrate more attention than they have on exploring continuities and similarities in child and adult abilities, skills, propensities, and understandings. In our research, we have demonstrated that children's understandings are often much more sophisticated and developed than most adults know or are willing to acknowledge.

From the vantage point of both the present day and the future, good research on children's lives is particularly important. Fortunately, this field of research has been growing slowly over the past decade or two. The intention of most research is to enhance knowledge and expand understanding of social phenomena. If we are to further enhance our knowledge about children's lives, we have to emphasize more than ever the social context, complexity, and sophistication of those young lives. This means sustained critiques of dominant theories that are condescending or too adultcentric in their understandings of children and childhood, and it means building new theories that attend greatly to the social, cultural, and interactive contexts of young children's lives. Accomplishing this will entail continued refinement of the research methods used to study children, which in turn will enable us to develop better ways of describing their realities. Our study provides a bit more insight into how children negotiate racial and ethnic worlds. The ultimate goal of additional research should be to understand further the meaning of race and ethnicity *to them* and its reality in, and implications for, their lives.

Theory and thinking do matter, and how researchers and educators think about children in regard to racial–ethnic issues can matter a lot in regard to how children and their behaviors are viewed and treated in the larger society. Indeed, the subversion of racial and ethnic oppression is, as we see it, an important part of theoretical work in the social sciences and in education (see Connell, 1985, 270). If we are ever to know fully what race and racism mean in the larger society, we must understand what they mean to children. We need to know more about how children "do racism," why they do it, when they do it, and with whom they do it. And we need to know about these things as early as possible in children's lives. By doing investigations mostly on older children, we in effect assist in allowing race and racism to become important operating routines for life. We can thereby provide few insights into the earlier years and thus few viable intervention strategies. Early patterns of behavior are often the most difficult to break. The research presented in this book shows clearly that early learning includes race and ethnicity as crucial interactive and interpretive tools for children. Racial–ethnic concepts inform much of children's social activity—from how children perceive themselves, to how they select friends, to how they explain social life, to the ways they develop understandings of social hierarchies and power. We need to develop ever more creative research projects that allow us entrée into children's lives and that focus on understanding the connections and similarities between adults and children. Perhaps in this way we adults can cultivate more insights into our own racial and ethnic prejudices, emotions, and practices.

Obviously, the realities of race and racism do not start with children, and programs to eradicate racism cannot begin there either. Our study of race and racism in the lives of preschoolers is intended to spark a greater awareness of the persistent and perverse racism that pervades, restrains, and limits all those who grow up in this all-too-racist society. It is not a mystery where children this young get their ideas: We adults are a primary source. And they are champions at showing exactly how masterful human beings can be in perpetuating racial–ethnic hatred, discrimination, and inequalities. Attempts to change their behavior, however, may be ineffective until we adults change our own. Watching children at work with racism is like watching ourselves in a mirror. They will not unlearn and undo racism until we do.

REFERENCES

Aboud, F. E. 1977. Interest in ethnic information: A cross-cultural developmental study. *Canadian Journal of Behavioral Science* 9:134–46.
———. 1988. *Children and Prejudice*. New York: Blackwell.
Addams, J. 1909. *The Spirit of Youth and City Streets*. New York: Macmillan.
Anti-Defamation League. 1993. *Highlights from an Anti-Defamation League Survey on Racial Attitudes in America*. New York: Anti-Defamation League.
Arce, C. A. 1981. A reconsideration of Chicano culture and identity. *Daedalus* 110:177–92.
Aries, P. 1962. *Centuries of Childhood: A Social History of Family Life*. New York: Random House.
Bachman, J. G., Johnston, L. D., and O'Malley, P. M. 1997. *Monitoring the Future: Questionnaire Responses from the Nation's High School Seniors*. Ann Arbor: University of Michigan Institute for Social Research.
Baillargeon, R. 1991. Reasoning about the height and location of a hidden object in 4.5 and 6.5 month old infants. *Cognition* 38:12–42.
Baillargeon, R., and DeVos, J. 1991. Object permanence in young infants: Further evidence. *Child Development* 62:1227–46.
Baillargeon, R., and Hanko-Summers, S. 1990. Is the top object adequately supported by the bottom object?: Young infants' understanding of support relations. *Cognitive Development* 5:29–53.
Baughman, E. E., and Dahlstrom, W. G. 1968. *Negro and White Children: A Psychological Study in the Rural South*. New York: Academic.
Bem, S. L. 1989. Genital knowledge and gender constancy in preschool children. *Child Development* 60:649–62.
Benokraitis, N. V. (Ed.). 1997. *Subtle Sexism: Current Practice and Prospects for Change*. Thousand Oaks, CA: Sage.
Biddle, B. J. 1992. Role Theory. In *Encyclopedia of Sociology* (vol. 3, pp. 1681–85), edited by Edgar F. Borgatta and Marie L. Borgatta. New York: Macmillan.

215

Bigler, R. S., and Liben, L. S. 1993. A cognitive-developmental approach to racial stereotyping and reconstructive memory in Euro-American children. *Child Development* 64:1507–18.

Blumer, H. 1969. *Symbolic Interactionism: Perspective and Method.* Englewood Cliffs, NJ: Prentice Hall.

Bobo, L., and Suh, S. A. 1995 (August 1). Surveying racial discrimination: Analyses from a multiethnic labor market. University of California, Los Angeles, unpublished report.

Bonilla-Silva, E., and Forman, T. A. 2000. I am not a racist but . . . : Mapping white college students' racial ideology in the U.S.A. *Discourse and Society* 11:51–86.

Borke, H. 1971. Interpersonal perception of young children: Egocentrism or empathy. *Developmental Psychology* 5:263–69.

Branch, C. W., and Newcombe, N. 1986. Racial attitude development among young Black children as a function of parental attitudes: A longitudinal and cross-sectional study. *Child Development* 57:712–21.

Campbell, S. F. 1976. *A Piaget Sampler.* New York: Wiley.

Clark, A., Hocevar, D., and Dembo, M. H. 1980. The role of cognitive development in children's explanations and preferences for skin color. *Developmental Psychology* 16:332–39.

Clark, K. B., and Clark, M. P. 1939. Segregation as a factor in the racial identification of Negro preschool children. *Journal of Experimental Education* 8:161–63.

———. 1947. Racial identification and preference in Negro children. In T. M. Newcomb and E. L. Hartley (Eds.), *Reading in Social Psychology* (pp. 169–78). New York: Holt, Rinehart and Winston.

Connell, R. W. 1985. Theorising Gender. *Sociology* 19:260–72.

Connolly, P. 1998. *Racism, Gender Identities and Young Children.* London: Routledge.

Corsaro, W. A. 1979. We're friends, right? *Language in Society* 8:315–36.

———. 1981. Entering the child's world: Research strategies for field entry and data collection in a preschool setting. In J. Green and C. Wallat (Eds.), *Ethnography and Language in Educational Settings* (pp. 117–46). Norwood, NJ: Ablex.

———. 1997. *The Sociology of Childhood.* Thousand Oaks, CA: Pine Forge Press.

Corsaro, W. A., and Miller, P. J. 1992. *Interpretive Approaches to Children's Socialization.* New Directions for Child Development Series, Number 58, Winter. San Francisco: Jossey-Bass.

Cross, W. E., Jr. 1987. A two-factor theory of Black identity: Implications for the study of identity development in minority children. In J. S. Phinney and M. J. Rotheram (Eds.), *Children's Ethnic Socialization: Pluralism and Development* (pp. 117–33). Newbury Park, CA: Sage.

Cross, W. E., Jr. 1991. *Shades of Black: Diversity in African-American Identity.* Philadelphia: Temple University Press.

Damon, W. 1977. *The Social World of the Child.* San Francisco: Jossey-Bass.

Danielewicz, J. M., Rogers, D. L., and Noblit, G. 1996. Children's discourse patterns and power relations in teacher-led and child-led sharing time. *Qualitative Studies in Education* 9:311–31.

Deegan, M. J. 2000. Jane Addams and Max Weber on the spirits of youth and capitalism. University of Nebraska, unpublished research paper.

DeMott, B. 1995. *The Trouble with Friendship: Why Americans Can't Think Straight about Race.* New York: Atlantic Monthly Press.

Dickinson, J. 1986. *The Development of Representations of Social Inequality.* Dundee University, unpublished Ph.D. thesis.

Dred Scott v. John F. A. Sandford 60 U.S. 393, 408, 1857.

DuBois, W. E. B. 1989 [1903]. *The Souls of Black Folk.* New York: Bantam.

Dunn, J. 1993. *Young Children's Close Relationships: Beyond Attachment.* Newbury Park, CA: Sage.

Dye, T. 1986. *Who's Running America?* 4th ed. Englewood Cliffs, NJ: Prentice Hall.

Elkind, D. 1981. *The Hurried Child.* Reading, MA: Addison Wesley.

Emler, N., and Dickinson, J. 1993. The child as sociologist: The childhood development of implicit theories of role categories and social organization. In M. Bennett (Ed.), *The Development of Social Cognition: The Child as Psychologist* (pp. 168–90). New York: Guilford.

Erickson, F. 1977. Some approaches to inquiry in school–community ethnography. *Anthropology and Education Quarterly* 8(2):58–69.

Farmer, Y. 1992. Role models. In *Encyclopedia of Sociology* (vol. 3, pp. 1678–81), edited by Edgar F. Borgatta and Marie L. Borgatta New York: Macmillan.

Feagin, J. R. 2000. *Racist America: Roots, Current Realities, and Future Reparations.* New York: Routledge.

Feagin, J. R., and Feagin, C. B. 1997. *Social Problems: A Critical Power–Conflict Perspective.* 5th ed. Upper Saddle River, NJ: Prentice Hall.

Feagin, J. R., and Sikes, M. P. 1994. *Living with Racism: The Black Middle-Class Experience.* Boston: Beacon.

Feagin, J. R., and Vera, H. 1995. *White Racism: The Basics.* New York: Routledge.

Gelman, R., and Williams, E. M. 1998. Enabling constraints for cognitive development and learning: Domain specificity and epigenesis. In D. Kuhn and R. S. Siegler (Eds.), *Handbook of Child Psychology,* 5th ed. (pp. 575–630). New York: Wiley.

George, D. M., and Hoppe, R. A. 1979. Racial identification, preference, and self-concept. *Journal of Cross-Cultural Psychology* 10:85–100.

Goffman, E. G. 1963. *Behavior in Public Places: Notes on the Social Organization of Gatherings.* New York: Free Press.

Goodman, M. E. 1964 [1952]. *Race Awareness in Young Children.* New York: Crowell-Collier.

Gordon, L. R. 1997. *Her Majesty's Other Children: Sketches of Racism from a Neo-colonial Age.* Lanham, MD: Rowman & Littlefield.

Graue, M. E., and Walsh, D. J. 1998. *Studying Children in Context: Theories, Methods, and Ethics.* Thousand Oaks, CA: Sage.

Griffin, J. H. 1961. *Black Like Me.* Boston: Houghton Mifflin.

Gubrium, J. F. 1988. *Analyzing Field Reality.* Newbury Park, CA: Sage.

Halbwachs, M. 1950. *The Collective Memory.* Translated by F. J. Ditter Jr. and V. Y. Ditter. New York: Harper Colophon.

Helms, J. E. (Ed.). 1990. *Black and White Racial Identity: Theory, Research, and Practice.* New York: Greenwood.

Hirschfeld, L. 1995. Do children have a theory of race? *Cognition* 54:209–52.

———. 1996. *Race in the Making.* Cambridge, MA: MIT Press.

———. 1997. The conceptual politics of race: Lessons from our children. *Ethos: Journal of the Society for Psychological Anthropology* 25:63–92.

Holmes, R. M. 1995. *How Young Children Perceive Race.* Thousand Oaks, CA: Sage.

Horowitz, E. L. 1936. The development of attitudes toward the Negro. *Archives of Psychology*: 194.

Hughes, D. 1997. Racist thinking and thinking about race: What children know about but don't say. *Ethos: Journal of the Society for Psychological Anthropology* 25:117–25.

Jeffcoate, R. 1977. Children's racial ideas and feelings. *English in Education* 11:32–48.

Kaplan, Howard B. 1992. Social Psychology. In *Encyclopedia of Sociology* (vol. 4, pp. 1921–36), edited by Edgar F. Borgatta and Marie L. Borgatta. New York: Macmillan.

Katz, P. A. 1976. The acquisition of racial attitudes in children. In P. A. Katz (Ed.), *Towards the Elimination of Racism* (pp. 125–54). New York: Pergamon.

Kim, J. 1981. *Process of Asian-American Identity Development: A Study of Japanese American Women's Perceptions of Their Struggle to Achieve Positive Identities.* University of Massachusetts, Amherst, unpublished Ph.D. dissertation.

King, R. 1978. *All Things Bright and Beautiful: A Sociological Study of Infants' Classrooms.* Chichester, England: Wiley.

Kohlberg, L. 1969. Stage and sequence: The cognitive-developmental approach to socialization. In D. Goslin (Ed.), *Handbook of Socialization Theory and Research* (pp. 347–480). Skokie, IL: Rand McNally.

Kozol, J. 1988. *Savage Inequalities: Children in America's Schools.* New York: HarperPerennial.

Lakoff, G., and Johnson, M. 1980. *Metaphors We Live By.* Chicago: University of Chicago Press.

Lasker, B. 1929. *Race Attitudes in Children.* New York: Holt, Rinehart and Winston.

Lee, L. C. 1975. Toward a cognitive theory of interpersonal development: Importance of peers. In M. Lewis and L. A. Rosenblum (Eds.), *Friendship and Peer Relations* (vol. 4, pp. 207–21). New York: Wiley.

Light, R. J., and Pillemer, D. B. 1982. Numbers and narrative: Combining their strengths in research reviews. *Harvard Educational Review* 25:41–48.

Lorde, A. 1984. *Sister Outsider*. Freedom, CA: Crossing Press.

Lynott, P. P., and Logue, B. J. 1993. The "hurried child": The myth of lost childhood in contemporary American society. *Sociological Forum* 8(3):471–91.

McIntosh, P. 1988. White privilege and male privilege: A personal account of coming to see correspondences through work in women's studies. Wellesley College Center for Research on Women, Wellesley College, MA: S.E.E.D Project.

Mackay, R. W. 1974. *Words, Utterances, and Activities*. In R. Turner (Ed.), *Ethnomethodology: Selected Readings* (pp. 197–215). Harmondsworth, England: Penguin.

Mandell, N. 1988. The least-adult role in studying children. *Journal of Contemporary Ethnography* 16:433–67.

Maratsos, M. P. 1973. Nonegocentric communication abilities in preschool children. *Child Development* 44:697–700.

Marx, K. 1971. *Die Grundrisse*. Edited by David McClelland. New York: Harper and Row.

Matsumoto, D., Haan, N., Yabrove, G., Theodorou, P., and Carney, C. C. 1986. Preschoolers' moral actions and emotions in *Prisoner's Dilemma*. *Developmental Psychology* 22:663–70.

Mead, G. H. 1934. *Mind, Self, and Society*. Chicago: University of Chicago Press.

Miller, G. A., Galanter, E., and Pribram, K. H. 1960. *Plans and the Structure of Behavior*. New York: Holt, Rinehart and Winston.

Mills, C. W. 1959. *The Sociological Imagination*. New York: Oxford University Press.

Morland, J. K. 1966. A comparison of race awareness in Northern and Southern children. *American Journal of Orthopsychiatry* 36:22–31.

Myrdal, G. 1964 [1944]. *An American Dilemma: The Negro Problem and Modern Democracy*. New York: Harper and Row.

Oldman, D. 1994. Adult–child relations as class relations. In J. Gvortrup, M. Bardy, G. Sgritta, and H. Wintersberger (Eds.), *Childhood Matters: Social Theory, Practice and Politics* (pp. 43–58). Aldershot, Great Britain: Avebury Ashgate Publishing Limited.

Omi, M., and Winant, H. 1994. *Racial Formation in the United States: From the 1960s to the 1990s*. 2nd ed. New York: Routledge.

Orfield, G., Bachmeier, M. D., James, D. R., and Eitle, T. 1997. Deepening segregation in American public schools: A special report from the Harvard Project on School Desegregation. *Equity & Excellence in Education* 30:5–24.

Peterson, C., and McCabe, A. 1994. A social interactionist account of developing decontextualized narrative skill. *Developmental Psychology* 30:937–48.

Pettigrew, T. F. 1964. *A Profile of the Negro American*. Princeton, NJ: Van Nostrand.

Phinney, J. S., and Rotheram, M. J. (Eds.). 1987. *Children's Ethnic Socialization: Pluralism and Development*. Newbury Park, CA: Sage.

Piaget, J. 1926. *The Language and Thought of the Child*. London: Kegan Paul.
———. 1932. *The Moral Judgment of the Child*. Glencoe, IL: Free Press.
———. 1965. *The Moral Development of the Child*. New York: Free Press.
Piaget, J., and Weil, A. M. 1951. The development in children of the idea of the homeland and of relations with other countries. *International Social Science Bulletin* 3:561–78.
The Plowden Report. 1967. *Children and Their Primary Schools*, Vol. 1, HMSO, paragraph 179.
Porter, J. D. 1971. *Black Child, White Child: The Development of Racial Attitudes*. Cambridge, MA: Harvard University Press.
Radke, M., and Sutherland, J. 1949. Children's concepts and attitudes about minority and majority American groups. *Journal of Educational Psychology* 40:449–468.
Ramsey, P. G. 1987. Young children's thinking about ethnic differences. In J. S. Phinney and M. J. Rotheram, *Children's Ethnic Socialization: Pluralism and Development* (pp. 56–72). Newbury Park, CA: Sage.
———. 1991. The salience of race in young children growing up in an all-white community. *Journal of Educational Psychology* 83:28–34.
Rogoff, B. 1998. Cognition as a collaborative process. In D. Kuhn and R. S. Siegler (Eds.), *Handbook of Child Psychology*, 5th ed. (pp. 679–744). New York: Wiley.
Rotheram, M. J., and Phinney, J. S. 1987. Introduction: Definitions and perspectives in the study of children's ethnic socialization. In J. S. Phinney and M. J. Rotheram (Eds.), *Children's Ethnic Socialization: Pluralism and Development* (pp. 10–28). Newbury Park, CA: Sage.
Rutstein, N. 1993. *Healing Racism in America: A Prescription for the Disease*. Springfield, MA: Whitcomb Publishing.
———. 1997. *Racism: Unraveling the Fear*. Washington, D.C.: The Global Classroom.
St. John, N. 1975. *School Desegregation Outcomes for Children*. New York: Wiley.
Saunders, R. A., and Bingham-Newman, A. M. 1984. *Piagetian Perspective for Preschools: A Thinking Book for Teachers*. Englewood Cliffs, NJ: Prentice Hall.
Siegler, R. S. 1998. *Children's Thinking*. 3rd ed. Upper Saddle River, NJ: Prentice Hall.
Sjoberg, G., and Vaughan, T. 1993a. The bureaucratization of sociology: Its impact on theory and research. In T. Vaughan, G. Sjoberg, and L. Reynolds (Eds.), *A Critique of Contemporary American Sociology* (pp. 54–113). Dix Hills, NY: General Hall.
———. 1993b. The ethical foundations of sociology and the necessity for a human rights alternative. In T. Vaughan, G. Sjoberg, and L. Reynolds (Eds.), *A Critique of Contemporary American Sociology* (pp. 114–59.). Dix Hills, NY: General Hall.
Smetana, J. G. 1985. Preschool children's conceptions of transgressions: The effects of varying moral and conventional domain-related attributes. *Developmental Psychology* 21:18–29.

———. 1993. Understanding of social rules. In M. Bennett (Ed.), *The Development of Social Cognition: The Child as Psychologist* (pp. 111–41). New York: Guilford.

Smetana, J. G., and Braeges, J. L. 1990. The development of toddlers' moral and conventional judgments. *Merrill-Palmer Quarterly* 36:329–46.

Smith, L. 1949. *Killers of the Dream*. New York: Norton.

Sniderman, P. M., and Piazza, T. 1993. *The Scar of Race*. Cambridge, MA: Harvard University Press.

Soteropoulos, J. 1995 (April 17). Skeptics put cops on trial: The American public isn't giving government or police officers the blind trust it once did. *Tampa Tribune*, p. A1.

Spencer, M. B. 1982. Preschool children's social cognition and cultural cognition: A cognitive developmental interpretation of race dissonance findings. *Journal of Psychology* 112:275–96.

———. 1984. Black children's race awareness, racial attitudes, and self-concept: A reinterpretation. *Journal of Child Psychology and Psychiatry* 25:433–41.

———. 1987. Black children's ethnic identity formation: Risk and resilience of castelike minorities. In J. S. Phinney and M. J. Rotheram (Eds.), *Children's Ethnic Socialization: Pluralism and Development* (pp. 103–16). Newbury Park, CA: Sage.

Spencer, M. B., and Horowitz, F. D. 1973. Effects of systematic social and token reinforcement on the modification of racial and color concept attitudes in Black and white preschool children. *Developmental Psychology* 9:246–54.

Spindler, G. 1982. *Doing the Ethnography of Schooling: Educational Anthropology in Action*. New York: Holt, Rinehart and Winston.

Stacey, J., and Thorne, B. 1985. The missing feminist revolution in sociology. *Social Problems* 32:301–16.

Sullivan, K., Zaitchik, D., and Tager-Flusberg, H. 1994. Preschoolers can attribute second-order beliefs. *Developmental Psychology* 30:395–402.

Swidler, A. 1986. Culture in action: Symbols and strategies. *American Sociological Review* 51:273–86.

Tajfel, H. 1984. Intergroup relations, social myths, and social justice in social psychology. In H. Tajfel (Ed.), *The Social Dimension* (vol. 2). Cambridge: Cambridge University Press.

Thorne, B. 1993. *Gender Play: Girls and Boys in School*. New Brunswick, NJ: Rutgers University Press.

Troyna, B., and Hatcher, R. 1992. *Racism in Children's Lives: A Study of Mainly White Primary Schools*. New York: Routledge.

Turiel, E., Hildebrandt, C., and Wainryb, C. 1991. Children's reasoning about complex social issues. *Monographs of the Society for Research in Child Development* 56(2) (Serial Number 224).

Turiel, E., Killen, M., and Helwig, C. C. 1987. Morality: Its structure, functions, and vagaries. In J. Kagan and S. Lamb (Eds.), *The Emergence of Morality in Young Children* (pp. 155–243). Chicago: The University of Chicago Press.

Turner, M. A., Struyk, R. J., and Yinger, J. 1991. *Housing Discrimination Study: Synthesis.* Washington, D.C.: U.S. Government Printing Office.

Van Ausdale, D., and Feagin, J. R. 1996. Using racial and ethnic concepts: The critical case of very young children. *American Sociological Review* 61:779–93.

Vygotsky, L. S. 1978. *Mind in Society: The Development of Higher Psychological Processes.* Edited by M. Cole, V. John-Steiner, S. Scribner, and E. Souberman. Cambridge, MA: Harvard University Press.

Wardle, F. 1992. Supporting biracial children in the school setting. *Education and Treatment of Children* 15:163–72.

Weiland, A., and Coughlin, R. 1979. Self-identification and preferences: A comparison of white and Mexican American first and third graders. *Journal of Cross-Cultural Psychology* 10:356–65.

West, C., and Zimmerman, D. H. 1987. Doing Gender. *Gender & Society* 1:125–51.

Williams, J. E., Best, D. L., and Boswell, D. A. 1975. The measurement of children's racial attitudes in the early school years. *Child Development* 46:494–500.

Williams, J. E., and Morland, J. K. 1976. *Race, Color, and the Young Child.* Chapel Hill: University of North Carolina Press.

Willis, P. 1990. *Common Culture: Symbolic Work at Play in the Everyday Cultures of the Young.* Buckingham, England: Open University Press.

Wilson, A. 1987. *Mixed Race Children: A Study of Identity.* London: Allen & Unwin.

Woolley, J. D., and Wellman, H. M. 1990. Young children's understanding of realities, nonrealities, and appearances. *Child Development* 61:946–61.

INDEX

ABOUT THE AUTHORS

Debra Van Ausdale was born in 1954 and received her Ph.D. in sociology from the University of Florida in 1996. She is currently assistant professor of sociology at Syracuse University, where her research interests continue to center on children and racism. She is also conducting ethnographic research on the American motorcycling community.

Joe R. Feagin is currently graduate research professor in sociology at the University of Florida. He mainly does research on a variety of issues connected to racism and sexism. Among his many books are *Racial and Ethnic Relations*, 6th ed. (1999, with Clairece Booher Feagin); *Living with Racism: The Black Middle Class Experience* (1994, with Mel Sikes); *White Racism: The Basics* (1995, with Hernan Vera); *Double Burden: Black Women and Everyday Racism* (1998, with Yanick St. Jean); *The Agony of Education: Black Students at White Colleges and Universities* (1996, with Hernan Vera and Nikitah Imani); and *The New Urban Paradigm* (1998). An earlier book with Harlan Hahn, *Ghetto Revolts* (1973), was nominated for a Pulitzer Prize, and *Living with Racism* and *White Racism* have won the Gustavus Myers Center's Outstanding Human Rights Book Award. He is a recent president of the American Sociological Association.